On the Go for the
LORD

To Delorine
From Dr. Bailey

WILLIAM D. BAILEY, M.D.

CrossHouse

Copyright William D. Bailey, M.D., 2010
All Rights Reserved

Printed in the United States of America
by Lightning Source Inc.
Cover design by Dennis Davidson

Library of Congress Control Number: 2010942054
ISBN 978-1-934749-98-2

CrossHouse Publishing
PO Box 461592
Garland, TX 75046
1-877-212-0933

www.crosshousepublishing.com

Unless otherwise identified, all Scripture quotations are taken from the King James Version (KJV).

This book is dedicated to the memory
of my father-in-law and best friend
(next to his daughter—my wife—Vickie Chandler Bailey).

Mr. George Louis Chandler was indeed a true friend who was always there, especially when I needed him.

Acknowledgements

I want to thank all the missionaries, my mission teams, and the nationals I have worked with in several different countries. I appreciate so very much that missionaries have the permanent call to the Great Commission and live full-time in countries outside the U.S.

I thank my wife, Vickie, who goes on some of the mission trips with me and from home supports me on the rest. I always ask her to be my first recruit for any mission trip, even the ones she doesn't decide to go on. She has spent endless hours counting out pills when we "dose pack" the medicines before going on our trips. She also proof reads all my chapters that go into writing my books.

I want to thank the Rev. Harrell Shelton and Airline Baptist Church for supporting me with prayers and financial support through our mission funds. Harrell also goes with me overseas once or twice yearly. My Sunday School class supports me with prayer each time I go.

I continue to thank Stan Horton, Minister of (Intercessory) Prayer, for his daily prayer for me and my mission work.

I thank Blessings International, MAP, CrossLinks International, Alcon Labs and Kingsway Charities for the medicines they give or sell at very reasonable prices so I can take these medicines abroad.

I thank Wayne Browning, RPh, who frequently sends me "care packages" (money) to go on these trips.

I thank my Sunday School department and other church members who help support these trips with money or supplies.

I thank Dan Bivins who has been instrumental in getting me on several teams to exotic or hard-to-go areas.

I thank Heather Colabove of MTS Travel Service for helping obtain all the airplane tickets when I coordinate some of the mission trips; she has been very patient obtaining and keeping us straight with the travel.

I thank Katie Welch, Ph.D., and her staff at CrossHouse Publishing for their help and patience with my efforts at writing my books.

Table of Contents

Introduction 9
Chapter 1: The Journeys Continue 11
Chapter 2: Benin, Africa, 2006 13
Chapter 3: South China, 2006 25
Chapter 4: Philippines, 2007 37
Chapter 5: Rwanda, 2007 46
Chapter 6: Ukraine, 2007 54
Chapter 7: Cambodia, 2007 64
Chapter 8: Burkina Faso, 2008 74
Chapter 9: Not Just an Average Day in the E.R. 86
Chapter 10: Just Another Night of Prison Visitation 88
Chapter 11: Coron (Philippines), 2008 92
Chapter 12: China, 2008 101
Chapter 13: Uganda, 2008 111
Chapter 14: Rwanda, 2008 130
Chapter 15: "Put Me in the Middle Seat" 150
Chapter 16: Loss of My Buddy 153
Chapter 17: Baguio City, Philippines, 2009 156
Chapter 18: Togo, 2009 172
Chapter 19: Rwanda, 2009 188
Chapter 20: When One Door Closes, Another Opens 203
Chapter 21: Uttar Pradesh, India, 2009 205

Chapter 22: Kampong Cham, Cambodia, 2009 219
Chapter 23: Is There a Santa Claus? 229
Chapter 24: Are You Going to Haiti? 233
Chapter 25: Pampanga, Philippines, 2010 235
Chapter 26: 61st Angola Day 246
Chapter 27: North China, 2010 252
Chapter 28: Draganesti, Romania, 2010 260
Chapter 29: Ecuador, 2010 274
Chapter 30: Cairo, Egypt, 2010 283
Chapter 31: My Word Shall Not Return Unto Me Void 299
Chapter 32: What is a Soul Worth? 301
Epilogue 303
Appendix A 304
Appendix B 309

Introduction

You may be happy to know that I am writing the original manuscript with a pen given to me by Dr. Katie Welch, publisher of CrossHouse Publishing. She gave this to me after publishing my first two books: *You Will Never Run Out of Jesus* and *There's Something Better Than Going to Heaven*. I feel honored by her gift and will use this pen only to work on the last of my trilogy.

Important events like Israel's history began with a single individual and a command to go. The Lord said to Abram: Go out from your land, your relatives, and your father's house to the land that I will show you (Genesis 12:1 KJV). *Go* is a profound truth; Jesus commanded it in the Great Commission (Matthew 28:19-20): *Go ye therefore and make disciples of all nations . . . .*

Going is obeying. We facilitate fellowship with the Lord by choosing to obey Him.

Traversing the globe many times to do the work of the Great Commission has been for me a dream come true. My initial thoughts about this dream started in Viet Nam in 1969 when I was a medical officer (USN Lieutenant) serving as a Battalion Aid Surgeon. My passion has become a commission.

My first book was about my first 30 medical mission trips; this book will be about my next 21 trips and local missions. I continue to be blessed with opportunities to go many places in the world.

My passion to tell everyone about Jesus has been very intriguing and rewarding. I hope these journeys that I have been fortunate to be a part of give you, my readers, an incentive to want to do missions also.

I feel that missions should be done locally just as well as abroad; I expounded on that in my book: *There's Something Better Than Going to Heaven*. In this book I will add more of my local mission efforts as well as tell about when I am traveling outside the U.S.

Chapter 1
The Journeys Continue

Going on medical mission trips seems so natural to me now. When a friend or acquaintance who hasn't seem me for a while greets me, that person's first question usually is, "Where are you going next?"

My standard for living now is
* serving the Lord by going obediently,
* the thrill of a new adventure,
* working with old friends,
* meeting new friends, and
* sharing the Gospel with others.

Working to earn money to go on missions also has been my way of life for well over a decade. With that goal in mind, work has been a challenge and a way to keep up with the medical field so I could give my few talents to those who need them.

I have so many opportunities to go on medical mission trips. With all the possibilities and needs that exist around the world, many wonder how I choose where to go. The answer is simple: I depend on the Lord for guidance. Most often I seek to go where a real need exists and sometimes where only a few others are willing to go. As the years pass, I am trying to go back to the same places where I have been previously so I can work with people I know and try to help with their needs.

Working with the same missionaries, and frequently the same workers, has been a privilege and honor. My life has been enriched and blessed by those called of God and "the going crowd".

It is not infrequent that I am the only medical doctor on the trip; I do not let this deter me. I can often get excellent help using nurses as nurse practitioners. All I ask is a willing heart; then I will put them to work.

Leaving on a jet plane to many places is not the only thing we do; going to local and regional prisons in the States is a special privilege and adventure. Witnessing to people locally can be just as challenging—sometimes even more so—than going to the uttermost parts of the world.

The following chapters will take you from the far reaches of "the killing fields" in Cambodia, the islands of the Philippines, to an area out in the middle of nowhere, miles from anywhere (Burkina Faso), the land of the pyramids and sphinx (Egypt), and many other exotic places. The cultures and people may be different, but the universal need for the love of Jesus is everywhere. I want to share with you many of the adventures since my first book, *You Will Never Run Out of Jesus*, was first published

Chapter 2

Benin, Africa
August 2006

Going back to south Benin in August 2006 was my third trip there to work with Jeff and Barbara Singerman; I had been to Benin in 2000 and again in 2001. Being there had originated from another mission trip in 1999 when I first wanted to start doing medical missions.

I had called Dr. Jim Williams, director of the Baptist Medical Dental Fellowship, at the suggestion of Dr. Charles Walker. He had referred me to Dr. John Gibson in Nan, Thailand, who in turn notified Westside Baptist Church that I wanted to do a mission trip there. I got an email from Sandra Benton from Westside Baptist Church stating that she needed team members for a medical mission to Thailand. We visited on the telephone and discussed the trip. I ended up recruiting most of the team. We had a great time with Dr. John Gibson and his wife, Linda.

In early 2006 I got a call from Jenice Hughes from Westside Baptist wanting me to go with another group in June to south Benin to serve once again with the Singermans. I agreed to go and began procuring meds and supplies for the trip, but later Jenice changed the date to August. Fortunately, I did not have another trip at that time slot; I agreed to still stay on the team. I had to ship a good portion of the medicine and supplies to Gainesville, FL, because of the weight and volume.

The Singermans had returned to Benin after an extended furlough because of Barbara's thyroid condition. She ended up having to have surgery, radiation, and finally titration of meds to control it to an euthyroid status.

Due to the shortage of missionaries in Benin and most of west Africa, Jeff was made the coordinator for the Baptists in Benin, Togo, Burkina Faso, and Ivory Coast.

(Please read the email in the Appendix A about the job to which Jeff and Barbara are now assigned.) However, Jeff and Barbara had not forgotten their grassroots in Benin; they had plans there for us to work with two new churches, to start three new preaching points, and to help evangelization efforts in another church that had been decreasing in members.

I left Shreveport over an hour late on August 6 due to the flight from Atlanta arriving late. When we arrived in Atlanta we were on the tarmac for 45 minutes. That left me 20 minutes until my Air France flight was to leave for Paris. I literally ran to Concourse E inside the airport because I fortunately knew where the Air France terminal was.

When I got there, the line was almost completely boarded. At the desk, I found out that my ticket had been cancelled, but I told the agent emphatically I was going, so he made me a new boarding pass and I quickly scampered onto the plane almost last in line. I was a bit winded and perspiring from the jaunt across the airport.

By the time I got to the back of the airplane, I heard my name being paged. I found out that the team members were on board and wondering if I had made it. They had called my home and Vickie told them that I had left Shreveport. Then I recognized Jenice and could feel a little more relaxed. Jenice told me she had tried to reach me at home, so I borrowed her cell phone and called Vickie to let her know that I was on the flight and headed to Paris in a few moments.

Then I found out that the other doctor could not join us; he had an acute family emergency the day before leaving. I could understand a little better then about the anxiety the team from Westside had about not having a doctor on the team.

Our flight to Paris made for a long night, but I got to watch a couple of movies I had not had the opportunity to see before. Once in Paris, I got to meet all the team members and got to know them personally before we started working together. Jenice's husband and son were among those on the trip, and I thoroughly enjoyed their acquaintance..

Michelle McElroy, R.N., was accompanied by her mother. I heard an interesting story about how Pam McElroy didn't particularly want her daughter to go on the trip, so mother and daughter ended up going on the trip together. Isn't it interesting how God works?

Brenda Woody, R.N., was on her first mission trip. (Later I recruited her to go with me to the Philippines in 2007.)

Lauren Gibson, R.N., was engaged to another of the Hughes' sons. Howard Rogers and Mae Griner, R.N. rounded out the team.

We then flew on to Cotonou and were met by Barbara and Jeff Singerman, who were accompanied by Judy Miller, the Baptist coordinator for Benin. Wow! Seeing the Singermans was so good because the last time I had seen them was five years earlier in 2001. We loaded up our suitcases and trunks and headed for the Baptist Mission House, where we spent the night.

The next morning Jenice, Tom, Jeff and I went to meet with the Minister of Health to get our meds approved for our mission trip. The minister was very gracious and grateful that we were in Benin to help his people. The meds were approved without any problem, after just peeking in one trunk of meds.

Jeff and Barbara then took us shopping at the African Artisan Village, where we made a few purchases.

We next arrived at Calavi to check out the Catholic Conference Center. Jeff and Barbara had managed to get us rooms there for the next eight days; the facility was less than a mile from their home. It was really nice, but all the air-conditioned rooms had been taken; however the weather was so nice—70 degrees at night and 80 to 85 during the day—so we didn't need the air conditioner. That sure beat the temperatures of 95 to 100 degrees I had experienced on the two previous trips there. Fortunately this was not the season for the hamartan when dust from the Sahara desert is ubiquitous.

Each morning we would have breakfast, followed by fellowship in the Catholic Conference Center cafeteria. Then we would have a devotion given by members of the team rotating turns. This produced a refreshing start every morning. Shortly after the devotionals the Singermans would arrive to take us out into the field.

On August 9, we loaded up and went to Gbazoundkpa; this was a new church actively being built. When we arrived no one was there, so we all had prayer and divided into small groups or pairs and went prayerwalking in the surrounding village.

During our stroll down the village road, Jenice and I met several people going about their usual chores. We invited them to the clinic. Shortly after we returned, people started coming from all over the village to our clinic, which we had set up in the unfinished church. Jenice and one of the other nurses took turns seeing patients. I extracted teeth, did some minor surgery, and was medical consultant to the two nurses doing the nurse practitioner duties. I liked the arrangement; it worked out great all week. The spiritual station was staffed by our team on a rotating basis. The people were so friendly, receptive, and appreciative. We started out slow, but more and more people showed up as the news about the clinic spread.

On August 10, we went to Gbedoudo to work with a brand new church. This village consisted of mostly baked mud houses with straw roofs. We found that the young children there frequently had kwashiorkor (chronic deficiency of protein causing protuberant abdomens, swollen lower extremities, and stunted growth). We did the best we could by giving vitamins and meds for diseases we could treat. Again the people were very gracious and thankful to have us there. We got to see some of their very primitive ways of cooking, doing blacksmith work, and gardening.

On August 11 we went to Tori, where a new work was being started in hopes of forming a church there soon. People were there in fairly large numbers; this is an excellent way to get folks interested in visiting your church, particularly when many people accept the Gospel and Jesus Christ as Savior. We had made cards for treatment purposes which would then go to the pharmacy. At the spiritual station the cards were marked for follow up by one of the pastors. Those that had accepted Jesus could hopefully be churched then.

On August 12 we went to Toffo to work in an established church, where the attendance had fallen some. This is a village, where I had worked in 2001 and had seen several accept Jesus through personal evangelism. Cyprien, my interpreter, who I had worked with every time I have been in Benin, was disappointed when I sent some of the people who needed salvation to our spiritual station instead of presenting the saving knowledge of Jesus ourselves. But we had a good system worked out and my job being a medical consultant was seeing patients and extracting teeth as needed. Our spiritual team was very effective and doing a great job presenting the Gospel and having dozens accept Jesus as Savior every day.

On Sunday, we went to church near Ouida which is very near to the Atlantic Ocean; afterwards we went to the beach for lunch and then walked along the beach for a spell. The Bay of Benin was very refreshing. A rather steady breeze from the ocean was coming in from the direction of the constant breaking waves. All seemed to enjoy the break. Barbara looked as though she had fallen asleep in the warm sunshine. Hosting a medical missions team is exhausting for missionaries because their lives truly consist of late to bed and early to rise every day.

While in Ouida, we went to the Ouida Slave Museum (an old Portuguese fort), where in 2000 and 2001 I had previously heard the real slavery story. I was anxious for the group to hear the best explanation of slavery I have ever encountered . . . but . . . this time the guide (a woman) told us only of the Voodoo history and how the slaves influenced areas such as Cuba and particularly Brazil. I was very disappointed as I wanted the others to experience the real story of the slave trade and to see evidence of that truth. Jeff was also surprised at the emphasis on voodoo as he had heard the slavery story told many times.

On Monday, we went to Sedje, where a new preaching point-church was being organized. It was situated way out in the jungle, but despite its remoteness many folks attended. We continued our medical treatments, minor surgeries—I took off several lipomas and cysts—and extraction of teeth.

I was located out away from the thatch huts under a large tree similar to a mango. I had shade and light at the same time. A local pastor heard that I was doing surgery out in the village; he came for treatment. He had been given medicines on more than one occasion to make the relatively large lipoma (a benign, fatty tumor under the skin) go away, but to no avail. He couldn't afford to go to a surgeon to have it excised, but here, out in the middle of the jungle, surgical relief was offered free. Under local anesthesia a multilobulated lipoma measuring about 8 by 10 centimeters was excised. I had the man lie down for an extra 30 minutes to make sure he would have no extra bleeding. He spent the entire time praising God that he had been able to finally have it excised.

The following day we went to Menyotame, where a new work was being done. The group worked diligently to see a large number of people while I was quite busy all day excising more lumps and bumps and extracting teeth. The team worked so efficiently and with such cooperation that I can honestly say this was one of the very best teams with which I have ever worked. Jeff and Barbara kept busy coordinating all the stations. They saw to it that we had what we needed and kept things running smoothly. Barbara fed us great sandwiches every day at lunch.

On August 16, we went back to Cotonou to check our luggage at the airport; then we went back to the Singermans to inventory the left-over meds for the next group to arrive.

The Singermans then took us out to tour Ganvie, the stilt city, on Du Loc (the lake). The history was quite fascinating and the sites amazing. The people were placing trees, like I do at home, for the fish to bed up so they could catch them later.

Later, we returned to Cotonou to have a supper out together, then on to the airport for a flight that left close to midnight. We were so privileged to have had the opportunity to work with two of my "bestest" friends. We had a GREAT week. As a group, we saw 1,034 people during the clinics; 474 accepted Jesus as Savior—what a boost that will be for the local churches. We felt we were the most blessed of all by getting to serve with the Singermans.

We spent all day, August 17, in Paris and left for home the next day. Due to heightened security and delays in Paris most of the team had to spend the night in Atlanta before traveling on home the next day.

WHAT A GREAT TRIP!! I want to thank the Westside Baptist folks for asking me to go on the trip and the Singermans for being such great friends.

email FROM JEFF SINGERMAN
8/19/2006

Dear Westside,

I just wanted to let you know what a great team we had with us these past 10 days! It really was one of the best teams we have ever had. They worked extremely hard, were very flexible, and were true servants. Their demeanor and love for Christ was evident and they made a huge impact on our churches and villages here!

The medical folks were all great and they pitched in and moved around where they were needed at any given moment. Perhaps the most impressive thing though was the way they were organized for evangelism. It was absolutely the best medical team I have had that really made evangelism a priority and each person participated in that process.

Many came to Christ and that is a testimony to their organization and their love for the Lord!

Thank you so much for sending them our way! There will be many more Ayizo people in heaven because of this trip!

Blessings,
Jeff Singerman

email FROM BARBARA AND JEFF SINGERMAN
8/22/2006

Dear Ayizo and Beyond Prayer Partners,

God did tremendous things through your prayers and the presence of the Westside medical team!

~**1034 patients were seen** during 6 clinics, held in different villages

~**474 people prayed to surrender their lives to Christ** through prayer walking and evangelism by the team and African brothers during the clinics!

The clinics **aided the work in 2 new churches**

The clinics **opened the door to hopefully start 3 new preaching points**

And **helped evangelization efforts** of an established church.

One man from the Sedje (said-jay) area, named Dowe (doe-way) had attended the new preaching point several times, but didn't show any real commitment. He came to the clinic to see if Dr. Bill could do anything about a painful lump on his shoulder. Over the years he'd seen many doctors, had taken many medicines, and had tried the skills of many traditional healers. He could not even say how much money he'd spent for the healing of his lump.

When the sacrifice of Christ for his sins was presented, he gave his life to Jesus. Then he met Dr. Bill, who was using his surgical skills under the trees (where the light was the best), and in just a few moments the lump was gone!

Dowe is now serious about a relationship with Jesus Christ.

The removal of countless, painfully rotten teeth; the prayers prayed over the sick; the tender touch of a team member; the giving of medicines in Christ's name and even the cleaning of a foot that had been rotting away for 50 years due to a viper bite when the man was five years old, all resulted in people's lives being changed for eternity and villages touched by Christ's love.

That's what the people are saying—that the churches who hosted the medical team's presence in their village manifested to them the love of Christ. They are so very, very thankful.

And so are we, for your diligence in prayer for the eternal and physical lives of the Beninese people.

Yours in Christ,
Barbara and Jeff Singerman
Ayizo People Group Team

jeffsingerman@usa.net
Web page: http://dwmweb.com/ayzio
Barbara J. Singerman: author of *BEYOND SURRENDER*

Benin, Africa

Jeff and Barbara Singerman
"The Point of No Return" monument
Benin, Africa, 2006

Benin, Africa, 2006

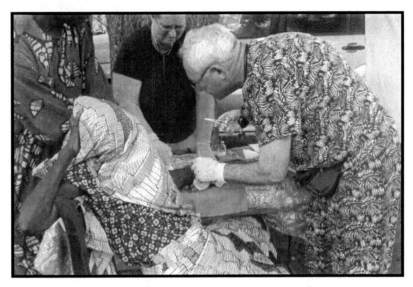

Dr. Bailey doing minor surgery out in village
Benin, Africa, 2006

Chapter 3

South China
Opening Doors
2006

While preparing all the final steps of getting ready for south Benin, I received the following email:

> Subject: Urgent: China Medical Team Needs Doc
> Date: 7/19/2006
> From: bmdf@coxinet.net (Baptist Medical Dental Fellowship)
> To: wandvlovejesus@aol.com
> Dear BMDF Members,
> We just received this urgent message from our ministry partners at MMR. A medical team headed to South China has had a doctor cancel out. If you feel led to respond to this need, please contact Dan Bevins at MMR (email address and telephone number were included).
> "Urgent Need
> Doctor needed for the team below. The original doctor for the team backed out. The team needs a new one. We would need a commitment by July 24th. If you are interested, please contact Dan Bevins at MMR. Thanks for your consideration:
> Name: South China Clinics
> Type: Village clinics

Date: (date was given)
Location: Rural clinics in South China
Tasks: Any primary care doctors (pediatricians, internists, FPs, OB/Gyn and GPs) to conduct mobile village clinics. Will conduct one clinic per village per day, with possibility over 100 patients each day. Days could be long and strenuous.
Objective: Through these clinics, doors and relationships will be opened in many villages through which the Gospel can flow. It is hoped that many will come to know the Master and a new church will be started in each village, where a clinic is provided.
Note: This is a mountainous area, rich in natural beauty, but poor in almost every other way. Very limited or no medical care is currently available for the people there."

Having always wanted to go to China, I was delighted that the opportunity finally had arisen; I thought about it, prayed about it, and discussed it with Vickie. Vickie is so understanding and such a good wife; she told me it was OK to go. I called Dan and told him I wanted to go, but I would have to try to rearrange my ER schedule. At this time in order to go on mission trips I was still working three to four 12-hour shifts at different hospitals.

After making a few telephone calls, I arranged to have my shifts covered by the emergency-room agencies. I felt jubilant and called Dan and told him all was go.

I had to wait until I returned from Benin to get my visa to China; This required my putting a "rush" on it. I filled out all the applications, sent my fees, and started getting mentally ready for that trip. I volunteered my dental skills, but I was told that an in-country dentist would be accompanying us.

Meanwhile, I did a little research on *www.google.com* and found many interesting facts about China, mainly from the United States Department of State web site:

China's population is now over 1.3 billion. It has 57 recognized people groups with the Han making up 91% of the population. Some 59% of the People's Republic of China are non-religious or atheist. Five main religions exist there: Confucianism, Taoism, Buddhism, Islam, and Christianity. Official records says the country has 15 million Protestants, 5 million Catholics, and 20 million Muslims. Many believe those statistics are under-reported.

Dan told me I had to have another email address as my current one: *wandvlovejesus@aol.com* had a no-no word in it; he said the address was certain to be scrutinized on China's cyberspace network, so I got a new email address at Yahoo.com; soon the field workers in China began e-mailing me. They were helpful in relating the what, when, and where about the logistics of the trip. I was told that we would get specific instructions in Hong Kong at the IHR when we had our orientation session.

Medicines were to be provided in-country; we were told shipping meds there would draw suspicions of what we were doing. However, I also was told that a few items were not available in the part of the country where we were going. I specifically was asked to bring some lice shampoo and solution, so I called Blessings International; they were very kind to work with me to provide the shampoo. Likewise, I also needed some containers into which to put the liquid, so they sent me a rush order of what I requested.

Information was forwarded to me about the enrollees in our team; I found out that the team included people from all over the U.S.; however at that time I knew none of them personally.

Departure day finally arrived. I flew to Memphis, then on to Los Angeles, and from there to Tokyo, and finally to Hong Kong. By then I had met a couple of the other participants; one was a dentist who the year before had been on a similar trip. I bombarded him with questions about what to expect and where we would go.

We were taken to the YMCA Hotel in Kowloon (Hong Kong). The next morning I met more of our group at breakfast; then we were off to the IHR headquarters for a full day of orientation. I met with several of the workers in the area and was introduced to the rest of our team. We found out we would be divided into two teams; one team would be in the west of the province we were assigned to visit; I was on the team going south.

From our orientation we knew the geography, a general picture of the culture of the people groups with whom we would be working, and what to do, say, and basically how to act around them. The session was interesting, especially the description of the food we might be asked to eat. We were told the people considered it a real honor to offer the head of a rooster or even chicken feet to guests to eat. Someone asked how to eat the rooster head; and this was explained somewhat humorously. That information set me to wondering what I really would do if I was handed a rooster head to eat.

We were told we could not use words such as God, Jesus, and heaven, as well as other theological terms that might confuse the people. We were warned against public evangelism; we were told this only could be done in private—like in their homes into which we were invited. We were reminded our purpose was to open doors and build bridges. The people in areas where we workers were assigned were described as friendly and very receptive to the good will of medical, dental, hygiene, and nutritional assistance, but we were forbidden at this time to do what many of us were really trained to do: witness to the redemptive power of God through Jesus Christ. However, we knew that in some parts of China open evangelism is permitted; regrettably this was not where we were going. Many hope that one day evangelism will be openly welcomed throughout China.

South China

Two of the doctors assigned to the other team were a husband and wife duo. They brought their 1-year-old son with them. They were a reminder that if one has a strong-enough desire, one can do whatever one wants. I believe their ambitions in the near future were to become full-time missionaries.

That night we ate at one of the better Chinese restaurants (Panda Hotel); we were shown the style of how we would be eating soon and with what tools—also known as chopsticks. Then we rode the MTR (Mass Transit Railway) to the Hong Kong harbor to see the laser-light show. The harbor at night with all the skyscrapers surrounding it was pretty enough, but when the laser show began, the scene was just magnificent. The lasers were shot from one side of the bay to the other in a concert of light and color.

The next morning our entire group then flew on a Chinese airline to one of the larger cities in south China. As explained, we had to be careful not to name people, locations, dates, etc., to protect the workers there. We were met at the airport by our leaders and workers; the other team went west and we went south by bus.

We met our interpreters and workers; we found bonding into a team easy and that we could work together easily all week. We drove on a large highway equivalent to an interstate. Along the way, we saw beautiful countryside. We were in the foothills of one of the larger ranges of mountains anywhere. Initially, we saw thousands of hothouses used to grow food in the cool weather; we were reminded that it takes a lot of food for a nation as densely populated as China. Further on, we found the mountainsides were adorned with terraces of rice fields, corn fields, and other crops; the varying shades of green and yellow made an astounding panorama. We gradually found the roads more winding as we got deeper into the mountain range. Often, the corn fields seemed to be at a 20- to 30-degree angle up the mountainside; I wondered how the farmers walked on those plots—much less cultivated and harvested them. Frequently, you could see workers out in the fields, but little of their work was for harvesting, as it was not harvest time yet.

Finally, we got to the capital of the province, where we were to work; it seemed fairly modern. Our hotel was nice and comfortable; we would go out from there daily to our work sites. The next day we prepared for our clinics by getting the medicines ready. We also listened to our coordinators as they gave us their policies and procedures. It was a good time to get to know our missionaries and the workers as well as what to expect from them.

At lunch and supper we had some real Chinese cuisine; I found it much better than I had expected. Two team members from Texas said they were there to discover what overseas missions was really like; they told me we presumed this trip would be temporary and only an adventure. However, they soon committed to a long-term lifestyle there sponsored by their home church.

The next morning we loaded up and headed for the mountains further south, where we were to work for the day. The people we saw were said to be the least-reached people of any in the whole area. After going up a steep, one-lane road, then up a winding mountain road I could see why people said this. For almost two hours, the bus climbed to an area above some of the clouds revealing the grandeur of the mountain terrain. As I looked down from the bus window, I could see several hundred feet straight down (at the time it looked like 2000 feet at one time). I grew weary holding on to the back of the bus seat grip—as if I thought by holding tight I was holding the whole bus on the road. I finally had to quit looking straight down, but the view was just as scenic and magnificent though still a little scary.

Soon we arrived near the village, but we had to approach it on foot. As we walked to the old school building, which was to be our clinic site, we could see all the houses on the mountainside forming a rather large village. They seemed almost isolated from the rest of the world. People in the village stared at us as we passed by; they clearly were taking in the strangers in their mist. Meanwhile we marveled at all the new sites we had never encountered. The children particularly were intrigued by our presence; we were an unusual sight and occurrence to them. A crowd was gathering at the clinic site. We quickly put up our equipment to start; we offered medical, dental, and nutritional clinics.

As we started the clinic, many people entered wearing their customary clothing which seemed very unique to me at the time; the people seemed to be wearing their very best. The mountain air was cool, so the people were dressed accordingly. The people were friendly and courteous but two of our big husky Americans, who towered over the people, had to stand at the doorway for crowd control or else we workers would have been mobbed. Children always peeking in the windows seemed unusual, but they reflected the general curiosity about what was occurring. Dr. Oliver and I covered all the medical needs while our in-country dentist did the dental clinic. I saw him using a pressure cooker to sterilize his instruments. This gave me the idea to do that on my next mission trip when I did the dental work. Our nutritionist had her work cut out; the food supply this high in the mountains was limited.

At lunch, we ate some real Chinese home cooking, much of which I had never seen before—but nevertheless was quite tasty. However, I can say I did not eat all the cuisine that was offered. I was careful to drink only the bottled water we had brought with us.

I was happy I got to choose my food like at a buffet rather than to be handed a plate and expected to eat all of it.

A local Chinese camera crew arrived to film the clinic activity; this was novel to most of the people there. The news clip was shown that night on a Chinese TV station. I missed it because I only watched the local English-language British TV station. A local hospital sponsored our clinic and had alerted the TV crew to our presence.

At this location we saw the usual health problems we see anywhere else, except for a few more nutritional problems than normal and a few exotic cases unique to the area. We would occasionally see people with bruise marks all over their abdomen or extremity. I asked what these represented and was told that a local health person would pinch the area(s) of the body to relieve the pain they were having. This caused a lot of bruising or ecchymotic areas on the painful part. (This was in comparison to all the cutting and marking of body parts I had seen in several parts of Africa.)

The following day we went over to the next mountain range to see more of the same people group. We arrived at a grammar school that was in session. We were openly welcomed there. For our use two relatively large rooms had been emptied. Again, we saw a variety of complaints and illnesses. The people were very appreciative and openly expressed their gratitude for our treatments and meds. During the lunch hour we mingled with several of the children who seemed fascinated by our presence. They loved for us to take their pictures with a digital camera and show them the images. At lunch we got to partake of more of the local cuisine.

I would have liked to evangelize like I do most everywhere else I go in the world, but I had to accept that we really helped build relationships that will one day lead to pointing others to Christ.

The next day our group went to a different mountainous area to another of the least-reached people in the area. We made provisions to stay up there overnight because the drive to our hotel in the city was about three to four hours. We traveled miles and miles into a range of mountains until we finally came to a city which seemed somewhat remote to me. I was amazed at some of the homemade vehicles they had built for transportation and local use; some were made from large tillers or small tractors into a vehicle like a truck.

On the way, further into the village, we passed a large common pool of water that was supplied by a mountain stream; some of the

South China

women were washing their vegetables or cleaning fresh-killed chicken that soon would be cooked. We were led to a local hospital, where we were allowed to use two of the hospital rooms for our clinic that day. Dr. Oliver at lunch the previous day had eaten some fried curdled beef blood and by mid-morning on this day became quite ill with nausea and generalized weakness. So I had to double up with the patients we saw that day. A large crowd arrived all day, but we managed to see most of the people that wanted to be seen.

That night we were invited to a town meeting, where the people put on a folk festival for us. Their costumes were the classical attire of their people group. Their music and dance were very unique and entertaining. At the event we were placed front and center like special guests or royalty. We were made to feel welcome; after their performances, they insisted we go on stage and dance with them. I felt like an elephant in a tulip bed.

By the end of the celebration, I was about to freeze because I was wearing just my scrub suit. By the time the festival was over, the cool mountain air and gentle breeze chilled me to the bone. I was happy that our hotel was next door. I went to bed as soon so as I could get in the room, cover up, and get warm.

The next morning we ate a breakfast of noodles and hot tea at a local restaurant. The dentist that lived in-country told us we could eat three meals a day in rural China for less than $2 per day. Then we proceeded on to the next village to hold clinic all day. This was with a different group of people with their own identity and location; this was another of the least-reached people. Again, the crowd was so happy to see us; we tried to provide what dental, medical and nutritional advice we could. The work load of seeing a large number was difficult, but the people's appreciation and gratitude more than made up for the overload. When we arrived that morning the streets were empty. Soon after starting the clinic in one of the local school's rooms, we saw a large number of people. One of the school teachers there dealt with the crowd for us. We again saw a lot of the routine complaints that people have most everywhere in the world. Only occasionally would we see some exotic disease or problem.

Once again, we had lunch with the people. I asked why the chicken was cut up so differently. It was explained to me that when there were only a few guests, they cut the chicken in larger portions; but when the crowd was larger the chicken was cut into much smaller pieces in order to serve more people. More rice was offered to fill in the difference.

When we went left the school building, we were practically mobbed by the children; they found us to be such oddities. Whereas on arrival we found the streets empty, now on leaving the scene was quite different. A large crowd followed us to our van like our leader was a pied piper.

Along the path, I saw two men threshing rice. I went to take a picture of them. They insisted I thresh some rice so I could have my picture taken doing work like them. Indeed, the people were cordial and very receptive to our group.

Further along the way I saw a woman on two small roller boards getting around the best she could; I was told she had fractured a hip years before and never walked again. Her feet were extremely small from the long-term compression to keep them small—an old Chinese custom that is mostly extinct. Then we headed back to the city for a hot shower and rest.

On the last day of work we went to the local Women and Children's Hospital that was sponsoring our trip there. We went into a facility that resembled hospitals in the U.S. in the 1950s. The nurses and doctors were neatly dressed in their white uniforms; several had on white masks for their protection against respiratory problems. There we saw employees of the hospital and their relatives. One unusual event occurred when one of the hospital patients came in with an I.V. going to be seen for what he considered a second opinion of his condition. Otherwise, we saw several mundane conditions and complaints, but we always gave multiple vitamins, pain meds, or meds as indicated for the problem(s).

Next we were taken to a local facility for lunch and were honored to have several of the big local political authorities arrive and meet with us; they wanted to show their appreciation for our team's efforts. We tried to acknowledge our gratitude for the privilege to serve the local Chinese people. They tried to westernize the meal as much as they could by having such things as real French fries and fried onion rings. As another form of their appreciation a woman sang for us in almost perfect English.

We packed up that night for the ride back to the main southern city, but on the way our transmission went out and we had to call in another bus. I was extremely grateful that didn't happen way up on the mountainside, where we had been going all week.

We all met at the very modern hotel and went to a Kentucky Fried Chicken restaurant for supper. The next morning we got to shop locally and found a host of souvenirs to buy, but it was really more interesting people watching and seeing all the arts and crafts that were available.

The next day we flew back to Hong Kong. We were debriefed the following day. Our debriefers were extremely pleased with all our efforts to build lasting relationships that one day will lead to open evangelism and a real spiritual awakening in that great country.

I sincerely thank Medical Missions Response for inviting me and all the people I worked with in China. The volunteers I worked with bonded quickly and hopefully will be lifelong friends.

Once again let me repeat that I have been deliberately vague and restricted a lot of my descriptions (names, places, dates, and locations) as I do not want to jeopardize any of the workers or coordinators still working there.

At one of the local schools
South China, 2006

South China countryside

Chapter 4

Philippines
2007

Our first trip to the Philippines started when Bro. Chad Grayson arrived at my home in June 2004 to stay while looking for a home in Bossier City. He had been chosen as our new pastor of Airline Baptist Church. While Chad stayed with us, we got into the discussion of medical missions. Chad told me about a missionary pastor he knew in Pampanga, Philippines. He suggested that I should email the pastor and set up a mission trip to go there. Not long after Chad gave me Alan Guevarra's card, I emailed him. In a few days, I received an email from Alan replying that any time would be a good time to visit.

In order to give my readers a better idea of who Pastor Alan J. Guevarra really is, I asked him to email me a personal testimony so I could put it in this chapter. I received the following email from Alan on October 23, 2007:

> I am missionary Alan J. Guevarra, a former Catholic, born and raised here in the Philippines. I grew up in a large family of 7, with 4 sisters and 2 brothers. I was the third among the eldest. I was about to graduate in Bachelor of Science in Civil Engineering when a classmate of mine shared to me the Gospel of salvation. At first I felt awkward because I thought this was a foreign religion being introduced in the country (because most Filipinos

are Catholics). But as I continually heard the Gospel being preached, as the scripture says, "Faith cometh by hearing and hearing by the word of God", God's word kept pondering my heart and I came to realize that I was lost and I needed Christ as my Lord and Savior. Bro. Ernesto told me that Jesus loves me and he died on the cross to pay the penalty of my sins; that day August 26, 1988, I opened my heart and accepted Christ as my Lord and personal Savior. It was then that I realized the true meaning of life and the value of a precious soul.

I started attending a local church (Hurst Missionary Baptist Church), where Bro. Ernesto was a member. It was a mission work supported by American churches. For five years I attended the church and supported our pastor by handling home Bible studies and as a youth leader. Then, I became as assistant pastor and became actively involved in soul winning. In 1993 when God called me to enter the Bible School and become a missionary, I was still a freshman when I started a mission work in Guagua, Pampanga. With 7 pioneer members in a garage, we started our first Sunday worship service. In the afternoon, we would go to the plaza for soul winning. For almost a year, the number of those attending grew to 80. Then we moved from Guagua to Lubao. A property was donated by an American missionary to put up the church building. After 3 years, I graduated from the Bible School with a Bachelor of Theology. The ministry kept on growing and the church was able to put up two daughter churches. In 1998 I married Sis. Elnora Sendito. In 1999 I went on my first trip to the U.S. for deputation so that I could start a new mission work. For six months I was not able to raise my needed support; that's why I came back by the year

2000. By then I was ready to start a new mission, together with Bro. Ernesto's family. We started a worship service in their home with 11 people. Again, soul winning and home Bible studies were important. For almost two years we stayed in Bro. Ernesto's home for Sunday service. Even though the house was full of people, we could not afford to rent a temporary place of worship. With much prayer and faith in God, I went back to the U.S. to raise money needed for the property. (This was the time I met Bro. Chad Grayson at Lincoln Road Baptist Church.) Now, this mission is already a church, with almost 100 baptized members; our goal is to reach 300 in attendance. We also now have one daughter church under Pastor Zandro Tayco (Gospel Light Baptist Church).

Our ultimate desire is to do the will of God. We want to see souls getting saved and families being changed through the Gospel. We covet your prayers and continual support. Thanks for all the help of American churches and especially to the Airline Baptist Church.

Bro. Alan Guevarra
Faith Baptist Church

To more fully understand what I am saying here, please refer to my first book: *You Will Never Run Out of Jesus*. We made our first trip to the Philippines in February 2005. Our second trip there occurred in February 2006. On that trip Alan wanted us to go to Coron in the Palawan group of islands (southwest of Manila), but we were scheduled to dedicate the Airline Baptist Church of the Philippines with Rolly's church in Samal, Bataan, so we came back to work in the Pampanga region again.

Bro. Chad was too involved in church work in a growing church and was still going to seminary in 2006 and in 2007, so Bro. Harrell

Shelton, our associate pastor, made the trip with us in 2006 and again in 2007. Likewise, Rev. Scotty Teague from Chester, AR, was returning for the second straight year. Moreover, I had with me other Airline Baptist members: my wife, Vickie, Glen and Kay Carter, and Heather Frederick. (To show once again that one can go on a mission trip if one really wants to, let me tell you about Heather. She weaned her son from breast feeding at age 11 months and left him with her husband and mother-in-law while she went on this trip.) For a diverse team I invited Dr. Bud Young from Murfreesboro, TN, Robbie and Ashley Webb, and Justina Rivera from Antioch, TN. Brenda Woody from Gaineville, FL, had joined our team as requested from a previous trip I had made to Benin, Africa. My regular team member and pharmacist friend from Mabank, TX, Don Salyer, had joined us again. Although five states were represented, we all met in Detroit, MI, and flew together to Manila, where Alan met us at the airport. We drove from Manila to San Fernando, where we lodged at the Filipino Hotel.

After getting only a couple hours of sleep, we met in the cafeteria of the hotel to have breakfast and then proceeded to go by and see the new addition to the Faith Baptist Church. Airline Baptist Church had donated several hundred dollars, but Jeff Lowe donated several thousand dollars to make the addition a reality. The church had expanded the sides and had a new roof. Alan and his family were now living in the rear section of the church building in private quarters. (This was the custom of many of the churches in that area—to have the pastor and family live in the church building.)

Then we proceeded on toward our first work site. Along the way, we could see the rice fields which were in various stages of maturity. Occasionally, we could see a water buffalo and a few cattle out in the distance. The warm tropical day was beginning to heat up rapidly.

Philippines

We continued on to the Lighthouse Bible Baptist Church in Palihan, Bataan, and worked with Pastor Rowel Serano. All the members of the team took up stations in the church, but it was HOT compared to southern U.S. weather (it had to be in the '90s and very humid); however, Glen and I went outside of the church under a tree, where it was much cooler to set up our dental station. The team members inside about wilted; there was just no air circulation. Brenda and Ashley did the triage (sign-in area). Harrell and Scotty held the spiritual station; Harrell frequently used "Grandpa", the puppet, to get the attention of the people in the station. Vickie, Justina, and Heather did the eye station; many of the people came out with "new" glasses and a smile on their faces.

Dr. Bud Young and Robbie did the medical stations while Don and Kay managed the pharmacy. The group saw the usual complaints and diseases, but the people (church members and others invited to the clinic) were very appreciative and happy for our coming and caring. The intent of the clinic was to reward the members of the church with free treatment, meds, glasses, and dental extractions, but also to attract others to come to the church and have the Gospel message given to them at the spiritual station. Many accepted the Gospel when the message with the Evangecube was given. Many claimed to have accepted Jesus as Savior. These people would be followed up by the ministers later after we left. From these, many hopefully would become new members of that church.

On Thursday, February 22, we went to the Little River Baptist Church area in Masantol, Pampanga, to work with Pastor Jun Robies. We worked on the second floor of the building in a large spacious room. The word that we were going to be there had spread; crowds were flooding the triage area downstairs and we had to limit the number to be seen, but we tried to see everyone that came.

Glen had helped me the previous year and watched very closely. When allowed to start extracting teeth, he was very precise and correctly approached the technique to anesthetize and pull teeth. I must say he is a quick learner.

At lunch time, we placed our instruments off the tables and a feast was set before us. Barbecued chicken and rice were our main meal, but the fresh bananas and pineapple were very tasty.

By the end of the day, we had seen many people and the spiritual station was very productive of new Christians. The church should really expand with the new believers.

On Friday, February 23, we went to Mt. Vernon Baptist Church in Mexico, Pampanga, and worked with Pastor Marvin Edrosolam. This was a fairly new facility but still in the process of welcoming new members. Again the folks here really loved "Grandpa" and Harrell's talent at entertaining the group. Large numbers again occupied our time. Many eyeglasses were given out. We did a couple of minor surgeries; Glen and I both extracted teeth. The pharmacy was kept busy with all the patients coming through. The spiritual station again was both busy and successful at its task.

On Saturday, February 24, we went to Faith Baptist Church in Lubao, Pampanga, where Alan is pastor and lives. We had a relatively light crowd that day to treat and minister to. Rolly showed up to see if we were coming to his church to dedicate it as the Airline Baptist Church of the Philippines. By this time, Alan had told me that he and Rolly had split (in more ways than one; they were no longer sharing the same house and they considered Rolly an outsider, mainly over the use or demand of the money we had sent to expand the churches from our visit the previous year). When Rolly showed up, without an invitation from Alan, at his (home) church, sparks could almost be seen to fly.

(In my opinion there is no worse situation than when the church fights among itself.) After discussing this situation further with Alan later, Harrell and I decided it was not right to support something that was not done correctly.

We finished early that day, so we got to go get some much-needed rest; I think the heat, fast pace of the work, and the potential church rivalry was getting to every one.

On Sunday, February 25, we went back to the Faith Baptist Church, where Harrell and Scotty both got to preach and teach. The messages were very inspiring. The singing from the church membership was just outstanding. We on the medical team were presented plaques of appreciation for our efforts. I gave Alan a copy of my first book: *You Will Never Run Out of Jesus*. It was in the Philippines that I was inspired to tell Chad that statement one day when we were busy seeing patients in 2005.

On Monday, February 26, we went to work with the Freedom Baptist Mission Church people at Santa Rita to work with Pastor Rio Dematawaran; they did not have a building yet, so we worked, with permission, at the large Catholic church nearby. We worked out under the side of the church under the roofed area. Glen and I had an air-conditioned room for dental extraction. Harrell and Scotty got do the spiritual station inside the large church. They got to preach and give the Gospel with the Evangecube inside the auditorium. That was probably a first for both ministers. We all had a good day and an excellent lunch made by the church members.

In all the clinics, the people were so happy to see us and were very appreciative of the free medical, dental, and eyeglasses clinic care. In all, we saw about 1,300 people and provided much free medications, free eyeglasses (prescription and reading), and did many teeth extractions. One patient had four tumors cut off her forehead and lip. Most important of all at the spiritual station 646 accepted JESUS as SAVIOR.

On Tuesday, February 27, we went to Subic Bay and drove through the military base to the Zoobic Safari Zoo. There we had close encounters with tigers and many other kinds of animals. It was a very nice outing for the group.

On Wednesday, we drove back to Manila and went to the Asia Mall (the largest in all of Asia)—it was huge and still being built. It is a very westernized mall with up-to-date electronics, fashionable clothes, etc. We returned to the hotel to get a little sleep/rest before getting up at midnight to go back to Manila to catch the 6:45 a.m. flight back to the U.S.

Alan and his staff plus all the different pastors and assistants were so very helpful and attentive for all our needs for the clinics and touring. We owe more than appreciation to Alan and the group as they bent over backwards to be helpful.

The following year we planned to go to Coron, an island southwest of Luzon and work there with some new mission churches.

It is with deep appreciation to all 12 team members that I dedicate this trip to the glory and praise of Jesus Christ, our Lord and Savior.

Philippines, 2007

Rev. Scotty Teague presenting gospel with evangelists
Philippines, 2007

Chapter 5

Rwanda
The Land of Reconciliation
April 2007

In August 2006 former IMB missionary John Crocker called and talked with me about missions. He was busy as mission director at Whitesburg Baptist Church in Huntsville, AL. He wanted to know if I could join his group in April 2007 to go to Rwanda (central Africa) and Ukraine (formerly part of the USSR). I told him that I would try to make plans to go on each of the trips.

John made an exploratory trip in November 2006 to check out the possibilities in Rwanda and set things up with Kelly and Laura Sager, IMB missionaries there for several years. I was offered the chance to go on that visit, but had to decline as I had a lot of ER work scheduled. By November 2006, I was already getting the monthly newsletter from the Sagers called: Chronicles of Kigali. I could see from the newsletter that they had six children.

In late November John Crocker called and briefed me on the exploratory trip he had taken to Rwanda over nearly a week. He was full of excitement and anxious to proceed with plans to get things ready for our trip.

Soon I emailed the Sagers and introduced myself as one of the April team members. This was their first medical team that had come to Kigali. A deposit on the trip was made, then full payment proceeded as well as a request for my medical license and diploma copies. I was made aware that one of the doctors in Huntsville had

Rwanda

dropped out, so I was encouraged to invite another. Not long afterwards I had secured an internal medicine doctor from Natchitoches, Dr. Lori Rodriquez. She was thrilled about going to Africa. She had been to Africa at a younger age and had always wanted to be a missionary.

Then I was asked to contact Dr. Jeff Brassert, a pediatrician from Huntsville, who was the other doctor going. I called him and we discussed the medicines and supplies we would be using.

Meanwhile, I took my team to our annual Philippines trip in February; this was our third year to work with missionary pastor Alan Guevarra.

When I returned from the Philippines, I concentrated on the Rwanda trip. I gathered medicines and supplies I had left over and shipped them to Huntsville for the team to take. I would be unable to take all these supplies with just my one extra suitcase.

Knowing I did not have enough meds and supplies, I ordered more meds from Blessings International.

On April 13 Lori left from Alexandria, LA, and I left from Shreveport; the Huntsville team left going to Washington, DC, and we all were to meet in Brussels, Belgium. I met the Huntsville group in Brussels, but Lori was in another building and we could not leave our security section to go see her. Meanwhile, we found out that Brussels Airways was on strike secondary to the luggage personnel holding a strike, and we would not be able to get to Kigali via that airline. We were forced to seek another avenue. We found out that the only other airline going that way was Ethiopia Airlines. We had to reroute our luggage also and they wanted to charge us over $2,200 for that. Anyway, it was not long before we found our group heading for Addis Ababa in Ethiopia. We had a four-hour delay there, but it was interesting seeing all the people go by. There were obvious Muslims everywhere, but the distinct Ethiopian look was predominant.

Finally, we made it to Kigali overnight, but none of our luggage made it. (My dental chair came in the day we finished clinics, and my suitcase of clothes made it on the plane that we were leaving on one hour after its arrival, so I finally got my suitcase in Shreveport two weeks later.) Meanwhile, Lori had made it on Brussels Airways with all her suitcases. We went straight to the mission house in Kigali, where we were to stay all week.

Shortly after arrival, we all went to church to share services with the Africa New Life Ministries that Charles Mugisha Bureqeva had organized. Rev. Bureqeva had organized a tremendous ministry in hopes that the ongoing reconciliation in Rwanda will progress. He has started on the Dream Center, where church services and ministries to orphan boys and girls can take place.

Although Rwanda is a tropical country, its high elevation makes the climate temperate. The weather in Kigali was nice; it was about 4,500 feet above sea level, but only a few degrees south of the equator. During the time we were there, the temperature was 70 to 75 during the day and about 60 at night. The Baptist mission house had no air conditioners and fans were not often used, but for the most part it was comfortable.

According to *Wikipedia*, Rwanda is a land-locked small country in east-central Africa. It is home to approximately nine million people. Rwanda supports the densest population engaged in subsistence agriculture. A verdant country of fertile and hilly terrain, the small republic bears the title: "Land of a Thousand Hills." The country has garnered international attention most markedly for the infamous Rwandan Genocide of 1994. Rwanda's countryside is covered by grasslands and small farms extending over rolling hills, with rugged mountains that extend southeast from a chain of volcanoes in the northwest. Kigali, the capital, is built on seven hills.

Jerry and Cindy Prouty were there as missionaries to run the mission house and make things run smoothly. They said more and more people are coming to Rwanda, notably members from the Saddleback Church in Orange County, CA, recently.

The next day, after arrival, we were taken out to the Dream Home site. Three buildings have made their appearance on a large plot of land that can easily hold a large complex of buildings. Many street boys and girls come there up to two days a week for a good meal and exposure to the Gospel. We were entertained by a tumbling exercise group of boys that was quite an awesome site to watch.

Since my medical and dental tools did not come in, the medical team left for the Poly-Fam Clinic to hold clinic while I stayed at the Dream Center to present the Gospel to some of the boys. I witnessed to two groups of boys using the Evangecube and had 51 boys raise their hands when asked if they would like to accept Jesus as Savior.

I then went to help the medical team at the Poly-Fam Clinic, where Dr. Immaculate was so gracious to let us use several rooms in her clinic for three days. The medical team was swamped with patients. Dr. Ken Moultrie, optometrist, saw patients in great numbers; he was a "living machine" with his rapid sequence of seeing patients—but the eyeglasses had not come in yet on the airlines. (He ended up seeing as many patients as all three doctors in the medical clinic.) We saw many different maladies, including the universal complaints of pain in the back, neck, or all over, minor trauma, etc. We had to keep buying meds, as our meds had not arrived.

On the second day of clinic, I first went to the church and got to do more evangelism with the Evangecube before returning to the clinic to help the other doctors. At the clinic we did not have a spiritual station set up to evangelize to all the people there. We worked three days in the Poly-Fam Clinic while the evangelical team proceeded to go to schools, soccer fields, open markets, and other places to set up a site for direct evangelism. John said the people were very responsive to the Gospel at these sites; many were said to have accepted Jesus as Savior. Kelly and John had stopped one day to buy six new soccer balls as this was an excellent way to attract a crowd quickly.

During the last two working days we went to Kayonza, a city about 2½ hours drive east of Kigali. Along the way, we got to see a lot of the land of 1,000 hills; the lush green rolling hills were occasionally interrupted by a small village. A couple of the members of our group just had to stop and take pictures of the sign that said: KABOUGA. Several people were busy out in the fields working or traveling along the highway on bicycle or by walking, but no one seemed to be in a big rush.

On arriving in Kayonza, we proceeded to the African New Life Orphanage: the Rwandans realize that the children are the future of their country and they are desperately reaching out to them. A lot of these orphans are due to the genocide that took place in 1994 when the world seemed to turn its back on the situation. The people at the orphanage asked if we could do dental work, but I had to reply that my equipment had not come in.

Then the medical team went up the road approximately one mile to the Makavange Clinic, where we saw patients for two days. Again, we had not arranged to have a spiritual station, so I volunteered to go to the waiting room and present the Gospel with the Evangecube. I did not realize that the waiting room was for women scheduled to have an OB-GYN consultation, but I presented the Gospel any way and seven raised their hands to accept Jesus as Savior. The pastor then continued to be my interpreter and we went up to the big crowd in front, under the passageway roof, as it was raining there; we had 20 accept Jesus accept as Savior. We were well received by the people and they were very friendly.

We returned to Kigali again reviewing the beautiful countryside, hills, and valleys lush with greenery, trees, crops, and people everywhere.

The medical team got to go to Kelly and Laura Sager's home to visit and have an excellent home-cooked meal. After supper, we had a short concert by Laura and the three older children: Darby and Tegan playing the violin, and Brick the mandolin, while Laura played the guitar. They played three songs for us and we all agreed how talented they were. Then Darby, Brick, and Tegan put on a brilliant performance with spoons in perfect rhythm. What a performance! We also enjoyed the three younger ones by holding them in our laps and loving on them. The evangelical team went later in the week to enjoy the same outing.

During the work week, we saw approximately 1,600 patients; of those 800 were fitted for glasses. For the week, 405 decisions for Jesus as Savior were made. What a week! It was so nice to work with such good people there: the pastors, the interpreters, the clinic people and especially the missionaries: Kelly and Laura Sager.

Dr. Ken Moultrie left the last day to go up to the Volcano National Park to see the gorillas (where the movie *Gorillas in the Mist* was made). He was picked up at the Mission House by the tour guide, taken by jeep to the mountains, and then they trekked for about an hour to get to the location and feeding grounds of the gorillas. Ken said he got to within six feet of a large silverback male without any disturbance of their feeding or normal routines. He said he was sure not to use the flash on his camera when he took pictures. He thoroughly enjoyed the trip. I knew about the gorilla tours from exploring the Internet, but did not know anyone on our team was going—or I would have gone for sure.

Meanwhile, Lori was back at the orphanage for the second time; she had found an 18-month-old native Rwandan boy which she just fell in love with. She started making arrangements to adopt him and possibly a similar-age female. Some of the other folks went to the local market to shop. I chose to rest at the Mission House and found myself talking at length with Jerry Prouty about the 1994 genocide and the main thrust of the reconciliation. Please see the appendix for more details. Jerry said Rwanda was using the term "reconciliation" as a thrust to get people who had left the country to come back, a means to attract industry and investments, and to get past the stigma of the genocide.

John and Kelly had a full week evangelizing at the markets, schools, orphanages, and soccer fields or wherever they could draw a crowd. They had excellent results. John was so pleased with our results that he was already making plans to return.

Then the long trip back home occurred, but this time there was no strike in Brussels. It was a great trip and I encourage you to go sometime. The blessings will come from your work.

Thanks to John Crocker and the Whitesburg Baptist mission group, it was a memorable experience.

You will be interested to know that Dr. Lori Rodriquez went home and convinced her family that adopting the young Rwandan boy and possibly the young girl was the thing to do. The family loved the idea and months on months of paper work followed. Finally in April 2008, Lori, her husband (Dr. Brett Rodriquez), and two oldest children flew to Rwanda to pick up Kevin, who was now 2½ years old. More hassle followed and several days were necessary to finalize the adoption; the deal with the little girl had fallen through. The Rwandans wanted the Rodriquez family to stay in Rwanda to take care of Kevin, but they finally convinced them that they had to come back to the U.S. Now all are home with the young Rwandan boy who is extraordinarily full of energy. I know for a fact that he is a very lucky young man to have found a family that will finally give him the love and attention he will need.

Missionaries Kelly and Laura Sager and their children
Rwanda, 2007

Drs. Bailey, Rodriguez, and Brassert,
pharmacists and national doctor

Chapter 6

Ukraine
July 2007

Shortly after returning from the Rwanda trip in April, I got busy getting ready for my next trip to the Ukraine in July 2007. This trip also was with John Crocker and the Whitesburg Baptist Church, but with a different medical team. John's brother-in-law, Dr. Ron Collins, was going (he and I worked together in north Benin in 2005) and John's brother, Dr. Mark Pullig, was our real dentist.

I had always wanted to go to the USSR (Russia); Ukraine now was a separate nation west of Russia after the division in 1991. (The Ukrainians do not like to be called Russians.)

John asked me to recruit more members for our medical team, so I called Don Salyer, my faithful pharmacist friend from Mabank, TX, who said he would like to go; he just had to arrange to take two weeks off work. Then I asked Devin Jenkins, R.N., who works in the emergency room at De Soto Regional Health System, and he agreed to go. Meanwhile, Holley Furrow, whom I met at a Gideon supper one night when I was invited to give a talk on personal witnessing, had called and wanted to go on a foreign mission. The trip to Rwanda was too soon when she called, but she stated that she would like to go to Ukraine. Holly is a physical therapist at Shriners' Hospital in Shreveport, LA, where she specializes as a motion analysis lab physical therapist. Neither Devin nor Holley had been on a foreign mission trip before. Also, I recruited Rev. Scotty Teague in

Ukraine

Chester, AR, to be our minister in the spiritual station in the medical clinic. We did not have any ministers in the medical clinic in Rwanda and missed a lot of evangelical opportunities. Scotty is a retired New York street evangelist; he worked on the streets of New York for over 26 years.

After we got the prospective prices for tickets to Ukraine and back, Devin looked it up on *www.hotwire.com* on the Internet, procured our tickets, and saved us a few hundred dollars each.

Ukraine is a country in east Europe; it borders Russia on the west. It is north of the Black Sea and Sea of Azou. It became a separate nation in 1991 when the USSR (Soviet Union) split. According to the World Factbook (Central Intelligence Agency), Ukraine has a temperate climate, the terrain mostly consists of fertile plains and plateaus, but there are mountains in the west (the Carpathians) and in the extreme south. It has a population of 46 million people; 67 percent of the nation speak Ukrainian and 24 percent speak Russian.

Our group went to work with IMB missionaries Brad and Melissa Atkins; they had been in Ukraine for about 5 years. Melissa later told me that they had become quite busy bringing in evangelical and medical teams on a regular basis. The Atkins live outside the capital, Kiev. We were to work in a small town named Tetariv which is about 80 miles northwest of Kiev.

Different flights brought us all to Kiev by late Saturday evening; my group of four missed our flight in Paris. Our group did not get our luggage (familiar story as of recently). We had all packed a couple of days of work clothes in our carry-on just for instances like this. We met Melissa and Brad just outside the baggage room, then the medical team headed for Tetariv and the evangelical team to Kiev.

After loading what luggage that came in, Melissa had us get in the van; we crossed a good portion of Kiev viewing the ubiquitous apartment buildings and several very modern buildings including large churches like those built by the Seventh Day Adventists, Catholics, etc. Melissa said most of the young people from the area lived in these apartments as the city was the only place they could find work. We stopped for bottled water and Ukranian currency prior to leaving the big city which was getting heavy with traffic in the afternoon.

It was not too long before we got out of the city headed for Tetariv. I asked Melissa to tell me about their job and goals as IMB missionaries to Ukraine. First Melissa told me how she became fascinated with Ukraine. While still a student, Melissa came on a mission trip to Ukraine for a couple of weeks about 10 years earlier and she fell in love with the people and the country. She made a vow to return there one day—and to live there for a long time. Meanwhile she and Brad married and had started a family when Brad was offered a trip to Ukraine; he at first refused, but after encouragement from Melissa, he said they would pray about it. The Lord did impress on Brad that this was the place and time for them. They ended up applying and being sent to Ukraine over five years ago at the time of our mission trip. They still love the people and the country and strive very hard to make it a better place through the Gospel.

Finally we were definitely in the country; multiple pastures could be seen on the flat and occasional gentle rolling hills; only a few of these had cattle, mostly Holstein. The frequent sections of forest were adorned mostly with pine trees; a lot of these had lighter bark on the mid trunk. (Brad later told me that most all the trees were like that.)There was minimal traffic the further we got from Kiev. Soon we arrived at Tetariv, a town that looked like the U.S. in the 1950s, but frozen in time. There seemed to be little, if any, new houses or construction.

We were taken to the Baptist church, where Rev. Alexander is pastor; we were greeted with smiles and handshakes. The people present seemed very happy to see us.

Adjacent to this was the new but not completed church; it was going to be a very beautiful building when finished. We met several of our interpreters for the coming week; one was assigned to each group as we were divided up and sent to members' homes for our dwelling at night. Our group consisted of Don (pharmacist), Devin (nurse), Eugene Shatolov (our Ukranian interpreter) and me.

We traveled about two miles from the church seeing mostly old homes, many in disrepair. Most families had privacy fences and fruit trees were in just about every yard. Many of the apple trees were laden with nearly ripe fruit. We came to the home we were to stay in and found it on a small river, a branch of the Tetariv River. We were greeted by the man and wife of the home and they escorted us to their living room, where two couches were present; fortunately Don and I readily chose the queen-size one, leaving Devin and Eugene with one slightly larger than a single bed. The weather was slightly cool outside, but inside it was stale as Ukrainians do not like a draft in the house. We had plenty of windows, but the only one that was not stuck down solidly was a 6 inch by 8 inch open window. The owners had grandchildren staying with them and all of us were to share a small bathroom without a lavatory; but it did have a flushable commode and bathtub with hot running water.

We got to talk a lot with Eugene, our Ukranian interpreter for the week. We found out that he had been married for almost a year and lived in Kiev. He and his wife were teaching and taking courses at the university at the same time. Eugene was almost shy, but very polite and friendly. We all bonded rather quickly—a good thing since Devin and Eugene had to sleep together at night on that small sofa for a week.

The next morning was Sunday and we all met at the church for a delightful breakfast. We were to meet here daily for breakfast at 8 a.m., lunch, and then supper at 7 p.m. The ladies at the church went to great efforts to fix us a great meal three times a day. After breakfast, we had church there. Scotty gave a delightful sermon demonstrating some of his talents on keeping your attention, yet giving a great lesson in the Gospel. Then one of the other pastors followed with another sermon. By this time it was lunch, and the ladies put on another feast for us. After eating, we got to tour the new facility which is nearly complete except the last finishing work like dry walling, etc. At present, the project has stopped due to a lack of funds. It is going to be nice when completed, hopefully in the near future.

That afternoon we got all the meds and equipment ready for the clinic the next morning. By that time, Brad brought the rest of our suitcases that had come on the next flight from Paris. Shortly after that, we had Sunday night services at the church.

Monday morning our medical team was split into two groups; our team was taken to a local medical clinic to work; it was a medium-sized old house used as a medical clinic. They were gracious enough to let us borrow their facility. We saw many patients, mostly older citizens in their '60s to '80s with chronic complaints of joint and muscle pains from having to work hard all their lives. The people were happy to see us and graciously accepted our free meds. Scotty was outside on the walkway sharing the Gospel with the folks as they came in. Most of the people belong to the Orthodox Church and were not always receptive to our Gospel presentation. However, several prayed to accept Jesus as Savior.

Tuesday morning we returned to the same clinic but had no patients initially, so a group of us went out into the neighborhood and recruited several people to come to the clinic for free evaluation, treatment, and medicines. When we returned to the clinic we had

Ukraine

been evicted; the group said they needed the clinic for immunizations, etc. To me it was just professional jealousy—just another form of spiritual warfare. So we loaded up and went back to work at the church where the other team with Dr. Ron Collins (anesthesiologist from Huntsville) and Dr. Mark Pullig (dentist from Huntsville) were busily occupied seeing patients. We went over to the new church building and set up shop. Before long we were quite busy also.

Wednesday we went out to a nearby village, Raska, and worked in a church facility. We saw several people from there and the surrounding area. Scotty remained busy every day evangelizing; frequently he used the Evangecube, did some of his "street tricks", or just plain preached the Gospel through an interpreter. The people were very attentive and several accepted Jesus as Savior.

That afternoon, on the way home, we stopped by the Raska Memorial and graveyard to view the memorial dedicated to 700 people of Raska who had been lined up and shot during World War II by the German soldiers because they had resisted the Nazis so fervently; men, women, and children were all slaughtered and buried in a common grave. Only 18 families survived the ordeal. A very nice and appropriate golden statue of a child and a monument commemorated the event.

Thursday our group went to another village and set up our clinic in a theater, but a nurse also sees patients there during the week. According to that nurse we ended up seeing almost everyone in the village (90 out of 100 who live there). A twelve year old boy needed a circumcision for marked phimosis, so Rabbi Bailey did "his thing" in one of the exam rooms. After everyone had been seen, we had three house calls on some of the infirm elderly who could not leave home. It was delightful to be accepted so well; our visits were so well received. We got to view first hand some of the old homes and no open windows again. The temperature inside was surely above

59

90 degrees F. (the temperature outside in the sun was nearly 105 degrees F.) and the folks were dressed in 2 or 3 layers of clothing. We saw the colorful old blankets on the beds and pictures of soldiers and people during the World War II period; one of the older men was a captain in the army defusing bombs and artillery—he must have been very good at it. Friday we worked again at the church, while a few more house calls were made. Devin went with a small group to attend a lady who had been burned with hot water when a vengeful neighbor threw hot water on her lap. They went twice to check on the lady. All the people were so appreciative.

Friday afternoon Melissa and our group went to check on the young man on whom I did the circumcision. Initially, we went into the wrong house, where I was greeted by an intoxicated woman who immediately "fell in love with me", according to those accompanying me. She started hugging me and trying to kiss me and then pulled me by the arm wanting me to come in the house and dance with her. Eugene told me that we should leave now; this was emphasized by Melissa, so we left and went next door to where we were supposed to go. The young man was doing well and his wound was healing nicely.

Later that evening, we were also able to minister to a Gypsy village. One of the elder women there wanted to read our palms. We were able to tell her we already know our future with the King of Kings.

Through all this, we were still able to see over 400 patients and had many accept Jesus as Savior, after the Gospel had been presented to them.

We returned to the church for a late lunch, shared gifts, and went to our host homes to pick up our belongings. Then we said goodbye to our interpreters and host pastors before heading back to Kiev for the next two nights. This time we got to stay in a very nice hotel.

Ukraine

Saturday the whole group went downtown to the tourist souvenir area only to be greeted by a monsoon downpour for about 45 minutes; there were no drainage gutters and the street turned into a small raging river. We had to stay in the van, which was pulled up on the sidewalk, for several minutes after the rain stopped to wait for the water to abate. Then we got to go souvenir shopping. Along the way, you could see at least three large Orthodox churches in all their grandeur; they were very ornate and classical in their appearance with gold domes and steeples. At the nearest church to us, there was picture taking of a new bride and groom; Melissa told us that was just for pictures as the couple was most likely married elsewhere. Further down the street, more bride and groom pictures were also being taken.

Along the souvenir area, the street was crowded with vendor stands and many souvenirs typical of Ukraine. I ended up buying a Russian fur hat and Matrouska doll that had 20 pieces. Further down the street, there were a variety of paintings, some quite pretty and ready for purchasing. Scotty bought one. I could have purchased a few more things, but there has to be a limit. We all loaded up in the van and went for a big pizza lunch.

Then we headed for the World War II Memorial Park; two miles before arriving there we were greeted by the Monument of the Motherland Statue which is in the Pechers'ky Landshaftny Park. As we entered the park, one of the most significant statues was that of an Ukranian or Jew falling after having been shot by the Nazi; a symbol of the country of Ukraine was at the base of the hill showing that the country was being laid by siege. Many statues, old artillery, tanks, etc. lined the pathway to the main museum. Along the way were huge murals of scenes typical of World War II cast in bronze. Over the museum was the Monument of the Motherland; it was 203.4 feet tall and weighs 450 tons. It is a memorial to the Great

Patriotic War (World War II) given by Russia to Ukraine in appreciation for its support in World War II.

We entered the museum only 45 minutes before it closed, but we got to briefly tour the entire three floors of a well put-together "homemade" museum of the relics of the war with a unique story to match. One statute, at the front of the museum, was very significant: a Ukranian soldier standing over the broken Nazi symbol and eagle. Throughout the museum, it was very evident that the Ukrainians had suffered much, but they had risen and overcome, and finally drove the Nazis back to Germany.

We returned to the hotel for a night of rest before rising at 3 a.m. to leave for the airport at 4 a.m. It was a long way home. We were late getting from Paris to Atlanta, so we missed our flight to Shreveport; finally I got on the way four hours later on the second round of standby flights.

A separate report of the evangelistic team can be obtained from one of their team members. It was a very satisfying trip; I really appreciate the invitation by John Crocker, the excellent guidance by Melissa and Brad Atkins, our medical team members from Whitesburg Baptist Church, our host church, our host homes, our interpreters, and those I invited on the trip.

Ukraine

In front of Tetariv Baptist Church
Ukraine, 2007

Devin Jenkins, R.N.; Holly Furrow, physical theraptist;
and Don Salyer, RPh
Ukraine, 2007

Chapter 7

Cambodia
2007

This trip to Cambodia was our third; it would have been our fourth, but in 2006 Trish and Tony Pitaniello had their fourth child by C-section the week we were initially scheduled to go on our medical mission trip to work with them. The result was a beautiful baby girl (Adelaide) who was a year old during this visit; this complements the two boys (Nathan and Josh) and a girl (Isabella) they already have. Tony had asked me to hold the group to 12 because of the logistics and difficulty getting good interpreters.

Some of the group had been to Cambodia before with me, but new recruits were certainly welcomed. Five members from Airline Baptist Church in Bossier City, LA, went along with three members from First Baptist Church in Bossier City, three members from First Baptist Church in Mabank, TX, along with Dr. David McLaughlin from Bozeman, MT, (he had gone with our group in 2005).

On the Dragon Airlines from Hong Kong to Phnom Penh we had some authentic Cambodian food; believe me, it was some of the best airplane food I had ever had the opportunity to eat.

Tony and Trish, IMB missionaries, had been in Cambodia over nine years ministering to the Western Cham people. Tony has had several groups come to work with him in the villages, and he has started having large surgical teams come to work in Phnom Penh.

It is such a long journey there, but we arrived November 11 after 30-plus hours of flying. It was so nice to see Tony waiting in the airport for us; we had to get visas as soon as we got off the airplane. We all walked down the main building to find that all our luggage and supplies had made it. Because of Tony, we had no problem getting through customs. Sending the manifest of meds and supplies lists ahead of time and having Tony pre-approve them with customs was such a blessing. We headed for the Asia Hotel, where we were to stay the next 5½ days; it is in the middle of the capital, Phnom Penh.

Phnom Penh is a city of approximately 1.3 million people now; the population had been up to nearly 2 million before the Killing Fields in the mid-1970s. In the 1920's, Phnom Penh was known as the "Pearl of Asia". It was a significant global and domestic tourist destination for Cambodia. It is still influenced by traditional Khmer and French architecture.

The next morning as I went outside the hotel, I could see and hear the sounds of a big city. Like I was doing, Kevin and Glen were snapping photos. Outside the front door were the typical beggars: one a lady with a child on her back asking for money for food and then a man on crutches with one leg missing asking for money. Tony had asked us not to give alms. It was cool early that morning as we loaded our trunks of meds and supplies on the vans to head out to clinic.

Tony chose the village of Svaay Prey for us to minister; it is 60 kilometers north of the Phnom Penh. It is the home village of Abass, Tony's first convert and right-hand man now. As we went through the heavy traffic of Phnom Penh, we gradually traveled out into the country, where lush green rice fields, coconut and palm trees, banana groves, and the typical homes were seen. All too often, we saw Buddhist and Islamic temples; some of these were very pretty.

Finally we got off the main road and drove a few more kilometers to Svaay Prey. Tony had rented two adjacent houses for us to hold our clinic. The owners of the homes and other people immediately tried to make us feel welcome. Tony decided to place all the practitioners in one house and the pharmacy and spiritual station in the other. The lower floor of the second house was used for a gathering area for the clinics as well as a spot to repeatedly show the Jesus film via VCR for people waiting to be seen.

Jackie DePrang and nurses Kevin and Rosemary Andrews worked in triage while Dr. McLaughlin and Glen Carter, R.N. saw medical patients; I alternated between seeing medical patients and extracting teeth. Libby Horton and Lorene Salyer worked in the eye station, where many pairs of prescription and reading glasses were given out. Meanwhile, in the other house the pharmacy crew of Don Salyer and Kaye Carter worked along with Tony's pharmacist, Jessica, from his clinic site in Phnom Penh. Rev. Sonny De Prang and Robert Finley worked with Abass and others in the spiritual station. Each station had an individual interpreter; they were very helpful in work as well as translating.

The weather was quite pleasant at night and in the morning, but as the day progressed, it grew warmer and warmer. This was the dry season in Cambodia. It did not rain the entire week we were there. We were fortunate to have electric fans at our work stations; they were necessary to remain comfortable in the mid-afternoon.

The first day I saw a young boy about 6 years old with a very swollen face from an abscessed tooth. I proceeded to anesthetize and extract the two teeth involved. He was very cooperative in allowing proper anesthesia with a local block; I am sure he had been hurting for several days. He gave me a thumbs up sign when I was finished; this was not prompted and the event just made my week. He was given an antibiotic injection that morning and asked to return the next morning for repeat exam and more I.M. antibiotics. By the next morning, the swelling had gone down 60 percent.

The people were so grateful and gave us their hands-together-and-bowing symbol frequently. Some of the people were fairly ill; we treated them as best we could. Also several surgical cases were found; these were referred to the surgical clinic that Tony was having in January in Phnom Penh. One lady had a squamous cell carcinoma on her scalp that was the size of a thick plate. (A couple of months later I received a picture, showing where this lady had this large neoplasm removed in the surgical clinic that Tony held in Phnom Penh.)

Libby and Lorene kept busy the entire time at the eye glass station. This is the first time that Tony has had an eye station to offer to the public there. Most everyone wanted to have their eyes checked; it turned out to be our most visited station. Some people went for medical treatment, eye exam, dental extraction, free meds and then to the spiritual station.

In years past, we had a very large number of people stating that they wanted to receive Jesus as Savior. This year was a little different; Tony requested that our team ministers, Sonny and Robert, give the Gospel summary and salvation message, but they did not ask for any immediate decisions. Abass and an evangelical team would follow up in a week or so and request those who had been asked to pray about becoming Christians to do so then. Tony has found this is a better technique as so many that initially said they accepted salvation were later found to have a different opinion.

One day at noon, Kevin, Dr. McLaughlin and I walked down the road viewing all the interesting sites. Tony had told us the houses were on stilts mainly to keep livestock out of them and also to prevent flooding during the monsoon season. There were several small shops where you could purchase fruit or food. Down a secondary road we saw homes in the dense of the forest, but out in the yards of two, women were spreading out rice to dry in the sun. We could see bamboo shooting up toward the sky, some reaching to 50 to 60 feet tall. The folks did not mind us wandering past their yards; it would have been nice to converse lingually instead of just with a smile.

One afternoon in the eye glass station I saw a Buddhist monk getting fitted for glasses; he even went through the spiritual station, but no one could read his mind as to what he really thought.

By the second day, with word out that we were having big crowds at the medical clinic site, multiple vendors put out their food items for sale. I could recognize some of the fruit such as jack fruit and bananas (some were fried at the site), but I didn't know what the others were.

Marshall Clay worked with us a couple of days; he is Trish's dad. Marshall just could not understand why his daughter would want to come to a foreign place like Cambodia when she had all the comforts of home in the U.S.; but, after the last two visits he has gotten the vision and purpose of Tony and Trish's work and approves now. He likes missions now and wants to go to Africa with me some day.

Kevin brought two new soccer balls to give to the children; you should have seen their delight when they were given the new balls. All week they had been playing with an old, partially deflated ball. Kevin just had to be an ambassador of good will.

All the people appreciated the medical, dental, eye exams, glasses, and medicines so much, even the Islam chief. He said that the only thing that was wrong was that it was not held in the Islamic temple nearby. Tony told him that would not happen; Christians get the credit for these efforts, not the Muslims.

Riding back to our hotel that day Tony told us that Christians are slowly taking over the nation; when the need was so great during the period of the killing fields, who helped? Not the Buddhists nor the Muslims but the Christians. Now the people are learning who to turn to. The monks go, but beg from the poor; the Muslims are of no help, but the Christians are there to really care for the people's needs. Tony said he may not have built a lot of churches, but a network of Christians has become so strong among the Cham people to whom he is ministering that it will prevail.

Each night was an adventure; Tony took us to different restaurants to dine. One night we went to the mall to have pizza; there we found out it was his birthday—again; each time we went to Cambodia, it was always the week of his birthday.

It was a great week to have worked with Tony again. We saw 533 patients in four working days. Then on Friday he took us shopping in the Russian market for some real bargains. We got to see Tony and Trish's children again—and oh, my, how they have grown in two years plus the addition of another daughter; they are beautiful children.

Dragon Airlines cut into our time working for five full days; we had to leave Phnom Penh a day early because of their new flight schedule. We were to have a 25-hour layover in Hong Kong, so I took full advantage of this. First, I emailed some missionaries I know in the Hong Kong area and asked them to meet us at the Panda Hotel, where the airline housed us with vouchers for meals also. Second, through the magic of the Internet and a little research, I arranged a tour of the Hong Kong area for the day prior to flying back home.

Nancy and Don Mock were to take us down to the harbor to see the laser show, but due to a long and frustrating event of checking into the hotel, we missed the laser show. However, we got to eat at the Panda Hotel buffet; then, we got on the MTR and rode down to the harbor anyway. Nancy and Don showed us a few other highlights in the area. On the way back to the hotel, Kevin and Robert asked to be dropped off at the night market.

The next morning we were met at our hotel lobby by the Asia Tour people. We got to see a lot of the highlights of the bay area. We were driven through the main streets of Kowloon, the convention center on the harbor, and to the oldest temple in Hong Kong: the Man Mo Temple. It was very ornate but filled with thick smoke from many incense sticks burning. I asked Irene, our tour guide, to what religion she belonged; she said she had none or no preference. I told her we needed to talk; I planned on showing her my Evangecube and sharing its message with her. We then proceeded to Victoria Peak (we rode the electrical trolley up to the top), but the harbor was so overcast with smog we could hardly see the water or harbor from the peak. We continued to Repulse Bay and the Stanley Market, where we got to shop for 30 minutes. Then we went on to the Aberdeen fishing village and then to a jewelry factory. I tried to get Kevin to buy his girlfriend a wedding ring. (Ha!) We got back to the hotel in time to have a late lunch at the buffet. Once there, I took Irene aside and showed her the message of the Evangecube. She said she was intrigued about the message, but she kept changing the subject; at least she was told the message. I invited her to read the Holy Bible. We all ate a good lunch; then Irene made sure we made the shuttle so we could make it back to the airport in time for the long journey home.

I had a great team and appreciated all their efforts and cooperation. I appreciate the work and efforts Tony and Trish are making with the Cham and Cambodian people. It was a super trip. I thank all those who went and worked, those who helped prepare or contributed to the effort, and those who supported us with their prayers.

Cambodia

Tony and Trish Pitaneillo and their four children
Cambodia, 2007

Lorene Salyer and Libby Horton
Eyeglasses station

On the Go for the Lord

Dr. David McLaughlin from Boozeman, Montana

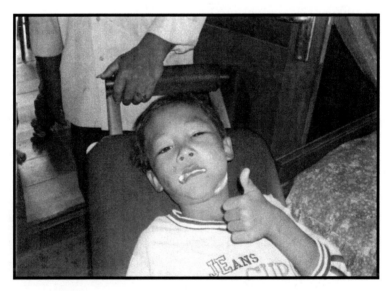

It's thumbs up after an abcessed tooth was extracted

Cambodia

The awaiting crowd in Saavay Prey

Chapter 8

Burkina Faso
Shattering Darkness
2008

Shattering Darkness, an organization founded by missionary Lynn Kennedy, Rev. Jamie Arnette, and others, sent out an invitation to help on a series of mission trips in January and early February 2008. Lynn, who lives and works in Burkina Faso, has worked diligently with a team of volunteers, prayer warriors, churches, and a very faithful team of Dagara people to get the dream to come true—all from a passion for the lost and a passion for His people. First Baptist Church of Orlando, FL, partners with Shattering Darkness and has been a very influential help; so has the First Baptist Church of Dillon, SC. These are only two of the many churches that partner with Shattering Darkness; together they have made a real difference that could not be done by a single church.

The purpose of Shattering Darkness is to reach the unreached; train, equip, and disciple the people and workers so they can do it on their own. The ultimate goal is to glorify and praise God's name.

I had made the trip in January 2004 and worked with Jamie (now president of Shattering Darkness); Paulette Holt, R.N. from McLeod, TX., had gone with me on the initial trip and had returned the next four years. She wanted me to go in early January when she went with the first wave of volunteers, but I had other obligations, so I made the next group. When Paulette returned she gave me a glowing report of how the organization had grown

Burkina Faso

through much hard work and prayer. Lynn has a network of national pastors, church planters, evangelists, and children's workers who have helped the churches there really grow.

By not checking the airport for up-to-date reports, I missed the fact that Delta had changed its flight schedule, so I missed my flight the first day when I was headed to Burkina Faso. I was fortunate and did not have to pay a penalty for flight-date changes. I traveled through Atlanta to JFK Airport in New York and on to Casablanca, Morocco. Because of my 13-hour layover in Casablanca, Air Morocco gave me vouchers for a hotel and food until the flight later that day.

On the way downtown to the hotel, Mohammed, the bus driver, offered anyone who wanted to have a tour of Casablanca to be in the lobby at 2 p.m. The two others that said they wanted to go did not show up, so I decided to go alone with Mohammed in his van and got a private tour. After seeing a couple of routine things, he pointed out the 210-foot new Islamic temple; this is an emblem of their religion; he seemed very proud of it. We drove close by and he offered to take me inside. I decided not to go inside (dummy me!). It was a beautiful building. He then drove me by the Mediterranean seashore and the popular resort area. He had me walk by the seashore to get a closer look. Not all was very pretty as he pointed out several slum areas in the distance. However, he then drove me through one of the nice residential areas and by a nearby office complexes.

I'm sure you will guess where I went next; he took me to the family-owned souvenir shop. I was escorted around the shop and saw many nice gifts, but I was most impressed with their leather goods, especially the purses—so I bought Vickie, my wife, a very nice one.

It was both a long and short night; I went to the airport about 8 p.m. to leave at 11 p.m. for Ouagadougou. I stayed up reading during the four-hour flight. When I arrived at the Ouagadougou airport at 3:30 a.m., I was so happy to see Jamie and Patrice Hien (Director of Ministry and Missions for Shattering Darkness); they were there to pick up several suitcases and trunks that arrived late and to pick up me, too. Then we drove five hours on to Diebougou (Lynn's home and headquarters), then on to Naro. At Naro (where we were to work Monday through Thursday) we attended church services; I was so sleepy and tired I don't remember all the details. But what I do remember was a real nice Sunday morning service in Dagara style.

Sunday, after church, I got to meet all the team members. Most were from the Dillon, SC, area. We had a break after lunch and most of the team members went to the *marchee* (open market); a couple of the women bought some material to make clothes when they returned home. Then the medical team got together and prepared the meds and supplies for the next day.

The weather on my first trip to Burkina Faso was warm to hot; the temperature would go up to 105 degrees F. during the afternoon. On the first day this trip was so nice; the temperature was about 75 degrees F. That night I was assigned a slot out on the screened porch to sleep; about 3 a.m. I awoke and thought I was going to freeze. The gentle constant breeze and the 59 degree F. temperature made me chilled to the bone. I got up and put on my coat, but to little avail. The next night I put a blanket and sleeping bag by my bed to cover myself.

For the next four days, we drove about 1½ hours to Naro to hold the medical clinic; this was the place we had church Sunday. Every morning after a crowd had gathered one of our team members would give a brief sermon; then the people would sing and dance in rhythm with their drums. During the session one of our team members would give his or her testimony; then more singing and dancing occurred until we were ready for clinic to start.

The millet stalk building (church) served its function well enough; it remained cool during the afternoon as most of the sunlight was filtered out, but the occasional breeze was helpful for a cooling effect. We had no tables, just benches on which to work. I claimed to really have a "low overhead office" (cost) as I had to put my dental tools as well as my supplies in trays on the ground, but we made out just fine.

The medical problems were significant though; for those that had any symptoms of malaria, we tested them with a malaria kit (it required one drop of the patient's blood). We found that at least 40 percent were positive for malaria. We never lacked for skin problems (open sores). One station was basically set up just to treat these problems; Tammy Allen and Gina McAllister did a great job all week in the wound-care clinic. Tami Wood (IMB missionary living in Bobo, Burkina Faso) and Jennifer Poston worked in triage. Linda Miller and Preston Moore worked in the pharmacy; Terri Holliday did the eye station; Mickey Fore and John Henry Williams prayed for individual patients before and after the clinic visits; Dr. Tim Fitzgibbon and I did the medical work. I offered dental extractions, but these people don't eat much refined sugars, etc., so few have dental cavities despite the lack of dental hygiene. I did end up pulling several teeth during the week, however. The team worked well together and was getting very proficient by the end of the week.

On Friday, we went to V-1. This is a territory divided into 10 districts by a large Project (VARENA) that had bought the land. We were in section 1. Just before we got there, I told Tami (the driver of our vehicle) that we were out in the middle of nowhere, miles from anything. She said, "It is not quite the end of the world, but you can see the end from there." Tami told us that the government had given these people 10 acres of land if they would come out and grow cotton for at least 10 years. At one point, I saw two large vats of picked cotton, the only cash crop these folks had; the rest was for food to subsist on. The whole territory was dusty and arid; dust was ubiquitous this time of year and the humidity was only about 10 to 20 percent.

On arrival we found another millet-stalk church like the one in Naro. We were welcomed by the people and after a brief period of their dancing and singing for us, we started clinic. Here we tested people with symptoms of malaria and found at least 60 percent positive for it. I wanted to treat everyone for malaria, but by this point we were running short of medicines. Once again the people were most gracious and thankful for our coming their way.

The classic picture of the week was a real sick young lady lying in a folding hammock with a temperature of 104.4 degrees F. One of the nurses was starting an I.V. to run in fluid and antibiotics while Lynn was at the end of the bed with her hand on one leg and the other raised to pray for the patient during treatment. That visual snapshot summarized the effort put forth the week we were there.

For the week we treated about 540 people, more than 400 eyeglasses were given out, more than 2,000 heard the Gospel, and most significant of all: more than 100 accepted Jesus as Savior.

Thursday afternoon we went to the Formation Center; at present it is a church, office, and baptistery, but plans have been made to build dormitories so that trainees will have a place to stay as they are tutored and trained in the Gospel ministry so they can take it back to their villages. Also, housing for Impact Teams from the USA is in the next phase. Buildings for a library and a youth activity building are planned soon to keep the youth out of local bars and "game" rooms. These are built only as they are paid in full before construction begins. The complex is situated atop a flat plain only 200 yards off the main highway and can be easily seen from the road. A recently dug well is out back and very functional; it was thought that it would have to be dug very deep as the complex sits on a hill, but it has a very adequate output at only 48 feet. The local people are encouraged to use the well at present to keep the flow fresh. The baptistery is nearing completion; it is called a "death pool" after the original baptisteries in Egypt right after the death and resurrection of Jesus Christ. The familiar saying that goes with this pool (baptistery) is very similar to that said in my church: "Buried with Him (Jesus) in death, raised to the newness of life."

On the living room walls of Lynn's home are two plaques: one is Matthew 19:26 WITH GOD ALL THINGS ARE POSSIBLE. (KJV) The other is: GOD WILL MAKE A WAY WHEN THERE IS NO WAY (paraphrase of Isaiah 43:19). This summarizes Lynn's life and testimony; see the following paragraphs.

I have been intrigued by Lynn Kennedy's story and testimony, so I got her to agree to give me a personal interview about herself; it took two nights of an hour each. I would like to share what I have written down while listening intently to her.

Lynn Kennedy's husband died when she was 35. The couple had come to a saving knowledge of Jesus Christ when she was 29 and he was 40. They didn't want other people to throw their lives away like they were doing, so they took Evangelism Explosion and started teaching college and career students at church. God continued to touch their hearts and they wanted to do more evangelism.

Lynn's husband Bob had decided to take early retirement, Lynn was to resign her job as well. The Master Plan was to sell their house, purchase a Winnebago and tour the US doing lay witness evangelism. The "For Sale" sign was ready to place in the front yard when they received the devastating news Bob had kidney cancer. In spite of surgery and follow-up, Bob died shortly afterwards. One month after her husband's death she participated in her first short-term mission endeavor, a leadership training effort in the Bahamas in 1985.

Later in 1985, she went to Indonesia; the Bahamas experience had truly convinced her God had called her to go international with evangelism. Not long afterwards she made two trips to Brazil. Then she went to Kenya. Each trip continued to emblazon on her heart the fire and passion for international mission service.

Guatemala soon followed, where God confirmed to Lynn that his call for her was to international missions. So she went to Baptist College of Florida, where she received her undergraduate degree in Religious Education and then to Southwestern Seminary in Fort Worth, finishing in May 1995 with a Masters of Divinity degree.

The whole time Lynn kept saying to herself: "Send me where no one else will go and where no one else has been." At that time, the IMB decided where you go from what requests come from the field. She was appointed to Burkina Faso. She stated that she was just miserable in Ouagadougou. Many missionary families were already there and a lot of them targeted the same group.

Then Lynn prayed: "I am too old. Time is too short. People are too lost. Hell is too real; you've got to send me some place where I will make a difference, and people will be willing to listen about You." Lynn started doing research, the IMB gave her some information, and then another couple gave her a lot of information about the Dagara. Then one day, during her research, she found out that Dagara means "**cross**". When she read that, she knew in her heart: "Lord, they are yours; they just don't know it yet!"

Lynn came to Diebougou not knowing any people or the language. Then her prayer was: "Lord, how are You going to reach 800,000 people (Dagara), 400,000 of them in Burkina Faso, and 400,000 in Ghana? There is no scripture, no radio, and no Jesus film in Dagara. Lord, how are You going to read to these people? They are only oral learners and all of them are village dwellers."

Then the Lord revealed to Lynn: you will need to: 1) have more prayer, 2) produce the Jesus film in Dagara, 3) do radio programs, and 4) use short-term impact teams (volunteer medical missions)

Now, after 2½ years the Jesus film is in Dagara, radio programs are in four countries reaching over 500,000 people each week; among those are four ethnic groups. Lynn has hosted 40 short-term voluntary medical mission trips, evangelism, church construction, leadership formation and even a marriage retreat. An area wide evangelistic crusade was held in the region of Dissin in November 2007, where 153 decisions for Christ occurred in that first-time-ever Crusade.

Lynn has had a separation from the IMB (International Mission Board of the Southern Baptist Convention). She said this was a similar situation to when Paul and Barnabas plus the team of Silas and John Mark split. They both wanted to plant. They both wanted new believers discipled. They both wanted viable, faithful leadership. However, they did not agree on the best way to accomplish their vision. History shows us that going separate ways did not hurt the work; in fact it expanded the work. Lynn feels the same about her resignation from the IMB. It has not hurt nor diminished evangelical work at all among the unreached groups of Burkina and Ghana.

At this point, Lynn asked herself: "Do I join a group, or form my own?" At that point she contacted a physician who had worked with her there, an attorney, and a pastor from the U.S. They all said to "form your own organization".

Next step: "What will I call the organization?" Immediately the term: SHATTERING DARKNESS came to her because that was what Jesus was doing in the area. During her quiet time the next two days God led her to these scriptures: Isaiah 9:2. *The people that walked in darkness have seen a great light: they that dwell in the land of the shadow of death, upon them hath the light shined.* (KJV)

Acts 26:16-18: *16) But rise, and stand upon thy feet: for I have appeared unto thee for this purpose, to make thee a minister and a witness both of these things which thou hast seen, and of those things in the which I will appear unto thee. 17) Delivering thee from the people, and from the Gentiles, unto whom now I send thee, 18) To open their eyes, and to turn them from darkness to light, and from the power of Satan unto God, that they may receive forgiveness of sins, and inheritance among them which are sanctified by faith that is in me.* (KJV)

Then Lynn contacted an attorney and formed a board of directors and filed for 501-(c)-(3) tax exempt status. In 2004, Jamie Arnette became the director of the board of Shattering Darkness.

Lynn gave me a summary of the organization: SHATTERING DARKNESS

PURPOSES: To reach the unreached. (Paul said he went where no one else had been.)

Train, equip, disciple people and work to teach them to do it on their own.

Glorify and praise God's name.

Shattering Darkness groups do not and will not go where other evangelical groups have already established work.

GOAL: Expansion into other countries and unreached groups.

Lynn asks that you contact or explore the SHATTERING DARKNESS website: www.shatteringdarkness.org.

One of the most significant encounters with the people was told to me that night.

Here is Lynn's brief account: "Here is something that happened about a year after I began the ministry in Diebougou. All the people, besides me, were new believers!!!

"One day I made a drop-off stop in the village of Kpakpara (mostly a Muslim village). A team of new believers and I had spent the day in the "bush" villages teaching the Bible. As I was dropping off the team, one of our believers came running across the road. It was evident he was coming with the news of some sort of emergency! He said we needed to pray. He said that someone in the village was dying. He said that we needed to tell God to heal him so the hard hearts in Kpakpara would know God was real and powerful.

"They grabbed hands (a new practice begun with my arrival). Oh! What a thrill, a band of men, all new in Christ, forming a circle of prayer in public! No shame. No hesitation. NO DOUBT. As they prayed beseeching God to show His power and glory and to heal this one close to death, I was praying, 'Oh God, they are so new in their faith! Please do not let them be discouraged when this person dies! Please don't let them lose their faith.'

"So, imagine my shock, incredulity, and SHAME when the next morning word came that the sick person was not only healed while the prayer team was at his house praying for him, but someone came and said, 'someone in my house is very sick; you must come and pray.' The first sick man rose up and followed the prayer team to the home of the second sick man whom God also healed!

"I went before the Lord and prayed; I asked Him to forgive me. I said, 'Lord, I have walked with YOU for many years. I know Your faithfulness, power, mercy, and grace. Yet it is this band of baby believers—new in faith—that prayed and believed! OH! Here I am back in Faith 101 class praying, 'Father, I believe. Help my unbelief!'"

Saturday we loaded up and went back to Oaugadougou. After a brief lunch we went out to the Artisans Village for souvenirs. That night we went to one of Lynn's friend's church that has hotel-type rooms and had a brief shower. Afterwards we went to a local restaurant for a very good meal and then to the airport for the long journey home. I sure found it better traveling with a group on the way back.

I highly commend the SHATTERING DARKNESS organization. It is doing a great job at reaching out to where other evangelicals don't go. Their goal is to reach other countries and unreached groups. Please log onto the www.shatteringdarkness.org site and explore what it is all about. And for those of you looking for a trustworthy ministry for financial contributions making an impact on lostness reaping incredible "eternal returns", I highly recommend Shattering Darkness.

Burkina Faso

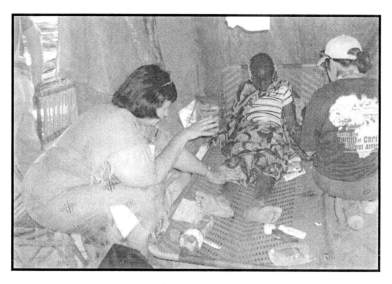

Missionary Lynn Kennedy praying for patient with high fever
Burkina Faso, 2008

Our thank you for holding the clinic in Burkina Faso, 2008

Chapter 9

Not Just an Average Day in the E.R.
February 2008

> Go ye therefore and make disciples.
> Matthew 18:19

In mid-February 2008 while I was still working in the E.R., I had a day that I will remember for a long time. Although that day was quite busy, it turned out to be very rewarding in more ways than one.

I was down the hall from the nursing station in a room examining a patient when I heard my name called frantically. I responded quickly and went to the cardiac room, where I saw a relatively young woman (age 52) in a serious predicament. She was pale, diaphoretic (sweating profusely), and looked gravely ill. The ECG (electrocardiogram) monitor revealed a huge ST segment elevation which meant an acute myocardial infarct (heart attack); her pulse was varying from 42 to 50; no P waves were seen. The lady was in complete heart block. Her blood pressure was 50 systolic at best (very low). I immediately ordered Retavase (a clot buster) and had the cardiologist paged.

About the time the cardiologist arrived in approximately 10 minutes, the Retavase had worked and a big emergency prayer had been answered: the clot dissolved sufficiently and her heart began to function much better; her blood pressure went up to 110/60, (normal) and she was out of complete heart block. Her pulse was up in the '80s. The cardiologist said we were lucky; she could have died any minute just prior to that; the cardiologist said her circumflex artery had been blocked but that she had responded to the Retavase. The lady continued to improve. She was admitted to the ICU for monitoring. Two of the nurses insisted I give them a "high five", but I really wanted to say that the event was an answered prayer.

I also offered another prayer that day, "Lord, please give me an opportunity to tell someone about You today." On that day I was seeing a 20-year-old woman about a recent onset of chest pain. During her history I picked up that she was studying journalism to become an author. I couldn't help but mention that I was an author and had two books published in the last year. I told her the name of my books and said they were available on Amazon.com. I asked her if she was a Christian. She related that her parents had given her complete religious freedom, and she had not decided to do anything about it so far. By this time she had introduced the person in the room with her as her fiancé. He stated that he was a Pentecostal. I asked him if he had rather marry a Christian (his fiancée accepting Jesus) and he said he would. I went on to say that after her lab and x-ray were complete I could show her how to become a Christian; meanwhile, I went out to my car and got my Evangecube.

At the appropriate time I presented the Gospel using the Evangecube. She accepted and prayed to receive Jesus as Savior. I asked her fiancé if the Pentecostals baptized people after accepting Jesus, and he said they did. I told them she needed to confirm her acceptance of Jesus by publicly acknowledging that and be baptized. Both seemed very happy about the occasion (she because she had accepted Christ and he because he now would be marrying a Christian); then, we had prayer praising Jesus for the decision. I felt like giving Jesus a "high-five" on that one—Praise the Lord for courage to do his Great Commission!

Chapter 10

Just Another Night of Prison Visitation

Our group of four still regularly gathers two or three times a month on various nights to do prison visitation. We go to the Minimum, Medium, or Maximum Security Prison in Bossier Parish rotating the prison site so that we make them all every four to six weeks. We have a tendency to go to the Minimum Security Prison a little more often as the turnover rate there is faster. Occasionally, we make trips in the afternoon when the prison rules allow it.

In the past, there seemed to be a set night we could visit, but with the help of the parish chaplin, the security guards, and the absolute delight of the men there, we are allowed to go more often and at any time visitation is allowed. We are not the only group that goes, but we are usually the most frequent group consistently going.

Another gracious thing also happens: the Gideons are happy to furnish us Gideon Bibles to distribute each time we go. On occasions, we take "used Bibles"—that is, we get some of the minimally marked up or damaged Bibles from hotels and motels and we take off the hard cover and refurbish them with a new soft cover. The Bibles look almost new; I have found that the prisoners are just as happy to have one of these as one of the brand new Gideon Bibles because they now have their own personal Bible to read and study. We usually distribute about 75 Bibles each visit.

Just Another Night of Prison Visitation

At the end of each quarter our Sunday School Department gives us their quarterly learner and adult-guide study books for distribution in the prison. The prisoners are always happy to receive these also. I encourage the prisoners to form a group and study the study guides on a regular basis. Also the *Open Windows* and *Daily Bread* that we take are highly sought after by the inmates.

Another serendipity has taken place too; a lady from our church volunteered to do prison ministry when I asked someone to start prison visitation while I was taking my recent F.A.I.T.H. course. She has started the ministry and is asking for help now. I have even had other people giving me Holy Bibles to give to her so she can distribute them when she visits.

One Thursday night I picked up Ron Hauser, Paul Vardeman, and headed to Dan Adams' house; we frequently arrive in time to chat a moment and then we pray that the prison ministry will go well that night. On this occasion we chose to go to the Maximum Security Prison; it had been almost a month since our last visit there. We were cordially greeted by the security guard at the controlled entrance. We showed all the Bibles and Sunday School literature that we had brought in boxes and a suitcase; we even offered the security guard a Bible. Dan and Paul went into the section that was marked minimum security; they usually invite all that will come into the conference room to hear a Christian message. Dan usually has a message prepared; Paul helps with the service by speaking also.

Ron and I headed for the other dorm in that section to hand out Gideon Bibles and proceed to ask if anyone would like to hear and see a demonstration of the Evangecube. Usually I get from one to three to listen. Some nights we are blessed more and get up to a dozen or so to listen to the message of the Evangecube. Ron goes off into one part of the open space in the dorm and I go to the other side. Ron and I handed out over a dozen Bibles; we each had three to accept Jesus as Savior. We emphasize that it is so important to follow up with their home churches, and be baptized, and follow through with their commitment to Jesus.

Ron and I headed to the Medium Security section. Again we gave out more than a dozen new Gideon Bibles; the prisoners are so happy to have their own private copy of God's Word. Again, we separated and presented the Evangecube to several people; more accepted Jesus as Savior. As Ron was walking toward the door to leave, he was approached by one of the men who wanted to talk with him. They sat at one of the tables and shortly more joined in. Within a matter of minutes, 8 more recited the Sinner's Prayer.

We were excited and headed to the Maximum Security portion of the prison. Again we were greeted by prisoners who literally ran to get a copy of the Holy Bible. We handed out almost a dozen more copies of the Gideon Bibles. Again, I showed the Evangecube to anyone interested. Several had already seen the Evangecube presentation from our previous visits. Ron and I both had at least one person to accept Jesus.

Ron likes to just go to one of the empty tables and sit there for a while. Like on other occasions, one of the prisoners brings his friend to the table stating that he needs Jesus as Savior. Ron is most happy to show him the Evangecube and lead him to the Lord in prayer.

Ron and I headed back to the Minimum Security section, where Dan and Paul were still preaching and teaching their lesson. We were fortunate to catch the end as Dan asked how many would now like to accept Jesus as Savior; several hands went up; Dan led them in the Sinner's Prayer. I noticed a couple of tears in the crowd. What a special moment to see the results of their efforts. Then we all had a prayer of thanksgiving for the victories won.

It was another good night; we felt exhilarated and planned to come again the next month to the Maximum Security Prison, but next week we planned to go to the Medium Security Prison across the road to give out Gideon Bibles and tell about Jesus to anyone that will listen.

I was once asked if I had ever been scared or uneasy in the prisons. My answer was, "No" because I have never been intimidated or threatened by anyone there. However, one of the prisoners in Maximum Security once threatened another member of our team stating, "I will cut your throat when I see you out on the street."

Recently while I was getting two chicken dinners at Popeye's Chicken, a young black male hollered at me as I was walking out toward my car. I walked closer to him; he came to shake my hand and asked if I remembered seeing him in the Maximum Security Prison two years earlier. He said I had brought him a Bible and witnessed to him. He further told me he had straightened out his life and he was doing well now. He had his wife and two children in his new truck with him. They all looked happy. That made my day.

Chapter 11

Coron (Philippines)
2008

Rev. Alan Guevarra, missionary pastor from Guagua, Pampanga (Philippines), had been inviting us to go to Coron, Palawan (Islands) for the past two years. His church, Faith Baptist Church of Pampanga, has four mission churches on the northern island of Palawan. Similar to what we have done in the past three years, Alan wanted us to go do medical missions there to help build the church crowd. On our last trip to Pampanga, Alan and I discussed the plans, then for a few months we corresponded via email and set up the trip.

First, that meant getting a team. I seemed to have little problem recruiting people; in fact, the number was limited to 8 because of the logistics of getting people there with adequate supplies. We would have to fly from Manila to Coron on a small plane (16 seater) with a very limited cargo (luggage). I researched, through the Internet, and found out that we would have to pay an "excess baggage" fee for people weighing over 86 kilograms (2.2 pounds per kilogram) and the luggage allowance was only 10 kg. per person. Alan told me he would take care of lodging, food, and the transport of our team on the island.

The first to volunteer was Rev. Harrell Shelton; he had been the last two years. Glen Carter, R.N. wanted to go also; he had been to the Philippines twice with us. I called Rev. Scotty Teague and he

Coron (Philippines)

wanted to go again; he had been the last two years also. My faithful pharmacist, Don Salyer, wanted to go as well as his wife, Lorene. Libby Horton, friend and church member to the Salyers, had been invited. She and Lorene did the eye station in Cambodia in November 2007. Libby said she would get the necessary eyeglasses from the Lion's Club.

My main quest was getting another doctor to go. Dr. Bob Rao had to turn down our invitation to go on our recent Cambodian trip, but he wanted to go again soon. So I even let him set the exact date he could be away from work. We discussed the trip over the phone. When I told him we had toured Hong Kong for a day on the way back from Cambodia, he wanted me to set up a day trip in Tokyo on the way back from Coron. I told Bob that I would take care of getting the meds and supplies.

Gracious companies like Alcon Labs of Fort Worth, TX, and Kingsway Charities of Bristol, VA, giving us free meds and supplies, and companies like Blessings International of Tulsa, OK, selling me meds at bargain prices are such great help in obtaining necessities for our trips. I ordered the meds and supplies for this trip with the knowledge that weight would be a definite factor.

Finally on February 23 our group from Bossier City and Chester, AR, met the Texas group at the DFW airport in Dallas; then we flew through Narita, Japan, to Manila. We made it through customs without a problem. Alan was there at 10:30 p.m. with a van to pick us up. We went to a nearby hotel and had a welcomed rest and sleep prior to going back to the Manila airport the next morning to go to Coron.

Then a problem arose. Despite my securing all the tickets three months earlier the weight issue became significant. We were immediately told we had too much luggage weight and two of our members were much over the limit. (I had told Harrell and Glen to bring a stash of cash for this leg of the trip.) I was sent to the SEAIR Air-

93

lines office and paid a considerable fee for the "excess baggage"; then, I was told that the two larger members would have to wait until the following day. Despite all arguments and pleading, Harrell and Glen had to be <u>left behind</u>!

At least the SEAIR was nice enough to give Harrell and Glen transportation to and from the hotel and give them vouchers for meals until the next day at flight time. While they were staying at the hotel and waiting for the next day they coined the following song: (Sung to the tune of "Leaving on a Jet Plane".

> OUR BAGS WERE PACKED. WE WERE READY TO GO,
> BUT OLD SEAIR SAID, "NO, NO, NO."
> GLEN AND I WERE OH SO SAD WE COULD CRY.
> OLD SEAIR SAID YOU CAN'T GO BECAUSE OF YOUR WEIGHT;
> YOU WILL HAVE TO GO ANOTHER DATE.
> THEY'RE LEAVING ON AN OLD PLANE,
> DON'T KNOW WHEN WE WILL SEE THEM AGAIN
> THEY'RE LEAVING ON AN OLD PLANE,
> DON'T KNOW WHEN WE WILL SEE THEM AGAIN

Meanwhile, the other six headed for Coron on a 70-minute flight. Coron is the scuba-diving capital of the Pacific. Ten Japanese ships sunk during World War II make for an amazing diving experience. As evidenced by the work we saw starting, Coron is in the process of having an international airport built for all the traffic; they have received grants from different organizations. There are several flights to and from Coron daily. When we arrived at the airport, we were welcomed by Pastor Lorwin Libarra and a few others who had a large banner like the previous missions which read:

Coron (Philippines)

WELCOME! AIRLINE BAPTIST MEDICAL MISSION
Headed by DR. BILL BAILEY, REV. SCOTTY TEAGUE, AND PASTOR HARRELL SHELTON.
Feb 25-March 1, '08

We drove on into Coron and had lunch at the very scenic marina; then we went to our hotel to put up our luggage and then back to the bay area. We crossed a large open area which had just been flattened out with soil brought in from elsewhere; a large hotel was going to be built soon to accommodate all the tourists, mostly for the scuba-diving interests. One of Alan's friends, a local pastor, took us on a tour of the multiple small islands about the bay. The water was a beautiful light blue. With the mountainous islands in the background, it made for a picturesque site. We passed many personal-size outriggers with people out fishing and then many larger ones with scuba divers.

Scotty, Alan, Libby, and I just had to go swimming; the water was just right for swimming or for other water sports. Getting a small amount of water in my mouth, I found the water to be very salty. While getting back into the boat, I found the coral bottom a little unfriendly; I scraped the top of my foot.

Alan pointed out a few houses and several people on or about the islands. The government pays these folks to guard the swiftlet nests which are numerous in the rocky crevices all over the many small islands. Once a year the nests are harvested and sold for $500 each. The nests consist almost entirely of the swiftlets' saliva. During the mating season, when the nests are built, the swiftlet's salivary glands hypertrophy and they are capable of making a lot of saliva. Once the saliva is excreted and exposed to the air, it quickly gels and the birds form it into the shape of a nest. The nests are harvested to be sold to the Chinese and Japanese who consider the soup that is made from them a real delicacy and aphrodisiac.

Tuesday morning we went to one of the largest churches in town: the Coron Central Baptist Church, where Pastor Venone Bihag and members greeted us with enthusiasm. Then, the work started. Our team of six saw nearly 300 people by the time Harrell and Glen arrived from Manila to help. I had helped Dr. Rao see medical patients all morning, but after a delicious Filipino lunch, I went to a different area of the church and proceeded to extract teeth for four straight hours; then I went back to help Dr. Rao again. When Harrell and Glen showed up, I readily turned over my medical clinic work to Glen; Scotty was exhausted also. He had presented the Gospel to well over 300 people with the aid of the Evangecube and had great results with many accepting Jesus as Savior.

Wednesday we went to Salvacion Fundamental Baptist Church, where Pastor Ludiunio Cabildo is pastor. We started with only a few patients, but many more showed up soon; the church put on a feast for us at lunch. We had fresh boiled crabs, many types of vegetables, and fruit. The medical team stayed busy all day and Libby showed us she is a <u>one woman army</u>; she was seeing about 90 patients daily for evaluation and glasses fitting. I extracted teeth all day. The people's dental hygiene must be non-existent with all the caries I was seeing.

Thursday we went across the island to Busuanga and went to the New Busuanga Fundamental Baptist Church, where Pastor Lorwin Libarra works. In the back of the present church are concrete pylons which already have been poured in hopes of expanding the building soon. A proposed picture was present in the church auditorium. We worked hard all day to see the seemingly endless lines of people. Even after the daily blackout about 6:30 p.m. that night and every night, we continued to work. (The electrical demand is just too great every evening until about 11 p.m. daily). Dentistry by Braille is a little difficult. Again we had both lunch and supper with the church folks; the food was very good.

Coron (Philippines)

Each day more and more people were seen in the spiritual station, even if they were not seen in the medical, dental, or eye stations; they were made welcome by Harrell and Scotty. The people are so receptive to the Gospel; many raised their hands when asked to accept Jesus as Savior.

That night we went out to a secluded peninsula with the electricity still off in town, but we were welcomed with the purr of a generator on our arrival. The cottages we stayed in were just a delight. We didn't realize it, but the next morning at the crack of dawn we were awakened by the birds chirping and a gentle breeze blowing through the numerous coconut palm trees. As I looked out the window I could see a beautiful lagoon approximately 100 feet from our patio and two outriggers on the sandy shore. I could see Glen out walking along the beach; then Alan and Scotty were returning from a swim in the lagoon. Unable to resist, I got dressed quickly and made a long stroll along the seashore. Only gentle waves made it evident that the tide was going out.

Friday we went several miles down the island to the Bulang Fundamental Baptist Church to work with Pastor Reuben Echagua. Soon the lines filled and seemed endless. With all the people attending the spiritual stations all week, we knew the pastors would have their work cut out for themselves following up on all the people who accepted salvation. The new believers would need to be churched which is why we came to Coron and Busuanga.

During the week, at least 1,175 people were seen as patients at the clinics in four days and 996 accepted Jesus as Savior. It was a phenomenal week.

We only know of the concept of <u>missions</u> like Alan and the pastors participate in daily. They truly follow the first and second Great Commandments. They truly love God with all their hearts and their neighbor as themselves. You would have to be as they are to truly experience the work of the Lord and the grace of His kingdom. We, as a group, were happy to be part of this. The four pastors we worked with are missionaries from Alan's church in Pampanga (Faith Baptist Church); they had worked diligently to grow their churches and we had really given them a big stimulus when they followed up on all of those prospects. TO GOD BE THE GLORY for the results of the week.

Saturday we flew back to Manila without leaving anyone behind! That evening we all went to the Mega Mall in downtown Manila to shop and eat. Early the next morning our group went to the airport to fly to Narita (near Tokyo, Japan) and spend the night.

Early Monday morning the Tokyo City Tours people came to our hotel lobby promptly at 8 a.m. (I had scheduled this 2½ months earlier on the Internet). We were allowed to place our luggage in the back of the bus; they agreed to drop us at the airport, saving us a trip back to the hotel and time and effort catching the shuttle. We headed for Tokyo which was 60 kilometers east along a freeway (much like our interstate highways). As we went, we could see many industrial sites, homes in the distance, and even the Disney World complex.

We crossed Tokyo Bay and soon were swallowed up by a large city. We made our way on to the Tokyo Tower and ascended to the observation tower. Tokyo is a big city (14 million people); you could see only city in all directions on the horizon. Four of us lagged behind the lead group and we were left to find our way down from the tower. I told Harrell, "Don't worry, they will not leave half the group here." Harrell commented, "I don't know; you left two of us behind in Manila."

Then we drove through the main Ginza shopping area on our way to the Imperial Palace; we toured part of the grounds and had our picture taken in front of the palace which is the symbol of Japan.

Coron (Philippines)

From there, we went to the ASAKUSA KANNON TEMPLE area, a famous cultural landmark of Tokyo. We toured almost all of the buildings, then ate lunch, and headed back to Narita straight to the airport to start our journey back home. By date and time, we would get home before we left; you have to remember you gain your day back going east over the International Date Line.

Coron (Palawan Island), Philippines, 2008

Rev. Harrell Shelton with "Grandpa"

Chapter 12

China
2008

When I was there coming home from Cambodia in 2007, project coordinators in Hong Kong invited me to go on the semi-annual medical trip to a chosen area in China. I had earlier emailed a previous coordinator and she referred me to the ones now assigned to her job. I got the email address and through a series of emailing we agreed to meet in the lobby of the Panda Hotel, where my group was staying. We were to go see the harbor lights and laser show at 8:00 p.m., but due to complications checking in we were made late starting out, so we would not get to see the laser show. However, we chose to have supper at the hotel and went by MTR to the harbor area. On the way Nancy and Don showed us several interesting sites. We still got to see the beautiful harbor that night.

A group recruited or invited from several locations in the U.S. (and one who located the event on the Internet from Australia) met in Hong Kong for orientation. We stayed at the YMCA Hotel in Kowloon while in Hong Kong. The morning after arrival we walked down to the office for our day of orientation. The day was quite informative as we were briefed of what to do, what to expect, and what not to do as we prepared to go "in country".

The oral surgeon that had come to Hong Kong then departed for a week of teaching and training at a large city in northeast China. The other seven then flew to a large city in north China.

This trip had been set up with two experienced coordinators, one living there and another in mid-China. We were the pioneer medical team to this city. I found out later we were unannounced; security was tight because of the Olympics coming to that area of China. The coordinators were quite worried initially thinking we might be thrown out of the country by the authorities.

Arrangements had been prepared for us to work in a trade school in the edge of the ghetto in the large city. MK's and PK's were being lodged and trained to enter the job market free of charge to them. They were given a choice of training in English, Korean, Bible, voice, instruments, dental assistant, computer, social skills, and Tae Kwon Do classes to name a few of the things available to them. The students will live at the school for two years and most likely will not go home because their parents are either too far away or are in prison because of religious activities.

We soon found the students to be a delightful group of young people who are all living under less than desirable conditions. They do not have showers and have only squatty potties for toilets. A building had been built for toilet/showers, but it was done incorrectly and now they lack funds to redo or complete it. Unlike children in the U.S. who go home after school and sit in front of the TV, computer, or go to football or cheerleading practice, they would each take their plastic wash bowl and hand wash and wring out their clothes; this was all done on the top of an old donated ping pong table sitting out in the courtyard.

The students had invited their families and house church members to come to the clinic we were to provide. Some traveled long distances as the MK's and PK's were from all over the northern part of China.

We had two doctors, two eyeglass workers, two working in the pharmacy and another R.N. working in the triage and/or pharmacy area. We could not bring medicines into China as we would be suspected of our intentions or activities. So, the first night we had to go to two local pharmacies and buy meds that were available. Fortunately, we could buy anything they had available; it is not prescription bound like in the U.S. We struggled to buy what we could, but made arrangements to buy meds at a pharmaceutical distribution center later. The following day we counted meds and dose packed them while one of our team members and one of the coordinators were out buying more meds.

Our clinic site in the large city was in the edge of a ghetto; the road into the clinic was horrible with deep ruts filled with water and unbelievable trash strewn about. The trade school had been set up not long ago for the MK's and PK's.

The first day at clinic started off slowly, but by the end of the day we were seeing more and more patients. The medical complaints and problems were fairly universal as in many parts of the world, but we certainly saw a few new and unique problems which presented a bit of a challenge. The eyeglass ladies stayed busy almost every day gauging and fitting glasses. One of their unique things was that every pair of glasses looked the same, so no time was wasted picking out a certain type. The people in the pharmacy stayed busy all the time handing out meds. Sonny, who is a preacher, was placed in the pharmacy and counted meds out into dose packets for days. His attitude was great; he said, "If you do it to the least of my children (people), then consider having done it to me." That is flexibility—that is what often is required on mission trips.

I had brought my dental tools but found few cavities, and even some of those did not want these teeth pulled; they wanted them fixed (I don't fix teeth; I only extract them.). I suppose the people have not experienced the western type diet. I found many with the molars ground down from their eating habits, but few caries. I think I extracted five teeth in five days.

The people were so friendly and appreciative. Many got free medical treatment, free meds, advice, reading glasses, but only a few got dental treatment. I learned a few Chinese words so I could relate to the people better, but most often a smile meant so much more. I am foreign-language impaired, and I found the Mandarin very difficult to speak.

We were very limited in doing evangelism. However, the first night a few from our group went out to the trade school and got to witness to the PK's and MK's. A strategy is in place for this and hopefully will be expanded very soon. We were there to build bridges and gain the respect of the people so the Word can openly be used in more places and hopefully soon.

The clinic was different in a way, as many of the patients were already believers, but there had to be some that were not. One day I was complaining to my interpreter (who at the time was one of the coordinators) about not being able to witness to the people. He turned around and asked the lady that had just finished being seen by us if she was a Christian. She said, "No." The coordinator then asked me if I would like to witness to her. Not being bashful or caught off guard, I quickly reached over and got my Evangecube that I almost always carry with me everywhere. Very carefully and with a bit of emphasis I went through the "cube presentation" and asked if she would like to pray to receive our Lord as Savior. She agreed to and did pray the salvation prayer. Naturally, I was elated and so were other people that were in the room. The lead coordinator later stated that he did not think a doctor could lead people to the Lord. I told my interpreter that I wish I could safely do that all day and all week.

Vickie, my wife, has the unique ability to bond with children so easily. I was told by one of the patients that she was giving her daughter (12-years old) to my wife. I was amazed, especially when I looked at the young girl; she was just beautiful and had an ever so gentle temperament. I can not explain the event as well as my wife, so I will use her own words; she personally wrote the next segment.

THE STORY OF LA LING

"My job on this mission trip was to work in the eye clinic. One day a young woman, probably in her late 30s, walked into the eye clinic; and with her, was the most beautiful little Chinese girl I have ever seen. For some odd reason, she and I were just drawn to each other. I told my interpreter to tell her she was beautiful. The mother overheard our conversation and told me, through the interpreter, that I could have her because she had another daughter at home. I looked at her (I'll call her La Ling for safety reasons.) La Ling had a confused expression. I said, "Your mother would be so sad if she didn't have you." La Ling stayed with me all day just watching my every move. By the end of the day, she would wrap her arms around me and hug me. She said, "I hope you will remember me always." I then told her I would never forget her. When she left that day I told her that I loved her. It was so sad thinking she may never become a believer and I would probably never see her again.

"The next day this precious tiny 12-year-old girl, along with her best friend of the same age, caught a bus and traveled all the way across town and came back to the clinic to see me. She ran up to me and the first thing she said in English was, "I love you." I hugged her and said "I love you too." She sang a song for me and did a little Chinese dance. She was so pretty and graceful. I told her that maybe when she was older, she could come to the U.S. and see me. She pointed to herself and made a walking motion with her fingers. I shook my head yes, gave her a big hug, and watched her wave goodbye as she left. I will always remember and pray for little La Ling."

Probably not understanding the full story at the time I told Vickie that she had done it now. The woman was bringing her child with her suitcase the next day at 5 o'clock for Vickie to take her home with us. SHOCK AND AWE!! Vickie did not know to be happy or frightened. She asked me how in the world we were going to get her through the airport.

The coordinator, at my medical station, told me that we would not be able to adopt Chinese children, especially ones that we chose. But Vickie and I would have adopted her in a heartbeat.

The clinics went well. Dr. Rollin and I saw a lot of pathology and had to refer some to a local hospital. One was a case of a young lady with thyrotoxicosis; she was almost to the point of having a thyroid storm. Dr. Rollin encouraged her to go to the hospital immediately. Many left seeing a lot better with glasses. And I know that relationships were enhanced—and that IS a big part of the future strategy to implement evangelism.

One of the children fell outside in the courtyard while playing and cut her ear and peri-auricular area and was bleeding rather profusely. She was brought to me and I stopped immediately to attend the problem. After examination, I anesthetized the area with local anesthesia and proceeded to suture up the wounds. The family was most grateful.

The next day after clinics were over we got to drive through Beijing on the way to the Great Wall. We got to see the Olympic Stadium from the highway, but more construction was being done. We drove through some pretty and mountainous country on the way to the Badaling section of the Great Wall. We paid for our tickets up the lift (like a ski lift) and proceeded up the mountainside to the Great Wall. It was just as grand and magnificent as I had pictured, if not more. It is so hard to picture what things are like sometimes until you really see or experience them. The stones were many centuries old, but the wall looked like it was built only 50 years ago. I'm sure the Great Wall is maintained and repaired regularly to keep it looking authentic. The Great Wall wound around the mountain tops for miles or as far as the human eye can see, and that is only a small segment of the remaining 1500 miles of the wall. The slots in the wall, where the archers would shoot their arrows were spaced all the way down the Great Wall. There were periodic housing every so far down the entire wall.

There were many people there, but it was not so crowded that we could not make our way westward to view a section of the wall. The weather was cool and almost nippy with the breeze blowing. We were glad we wore our coats. We made our way back to the souvenir area and purchased a couple of T-shirts and a model of a segment of the Great Wall. I took a picture of one young Chinese couple; then they wanted me to take a picture of them with their camera. On completion of this, they wanted to invite us to lunch as a gesture of their appreciation.

On the way back through Beijing, we got to go through Beijing and see the modern city and a tremendous amount of landscaping and beatification that was being done. We drove to the center of the city to see the Tiananmen Square and viewed the vast open space there. Although there were many people there, it was quiet and peaceful. It is hard to believe the events of the students protesting in 1989 had actually taken place there. Then we proceeded to walk under the street through a tunnel to the Forbidden City, the home of the former emperor of China. It was the imperial palace during the Ming and Qing dynasties. It is the largest palace complex in the world; if you were to walk through it as we did, you would agree. It covers 74 hectares (about 2 city blocks wide and 12 city blocks long). We were told that the southern section is where the emperor exercised his supreme power over the nation. The northern section or Inner Court is where he lived with the family.

The museum part of the palace complex houses numerous rare treasures and curiosities. Yellow was the symbol of the royal family and is the dominant color in the Forbidden City. We had to pay a fee to see the museum part; fortunately it is open to tourists from home and abroad.

Throughout the complex was much scaffolding for repairs and beautification for when the world would come to see the Olympics.

By the time I had walked through the whole complex and had seen a good portion of it, I had determined I was going to call 911 before I would walk back to the front; it was that big. But what a treat it was to see such a national treasure.

The following day we flew back to Hong Kong. That night we went down to the harbor to see the laser show and harbor lights; it was a magnificent sight and a real treat for those who had never seen it before. The next day we had a debriefing session and went over the events and happenings of the week. And what a week it had been; it was a very memorable time to work with the coordinators, and being with the kind and gracious people of China (they were so appreciative).

Not long after we returned from China, a devastating earthquake of 8.6 magnitude struck Sichuan Province. Many thousands of people lost their lives and the devastated people were dealing with loss of families, homes, farmland, and all that was familiar to them. The psychological impact will continue for years, but at the time, all types of help were being asked to come to China to give aid. I was emailed at least four times in a short period of time asking me, as a surgeon, to obtain a visa to China and come help as soon as I could. Although my heart bled for the people, I could not go at the time as I was scheduled for several shifts in the Emergency Room which I was obligated to fill. How I would have liked to have responded immediately to such need.

China

China, 2008

"La Ling" as drawn by teammate, Deborah

On the Go for the Lord

Vickie and Bill on Great Wall
China, 2008

Chapter 13

Uganda
Faithful Servants
2008

His lord said unto him,
"Well done thy good and faithful servant."
MATTHEW 25:21

From a private interview I scheduled with Tommy and Teresa Harris, I found out much information about their lives, what motivated them to move to Uganda, their work there, and their future dreams for ministry in that country.

The Harrises have been married since 1981. Teresa became a Christian on January 14, 1996; the next week Tommy became a Christian on January 21. Approximately six months after their salvation experiences their pastor asked them to attend a Southern Baptist Associational meeting. At the meeting a man from Uganda spoke about the needs of that country. They went back and told their pastor about what they had heard.

Their pastor was going to Uganda with another man, but the man backed out. Tommy volunteered to go and within three weeks he had gone to the CDC in Atlanta and obtained all his required immunizations. He also had to obtain a passport in three weeks; he even paid $65 to get it expedited. On the day planned for the departure to Uganda, Tommy still did not have his passport, so he said he would just ride along with the group to the airport—all the while knowing he would not be going with them.

Thanks to their Carrollton postmaster Tommy was handed his passport as he walked into the airport. Suddenly he was on his way to Uganda.

Tommy stayed in Jinja the first day, but soon went to Mbale, where he stayed three to four days. He and the team went to several villages in the area; he preached his first sermon on a mountain there. From there, he went to Tororo for two days, then back to Jinja. Tommy's heart was touched by the living conditions of the people, but especially by the condition of the Ugandan children. Tommy was forever impacted by the receptiveness of the people and their accepting the Gospel for salvation. At night, Tommy taught disciple prayer life in the hotel. A lot of young evangelists also attended for training.

At the trip's conclusion Tommy felt a great desire to help the Ugandan people, especially the children. The number of people who accepted Jesus while he was there made a real impact on Tommy. When Tommy returned from the trip and told Teresa, he related a lot about the people, but did not reveal his real desire to help the children.

In June 1997, Teresa traveled to Uganda with a group from New Vision Baptist Church to evangelize door to door, mostly out in the villages near Jinja for two weeks. After her two-week stay there, she felt the desire to help the children and return again.

The Harrises started raising money by having barbecues, etc. so they could go again.

In 1998 and following, the Harrises traveled to Uganda working with medical teams and did door-to-door evangelism in and about Jinja.

In 2001, Tommy and Teresa went to EMT school while still working; this was in preparation for further service.

In 2002, Tommy felt the direct call from God to go to Uganda to stay. He went and discussed this with Teresa. She asked if he was sure. He answered, "Without a doubt!" The next day both went and gave notice of resignation from their jobs so they could go to Uganda. Within two months, they had leased out their home and told the family of their plans. Some said, "You are crazy!" Teresa's mom said, "You need to think about this." However with some of the recent events no one was really shocked.

Late in 2002, the Harrises moved to Uganda for three weeks, but they had little financial support. He was getting only about $300 from churches. They came back to the U.S. and over the next three months started gathering support, initially by child sponsorship. Not long after that they set up a non-profit organization [a 501 (c)(3)]. They had to come up with a name of the organization; so they prayed and read the scriptures for a title. It seemed natural to select Matthew 25:21: *His lord said unto him, 'Well done thy good and faithful servant.'*

Within one month after coming back to Uganda, the Harrises started hosting medical and evangelical teams, usually eight to 10 in a group because of the accommodations and travel. About five to six teams went there each year.

While helping other schools, which were not cooperating, the Harrises thought they should start their own school. The Harrises bought 5½ acres in what was part of an Indian Sugar plant; it was basically just farm land at the time of purchase. The people in Uganda from India as well as thousands of other internationals that had taken up residence in Uganda prior to his regime were run out of the country by Idi Amin when he was in power from 1977 to 1979.

Only a few buildings were on the site the Harrises selected. They started renovating these so they could start school in February 2003. They started off with two nursery classes and grades 1 through 5 primary classes. All the staff they hired had to be born-again Christians. They started out with seven teachers and a headmistress. More support from home started arriving and helped the school develop. Prayers were being answered. The Harrises went home at least two times a year for two to three months at a time to garner more support. More is needed all the time with growth and added facilities.

They started a church in the largest classroom in 2005. They now have a separate church building with a 300-person capacity; it has 28 benches 14 feet long each; a baptismal fount is in front of the church. There is room for a standing choir and a youth choir as well as drums and rattlers for accompaniment.

With the help of the Lord, the Harrises' vision now consists of full high-school components; they have two classes of S-1 and S-2 now, but planned to add S-3 in February 2009. The next step was a separate building for a seminary that has already lasted three terms. The Georgia Baptist Theological Seminary out of the Harris' home church, Holy Ground Baptist, is backing this program. The seminary will grant a diploma for two years of study and an associate degree for four years of study.

The Harrises are also involved in several other ministries besides the school. With the help of the Ugandan team, they have a children's hospital ministry, two hospital ministries (adults), two prison ministries, they help in four different high schools, they do door-to-door evangelism, and they hope to start doing island ministries out in Lake Victoria soon. They are praying for a younger couple to come alongside them and share the same vision they have with all the ministries. They also hope to start new ministries in hospitals, in other areas, and also in the HIV Center.

Deborah Johnson of Villa Rica, GA, and I were on a mission trip to north Benin, Africa, in 2005 when she asked me to go to Uganda with their church (Middle Macedonia Baptist Church of Villa Rica, GA). I told her I would sometime in the future. Well, after a couple

Uganda

of more invitations, I finally said yes in early 2008. I was asked to call David Anderson, R.N., the medical director and discuss the trip with him.

After a nice conversation with David, I started preparations by first offering a great evangelical assistant, Rev. Scotty Teague. David said they would make room for him on the trip. I also agreed to procure some meds and supplies that were not available in Uganda, particularly children's vitamins.(The Harrises had requested enough children vitamins for a years supply for the school children and for all the clinics we were to hold.) I just happened to have a LOT of chewable vitamins left over from my previous two mission trips. Fortunately, about half of the 15,000 vitamins had already been "dose-packed" by my sweet wife into a bag that contained a month's supply; she usually does as much dose packing for me as possible so that the packs will be ready to hand out in the pharmacy. (The pharmacy just does not have enough time to dose-pack all the meds during the clinic.) I shipped the vitamins, meds, and supplies that I could not take in my extra suitcase to David for the team to take in second suitcases.

Not long after that, I was contacted by Todd Camp; he told me he was taking over the medical team leadership by default. David and his family had run into some problems and they were unable to go. Likewise, Deborah Johnson had recent total knee surgery and was incapacitated during the trip. Todd and I had a few rather lengthy conversations; I offered to help in any way I could.

Between David and Todd, I had found out a fair amount about the Faithful Servants International Mission Organization Tommy and Teresa had founded a few years earlier.

Scotty came from Chester, AR, and I came from Bossier City, LA, to meet the group at the Atlanta airport. While waiting for the group at the KLM counter, I saw a man in green scrubs. I went up to him and asked if he by chance was going to Uganda. With an affirmative answer, I knew I had located the group. Todd recognized Scotty and me as he had a copy of our passports. We met the group as they were checking in their luggage. Scotty had volunteered the use of his second suitcase allotment to the group so more meds and supplies could be taken to Uganda. We all talked and got familiar with the group as we headed for the concourse, where we would leave for Amsterdam. We flew overnight on KLM to Amsterdam. It sure is helpful to "fly with the butterfly"; i.e., it sure helps to have a sleep aid like Lunesta. We then flew through Nairobi on to Entebbe, where we were met by the Harrises. We spent the night in the nicest hotel in Entebbe, the Imperial Botanical Beach Hotel.

The next morning after a good breakfast at the hotel, we loaded up and headed out for Jinja, about a four-hour drive. As we drove by the airport, Tommy pointed out the old airport site, where the Israeli commandos invaded and got their hostages back in 1976; this was called Operation Entebbe (made into three or four different movies). Two old airplanes still sit at the airport. The new airport is so much larger and nicer.

As we drove along the road through Kampala, the capital of Uganda, the green countryside was very pretty. There were many people moving about, especially near the cities; motorcycles and bicycles were plentiful. The countryside had many groves of banana trees and crops of vegetables everywhere. The dust was ubiquitous and the air seemed full of pollen. Finally, we arrived at the Harris' home (mission house) just one long block away from Lake Victoria. The yard was striking with its palm trees, bougainvilleas, large green trees, and many other pretty flowers; it was well manicured. The weather was so pleasant; it was in the 70's. We were only 23 miles above the equator, but at an elevation of 3,700 feet above sea level.

By this time our team had become familiar with each other and every one knew working with the Harrises was going to be a pleasure. After breakfast the next morning, we went downtown to purchase more meds; we had brought a lot, but more meds were needed. The people at the drugstore were friendly and compliant with our wishes. Meds in countries like Uganda are so much less expensive than the U.S. The remainder of the day we dose packed meds for the clinics.

Wednesday morning we drove out past the Lake Victoria dam, where there is a large hydroelectric complex. Just below the dam is the beginning of the Nile River which flows due north. Tommy pointed out all the water hyacinths collecting at the top of the dam, where the water goes into the turbines that turn the electrical generators. Two boats of men were manually removing the water hyacinths. Further back was a machine on a barge that is used to remove the hyacinths, but it was apparently unusable. Tommy said they were building another dam down the river another mile as the need for electricity was growing exponentially.

From a man sitting next to me on the way to Nairobi when I was flying to Kenya in 1999 I first heard of this problem with the water hyacinths. He told me he was trying to figure out a way to contain this pesky ecological problem.

According to *Wikipedia*, the water hyacinth in Lake Victoria is Eicharnia crassipes. The plant was introduced by Belgium colonists to Rwanda to beautify their holdings and then advanced by natural means to Lake Victoria, where it was first sighted in 1988. There, without any natural enemies, it has become an ecological plague, suffocating the lake, diminishing the fish reservoir, and hurting the local economies. It impedes access to Kisumu and other harbors. It also interferes with recreation, irrigation, and power generation.

I told Tommy that if I could invent a way to turn the water hyacinths into food for animals (cattle) or if they could be used to burn as fuel, then I could become wealthy.

About six miles from Jinja, we turned off the main highway and drove two miles to the FAITHFUL SERVANTS compound. On arriving, we had several dozen uniformed children waiting in groups; they cheered acknowledging us. Soon they disappeared into their classes. We set up our supplies and meds in the clinic that had been built by supporters of the organization. It was a nice building with three exam rooms and an exam tables. Another room was for the pharmacy. We started the process of doing well over 300 physicals on the school children. The children were extremely well mannered and seemed quite shy. (There was none of the giggling and laughter like children many other places, especially the U.S.)

However, during the exams we saw a fair amount of Tinea capitis (ringworm of the scalp) and gave each child cream to treat this. Unfortunately, I was also asked to see a young child with eye problems. The toddler had one eye with the anterior chamber bulging out from increased intraocular pressure; the other cornea was opacified from scarring; apparently from the child scratching the painful eye. The child was obviously completely blind (apparently from intraocular parasites). We referred the family to an eye doctor in Jinja.

That evening we had Wednesday night church services before we left the compound. There was not a big crowd as many of the people may have still been working out in the fields. The people were energetic in their singing, and the pastor preached a nice sermon, through an interpreter.

The following morning we went back to the health clinic at FAITHFUL SERVANTS and saw nearly 200 relatives of the school children; they brought even more children for us to see. A myriad of problems were treated as best as we could. Meanwhile, the spiritual team with Rev. Scotty Teague, Rev. Hal Waters, and Clyde Bolden were out under the mango trees presenting the Gospel as frequently as they could. Scotty used the Evangecube often. Many heard the good news and a harvest of souls accepted Jesus as Savior. Clyde Bolden has one of the most direct evangelical messages I have ever heard, "Are you saved? If no, you need to be; I will tell you how. If yes, then you need to tell someone else how to be saved."

Late that afternoon Tommy showed Ken Boss, M.D., and me around the 11-acre compound; another couple of acres was being added the next week. Just that day, another Holstein cow was added; they would soon have enough milk to give many of the children a nutritious meal every school day. At present there are buildings for nursery and kindergarten through most of high school. New buildings will be opened soon to provide most of the room needed for high school. Tommy said with the help of the Lord, he soon wanted to build a seminary building there; seminary school has already been started. In the future, it is a dream to build a trade school for those that cannot go to the colleges available.

On Friday, August 22, it had been pouring rain for hours. Then it completely stopped, so we headed out for Busaana, along the shores of Lake Victoria. We went to the Busaana Baptist Church, where we worked with Pastor Timothy. We worked in a mud-hut church and saw and treated many. Toward the end of the clinic, I walked with my interpreter, Stephen, down to the lake shore and got to admire the many boats, myriads of small fish drying on the ground, and people milling about—just coming in, or getting ready to go fishing or loading up to travel to the other side of the lake. There were several different types of birds also to admire.

Out under the trees the spiritual team had a harvest of souls with their evangelism, while we worked inside the church. Pastor Timothy was present and was so happy for our presence and for our medical team coming way out on the lakeside to treat his people and the surrounding villages. I wondered about the "glow" on Pastor Timothy's face and remembered what Tommy had related to me on the way out to Busaana. Later, I got Tommy and Teresa to get a written biography from Pastor Timothy and perhaps I can share with you why the reason for that "glow" and why it will be there for a long time to come.

THE WRITTEN TESTIMONY OF PASTOR TIMOTHY:
(used by permission)
SENTINGO TIMOTHY – MUKONO LAKE SIDE
MY TESTIMONY:

I grew up in a home where my father was an Anglican by religion. We were twelve in our family; both parents claimed to be Christian by religion, so we grew up believing that we were saved and baptized. I was the youngest in the family; my father was a Judge (grade III). In the 1970s many things happened in the country. Many people were killed, tortured, and were disappearing forever.

My dad refused to work for the government of Idi Amin because of what was happening. Army men came to our home frequently threatening him in May of 1977. I can not forget June 22, 1977, when his friend came and broke the news to my Mum that he had been taken and we traced (searched) for him, but all in vain. My mother broke down in tears and we all started crying. Since that time things changed in our home; we were separated, and my brother had already joined rebel activities in order to fight Amin. We had no peace in our home and this forced me to leave our home and go into town and find work.

I started playing the sport of boxing, where I met other boys and we started drinking alcohol due to group influence. I became a real drunkard, rebel, and was behaving badly. This worsened when they removed my passport from me when I was going to turn into a pro-boxer. Time came when I was controlled by alcohol. In the '80s and mid-'80s, I found myself looking for my mother in the village, where she had gone after the death of our father. I found my mother and we stayed together, but I still had the bad behaviors. I was not controlled and very disobedient.

For God loved the world and that is why He gave His begotten child. God brought me in the village to know Him. A friend of mine, a fellow drunkard, preached the Gospel to me. In 1987 I accepted Jesus as my savior. That same year, when I was a three-month-old Christian, I was chosen by my fellow believers to lead them as their pastor. I loved the Lord and served Him. Many churches were opened, many souls were saved. I was already married in 1984, and by 1991 I had three children. Pastoring in Uganda is voluntary work, so I did not have support for my family. As an experienced man on the lake, I decided to get a job and stop the pastoral work. I got a job to help the government stop the smuggling of goods and other things from Uganda to Kenya.

Before I got this job, I had a dream three times in one week—always the same dream. I dreamed we had built a concrete building and this building was surrounded by people. I was not allowed to say anything. When I woke up, I thought I was dreaming of a grave, so I thought I was going to die. But how? I was not sick. I kept quiet, but I was very weak even in my prayers. On December 9, 1991, I was with four other men in a boat making a survey tour on Lake Victoria to the islands bordering Uganda and Kenya to find a place where we were going to form a station. A former pastor, I was now thinking of money instead of serving God and no longer talking the Word of God. On December 11 when we were in the middle of the lake, we saw a boat coming toward us. We did not know that these were thieves expecting to steal what we had. As they came near they realized that we had army men in uniform in our boat. By surprise, they started shooting at us. Within a few minutes, my fellow crew companions were killed. During this time I said to the Lord, "In Your hands I put my life, please help me; I have realized my sins." All of a sudden the thieves took off, leaving me with dead bodies, which I took to the nearest police post. I was not helped, but I realized that the case was being put against me.

I was put in a police cell for eight days. By then I had started preaching the Word of God to my fellow prisoners. On December 19, I was taken to court and imprisoned on remand for 1½ years as they began to search for more evidence against me, thinking I had killed all my fellow crew. But after 14 days I had to report to court. During this time, many prisoners received Christ. I saw the hands of God moving in the prison. Many prisoners were released and God was always near me. By the end of three days in prison, I was chosen as a leader of my fellow prisoners, a post which was always given to whom was given a long remand.

On the 26th day of my remand, when I was coming from the chapel, I went to the dormitory, where I was living, to sleep on my mat. Prisoners had bad treatment; we were not even given blankets. God knows how He can keep prisoners. Now a word came to me, and I said, "Lord I have finished the work You have sent me to do, open the doors of prison and let me out." I was astonished where the word came from; I looked around as if some different person had spoken it. I prayed and kept quiet. Many things happened in prison. Prisoners were released, the sick healed, and I saw the work of God's hand.

On the 27th day, the following day I had to report to court, for the second time. At night I had a dream, where the prison walls were falling on me, and I shouted saying, "Lord, I am dying out of air." I woke up very much frightened. The following day as I was going to court, three of our fellow prisoners had a dream that I was released. They came in that morning saying farewell, but I told them of my dream and promised I was coming back—for I had 1½ years to be in prison. That day in court I was released.

Since that time, I shall never stop serving my Lord whatever the situation I might be in, I shall serve the Lord. I was disobedient and the Lord brought me back in the field to serve Him. This experience has helped me to open new churches and I hope, if God willing, I shall continue serving Him.

May God bless you.

SENTONGO Timothy

Saturday was a "down day" for our team. The group went to get the African clothes they had been fitted for on the first day. Several bought new clothes. The clothes were colorful and bright. With the head scarves on, matching the clothes, I couldn't help but chuckle at a couple of the people; they were gringos in Africa. In contrast to our clothes, this was quite a change. Most folks in the U.S. just aren't this colorful.

Then we went downtown to do some souvenir shopping. It was so hard not to buy a bunch of things; they were so cute and also fairly inexpensive. While eating lunch, Scotty and I got into a conversation with four young women from London who were on vacation there. We got into a religious conversation quickly and found that they claimed salvation by works, so we tried to relate salvation by grace through faith in Jesus Christ, but they were not buying it. One of the ladies said her main function in life was to procreate. At least, they will think about what we had to offer next time they think about religion.

Then the entire group went out to the Nile River just below where it was coming out of Lake Victoria. WOW! What beauty the Lord does make! Talking about some picturesque scenes, they were around every bend, especially at the place called Bujagali Falls. It was a series of tons of water cascading down from Lake Victoria into what was now called the Nile River. We watched a balanced pole act put on by some of the locals accompanied by drums and beating on various sizes of gourds. It was truly amazing that someone could balance in mid-air on a bamboo pole several feet off the ground.

Then we got to see more amazing stunts; there were at least four young men who braved the rapid falls coming down the river on five-gallon plastic cans at great risk to themselves. It was quite a feat to watch. Someone said that a young man had been killed the week before doing this very stunt. I know one thing for certain, I would not try that—at least not without a life jacket. Todd rented a fishing pole and fished for an hour in the river without so much as a bite, but I admired him for trying.

Then most of the group went four-wheeling along the shores of Lake Victoria and through several of the nearby villages. It was a thrill, especially since I have never been on a four-wheeler before. (I was very cautious as not to show off.)

The next morning was Sunday, so we all went to church. I had been asked to give the men's Sunday School lesson in the auditorium. I gave a short program on faith from the book: YOU HAVE TO GET OUT OF THE BOAT TO WALK ON THE WATER. This is about the passage from Matthew 14:22-34. (John Ortberg wrote an entire book with this title; it is a fabulous book about faith.) I finished the 45 minutes with my personal testimony. For the morning worship the church was packed with people from all age groups; they were in a very worshipful mood, as I have not heard much more meaningful singing and the pastor gave an excellent message through an interpreter.

Immediately after church, we loaded up and went to the Bufalubi Prison. On the way to the prison, we passed several dozen men working out in the fields growing vegetables for their own consumption. The women of our group stayed outside the walls and had a program with the security guards' wives and children; some there accepted Jesus. Inside the men were welcomed by the prison staff and warden. A very impressionable and profound statement was made by the warden, "These men came here as common criminals, but most will leave as kings; they have accepted Jesus as Savior of their lives." Scotty then gave a very inspirational message with visual aids with his magic tricks he had used for years while a street evangelist in New York City. Everyone was very attentive. As the service ended at least a dozen or more prisoners accepted Jesus. We got to tour the prison and saw what meager lodging and food they have; the beds are just blankets on a rough concrete floor with no pillows. Most of the food apparently is fixed in a large vat; it looked mostly like vegetable soup. The prisoners grow a lot of their own vegetables; they have little meat. We were allowed to have cameras inside, which I thought was very unusual. The men seemed very cordial and were very happy for our presence.

The next morning we had to procure more meds for the prison ministry the following day. Then we went back to the FAITHFUL SERVANTS compound for everyone to tour all the facilities.

That afternoon we all went to the Jinja Hospital to visit and witness as the occasion arose. The first thing my group ran into at Ward 2 was a Muslim family waiting outside for their 20-year-old daughter who was inside the hospital ward. She was described as very ill. We asked to go inside and see her, so the family accompanied us. On approaching her bed, she tried to hold up her right hand, but was not really able to keep it up, so I gently grabbed it and shook hands; she was so weak. She could barely hold her eyes open and move them. A nasogastric tube was in place for feeding and a saline lock was in place for apparent IV antibiotic treatment. Her chart was on the bed, so Stephen handed it to me. I was reading the chart and was amazed that it was all in English. I was getting to the interesting part when the nurse came in and grabbed it out of my hands. From the family and the chart I had gleaned that the lady was two weeks postpartum of a natural childbirth at the local dispensary, but had become quite ill and had to be hospitalized. Their impression was full of question marks, but there was something about sepsis and her being anemic. I wondered if she had a retained placenta. Anyway, the lady was almost moribund (near death).

We all returned outside the ward and got to talking with the family and found out they were Muslim. I asked them if we could talk with them about Jesus and they were very cordial and allowed us to share with them. Over the next 45 minutes, I meticulously used the Evangecube and Todd answered many of their questions. The man (dad of the patient) insisted on having Todd's Bible, so Todd graciously gave it to him. The family was asked if they would like to receive Jesus as Savior and they all prayed to receive Him. Hallelujah! What a blessing! Tommy took a picture of Todd and me with the family—and that just happens to be my picture of the trip.

On Tuesday, August 26, we went back to the Bufalubi Prison and saw several prisoners at the dispensary, but we saw many more security guards and their families. I finally got written permission from the warden and state officials, so I pulled five teeth of prisoners that needed it. Many accepted Jesus at the spiritual station. Scotty later told me, "I was just physically tired, but what a great week of evangelism."

The next morning we headed back through Kampala to Entebbe, where we dined at the Imperial Botanical Beach Hotel. We got to walk out in the garden area and see several monkeys playing. In the foreground was beautiful Lake Victoria. Across the garden area was the Clinton Pavilion; this was the hotel that President George H. Bush (Daddy Bush) and President Bill Clinton stayed while they were in Uganda. Apparently, the pavilion was named after Bill made his visit there. After a good supper, we went to the airport and waited a few hours to start our long journey back home.

It was a delightful and gratifying trip. The people of Uganda were very receptive and friendly, and seemed very grateful for our treatment and the Gospel message. We saw over 1,250 patients and of those 288 accepted Jesus as Savior. Praise the Lord! Great things He has done! I appreciate the Harrises and the group for a great trip. I was happy to have been a part of a great ministry for a week. They showed me what willing hearts can do when the Lord leads you from your obedience to Him. They truly are faithful servants to Uganda from the Lord Jesus Christ.

Many Baptist churches are supporting the FAITHFUL SERVANT program and visions. A lot of the support comes from the $20-a-month-per-child sponsorship for the school.

The Harrises show their work to many churches near home to allow people to be a part of their ministries. You are encouraged to go to their website: *www.faithfulservants.org* and find out more about them and the opportunities for sharing in their ministries. They also request prayer, participation in Uganda, or your financial support.

Village near Lake Victoria
Uganda, 2008

Rev. Scott Teague doing newspaper trick
Uganda, 2008

Uganda

Five members of Muslim family who accepted Jesus as Savior
August 25, 2008

Chapter 14

Rwanda

Africa New Life (Ministries)
2008

In April 2007 I was in Rwanda with Rev. John Crocker, missions director from the Whitesburg Baptist Church in Huntsville, AL., his evangelical team, and a medical team from his church. John is just about the most enthusiastic minister with whom I have ever worked. I am sure all his energy has to come from the Lord.

While still in Rwanda, John started making plans to return in 2008. He loved the mission, the country, and the people so much that he stated that he would probably make this an annual event. The people had been so responsive to the evangelism and the medical team. I enjoyed the trip as well and determined to go again some day. We worked with the New Africa Life Ministries; this is a ministry led by Rev. Charles Buregeya with a growing number of staff. From what I had been told, the ministry had really grown since our previous trip there.

John called me in May 2008 stating that he was unable to get a medical team from Whitesburg Baptist Church; he wanted to know if I would gather a medical team to go along with his evangelical team. I told him that I would certainly try. This time I wanted a couple of ministers to have a spiritual station. The previous year we failed to have one and probably missed a lot of opportunities to witness about Jesus; the group was just too busy seeing patients to witness sufficiently.

Rwanda

I got out my medical-missions list and "long" email list and sent the message that I needed a team to go to Rwanda in September. As usual I had a difficult time recruiting physicians. They are "married" to their practice if they are still actively practicing medicine; I know because I did that for 25 years. I began to get volunteers from people who had been on previous medical mission trips with me. My goal was to get about 10 people.

Ann McConathy, R.N., told me that I should call and ask Dr. Jan Soapes of Stone Mountain, GA. She was in Burkina Faso when I was there in 2004; we had talked and she indicated that she wanted to start going on medical-mission trips soon. I had contacted her about other trips, but her husband and parents had gotten very ill and she had to postpone earlier trips. I was delighted when I called and she said she would like to go; she verified this soon afterwards with an email.

Rosemary Andrews, R.N., one of my most reliable and frequent volunteers, signed up as well as her son, Kevin Andrews, R.N.

When I called Dr. Michael Biddle in Griffin, GA, he was a bit surprised but delighted that I asked. He said that I had called at a good time and that he would go. He wanted to know why I had called him. I told him I was thinking of any good doctor that could go with me, and I had remembered what a good roommate he was in Rio de Janeiro, Brazil, in 2002.

Soon I had a team of 10; then one Sunday morning in June 2008, immediately after worship service at Airline Baptist Church, a young couple approached me, telling me their names and that they wanted to go on the next mission trip I was going on. I told them I was going to Uganda in August and that team was already complete, but I was assigned as the medical director on the trip to Rwanda. I hired them on the spot; that is the first time a couple had approached me <u>asking</u> to go on a mission trip. Julie Weatherall is a R.N. and Billy, her husband, works in the oil/gas leasing business for an oil company. I could tell Billy was quite enthusiastic. He said he would do any job that was assigned to him. I was told later that Julie was a new Christian; I really admired both of them for stepping forward in faith. Vickie, my wife, and I had lunch with the Weatheralls so we could get to know them a bit better. I found out that I had two jewels in hand.

Meanwhile, I asked Rev. Sonny DePrang and his wife, Jackie, to go; I needed a good spiritual leader. About that time, Bill Mc-Conathy and wife, Ann, R.N., joined. Bill works as a minister and would help in the spiritual station with Sonny. Libby Horton volunteered to go and do eyeglasses; I told her I would get her help as she was swamped when we were in the Philippines in February. My wife, Vickie, agreed that this was a great team and almost wished she was going. Not long before we left, John Crocker called me and asked if it was OK for Jan Massey from their church to also join. What a great team had volunteered!

Dr. Jan Soapes emailed me and asked me to inquire about getting less expensive tickets with a different travel agency. With a little research, I called and got information emailed to me about different flights at a considerable savings, but we would have to drive to Dallas to catch the first leg of our flight. John ended up using the same agency to get the evangelical team tickets also.

In 2007 we had trouble getting our medical supplies into Rwanda, especially with the two-year expiration date on the medications. Cindy Prouty, IMB missionary to Rwanda, had informed me that I could get in touch with the Kigali branch of the largest medicine and medical supplies distributor, Sun Enterprises. I was given the email address and arranged most of the medical supplies being ordered while I was still in Uganda on a medical-mission trip. We were told that it was cash on delivery, but I emailed a proposed list of meds and supplies and found out what they had available of the list I sent.

Rwanda

We found out that we had a 14-hour layover in London; so, being the opportunist that I am, I got everyone to agree to go on a day tour of London while there. I arranged all of this by email and payment by credit card. I missed the gorilla tracking in 2007, so I called my previous roommate, Dr. Ken Moultrie, and got the information to do this online, but I changed the numbers as more and more of our group wanted to do this also. I ended up getting Kelly Sager, IMB missionary to Rwanda, to go personally and get the permits. I had to wire the money immediately if I wanted to hold those reservations.

I did take one suitcase of supplies that I had left over from recent mission trips. Jim Renz, my brother-in-law, volunteered to drive our group of nine from the Bossier City/ Haughton area. We picked up Libby Horton in Canton, TX, on the way to the Dallas Fort Worth Airport. We met the two doctors from Georgia in Washington, DC; then we all flew to London overnight. I asked the group if they would like to "fly with the butterfly" (Lunesta) so we would be rested to take our tour two hours after arrival in London.

The Premium Tours of London met us with an appropriate-sized van to take the 12 of us to tour. Our driver then started downtown and picked up our host, Barry. He turned out to be very witty and very knowledgeable about all aspects of London. Barry pointed out many of the landmarks as we approached the Tower of London. The Tower of London is now a museum relating much of the past history of London; it even houses the crown jewels there. We took a brief cruise on the River Thames and went to Buckingham Palace. From there we went to see St. Paul Cathedral; it is a beautiful and very large church with a long complex history. We then went to the London Eye, a huge Ferris wheel, with compartments big enough to have a wedding or party in. As we approached the top we could see the most beautiful panoramic view of London and the River

Thames. Then we had to scurry to get to the airlines in time to fly to Nairobi overnight.

We had to stay in Nairobi for about six hours before flying on to Kigali. Julie and Billy Weatherall did not have the proper tickets to fly on to Kigali; I did not want them to be "left behind", so I had to purchase new tickets for that leg of the flight. We were met at the airport by Pastor Emma, our Rwandan sponsor for the week.

We were greeted by Cindy and Jerry Prouty, IMB missionaries to Rwanda, at the Baptist Mission House. We had a meal prepared for us almost immediately; then, we counted out what meds I had brought to get ready for the clinic the next day. The guest house is relatively large for a home; but, it was the home of the Rwandan delegate to the United Nations in 1994. He was accused of abetting the genocide, so he had to take refuge in the United States. The mission house is only three miles from the airport and three miles from the center of town. It is a beautiful place with well manicured lawn, shrubbery, and trees. From the front porch you can see a good portion of the city; at least two or three of the hills; Kigali is a city built on seven hills.

The weather was so <u>nice</u>, and it remained that way all week. It was about 65 at night and up to 72 to 75 during the day. This had to be the nicest weather I have ever encountered for a mission trip. It was two weeks before the rainy season, but Rwanda is a country of eternal spring; there is always something growing there and remains green all year.

I talked with Pastor Charles and he told me that I could interview him Saturday evening; I had told him that I wanted to feature him in my 2008 Rwanda chapter.

After a good breakfast, a few of the team members went with me to Sun Enterprises to get the meds. I had been told by Pastor Emma that we would be seeing a lot of people in Kagayo; so after meeting Sunjay, I ordered 50 percent more meds. This would take about an hour or so to gather the meds, so Cindy took me to the Primate Safari office to get a refund that I had paid for Dr. Biddle. Mike had decided not to go after they were charging him so much for the journey up to the rain forest and back; it was the same price that all eight of us were paying for transportation for the same trip. We returned to Sun Enterprises and got all the meds and supplies.

Then we returned to the mission house to get the rest of the team. By this time, the evangelical team had arrived and looked worn out from the two-day journey getting there. Next we headed for Kagoyo. It took 2½ hours and we would have to go this route to and from the clinic site at Kagoyo for the five days. Along the way, we got to see the lush green countryside with terraced rows of crops on the many hills; Rwanda is the country of 1,000 hills. We saw a lot of smoke coming from fires out in the fields. Carol, our coordinator for African New Life Ministries, told me that they were clearing the fields to plant new crops; it was close to the rainy season within two to three weeks. Several people could be seen out on the terraces and valleys preparing the soil for planting. There were a lot of banana trees along the way also, especially near many of the dwellings.

Kagoyo is one of three refugee cities near the Tanzanian border; we were assigned to work there the rest of the week. These Rwandans escaped to Tanzania in the 1994 genocide; they were in a refugee camp initially, but soon blended into the population getting jobs, property, and settling into a routine; they had become good citizens when the Tanzanian government decided in 2006 that it wanted ALL the Rwandans to go home. They were identified by their cards. Those that didn't volunteer to go home were beaten and forced to leave with just the clothes that they had on. The Rwandan government did not want them either; Rwanda is the most populated country in Africa per square mile, so there was no place to put them except a few miles from Tanzanian border miles from anywhere, out in the middle of nowhere. The land there certainly was not satisfactory for crops, and the scrawny bushes and trees were unwelcoming. The people were given no choice but to settle there. Carol said they had no hope, but the African New Life Ministries is trying to reach out to them in every way it can.

On the way into the village, we noticed that many were filling "jerry cans" (five gallon plastic cans) with water from a shallow pond on the road side. Cows were also drinking from this. We were later told that this was their only source of water. Clothes were washed here and laid out to dry in the sun. We were welcomed by the nurse practitioner and his assistant at the clinic at the edge of the village; the government had built this six-room clinic, but had no one to staff it but the nurse and assistant. One room was reserved for up to two "admitted patients". There was no electricity. Their pharmacy consisted of one table with just a few meds that they had; all of these could be placed in a relatively small bag.

The group decided how to divide up the rooms for triage, a pediatric room was to be used by Dr. Jan Soapes, a pediatrician, an eye clinic, a pharmacy; two more rooms were to be used for general medical patients and dentistry as the occasion arose. We scrubbed the floors and a few pieces of furniture. We asked for more furniture and this was brought in from the nearby school. The government also had built this and staffed it with teachers. There was no doctor available so one had to be sent several miles to a regional hospital if needed. We were told that we were only the second medical team to have visited this village.

We returned back to the mission house to really count pills in earnest this time as the clinic started the next morning. We were fortunate that many of the evangelical team also counted meds; within four hours we had counted out half of our supply. The meals at the mission house were always fresh and tasty. With the evangelical team the mission house was full; we had near capacity with the rooms and beds, but all was prepared for us and we felt right at home. We had four bathrooms to share. Although we had electricity most of the time, occasionally we had a blackout for a few moments. Brownouts were frequent at night. This time we had computers and "Skype" to communicate to home; that was so nice. At the Proutys' request I brought an Apple McIntosh laptop for them that I got off eBay.

On arrival back to Kagayo we were greeted by several dozen people; word had been passed that we were having free clinic. Initially, we had a bit of control problems with the crowd, but Kevin was able to get the crowd away from the clinic and they were asked to sit in the area in front of the clinic while the numbers were passed out to be seen numerically in the clinic. Bill McConathy later took control of the crowd and did an excellent job with this.

We saw many universal things like backaches, headaches, and colds; but we also saw a lot of nutritional problems and hygiene problems. Several had the symptoms of malaria and were empirically treated with quinine. We treated everyone for worms; the pharmacy personnel (Rosemary and Julie) had everyone to swallow their worm pills right there, with a sip of water. Occasionally, we saw oddities like rickets or massive spleenomegaly from chronic malaria. We also treated a fair number of wounds—and yes, I pulled several dozen teeth during the four days of clinic. Libby and Jackie ran the eye clinic. Ann and Jan did triage, but were joined by Kevin when the lines got so long. Dr. Biddle saw the adults like I did. Occasionally I could hear through the door when he was evangelizing to the individual patient.

Deborah was my interpreter for the first day, but later had to manage the whole clinic as Carol had been assigned elsewhere. She was most helpful and really aided with the people. Stephen was my interpreter the remainder of the time and was most invaluable in assisting and interpreting for me. He had such a sweet spirit everyday when working with me.

I saw one older man who said he had tuberculosis as diagnosed at the hospital several miles away. He apparently did not have the money to buy the meds for a cure. I insisted he return to get the meds as we did not have it. The next day the same man returned for tooth extraction and did not have his registration card or identification; I pulled his two necrotic teeth only to find out that he was the guy with tuberculosis, and I had spent 10 minutes in his face. Needless to say, I was not a happy camper about that.

Bill McConathy was on the spiritual team, and I asked him to comment on their work. The medical team was too busy to participate in the group meetings with the people for evangelism. Bill said that from the beginning, it was evident that the locals in the village were going to be a very attentive, mannerly group of people that were eager to hear about Jesus. It was the main goal of our whole team to present the saving Gospel of Jesus Christ to the lost people in the village. Each morning the spiritual team would gather the men, women, and children into groups as they waited to see the medical staff. Frequently the Evangecube was used as a tool to provide a clear depiction of the plan of salvation. The interpreters played such an important role in the presentation because they were able to make the story come alive with the use of the native language. An effort was made to make sure that everyone got to hear the Gospel. In between the presentations the team would pass out tracts and mingle with the people, engaging them in conversation and praying with them as they requested. The people were extremely friendly, had very sweet dispositions, and exhibited an infectious sense of humor. They were a real joy to hang out with!

The spiritual team was also given the opportunity to go into the school classrooms and present the Gospel to the school children. The team was very impressed with the receptiveness of the kids as they listened to the story of Jesus. Rev. Sonny DePrang said they started with the fourth grade presenting the Gospel and had many decisions for Jesus. When they got to the eighth grade and presented the Gospel, they asked if any of the students wanted to receive Jesus into their hearts, no one raised his or her hand, so Sonny asked the teacher why no one wanted to accept Jesus. The teacher said that all the students in the room were Christians; but just then, one little boy raised his hand; he came to the front of the room and said the Sinner's Prayer and gave his heart to Jesus. That really took some courage. All the boys and girls in the ninth grade were Christians. The response was tremendous as they saw numerous children throughout the school give their hearts to Jesus.

The spiritual team presented the Gospel to virtually every single person that lived in the village of Kagayo. The response to the Gospel was overwhelming with hundreds coming to Christ. The love of Christ was evident throughout the village. All of these entities added up for this trip being a tremendous success.

The people were very gracious and thankful; they wanted us to return again. We saw 649 patients that were registered, but there were so many more to be seen. People were walking from miles away to come to the clinic. We left all our remaining meds and supplies with the nurse practitioner to give out later.

The spiritual station was run by Rev. Sonny DePrang, Bill McConathy, and Billy Weatherall; they had fantastic results with people accepting Jesus as Savior. The Gospel was presented to 1,034 people and 598 of those accepted Jesus. Also several Bibles in the native language were given out. Africa New Life Ministries followed up with these people and hoped to start a church there soon.

On the way home that evening, we stopped to see the fruit bats near Kayonza. Kevin and I walked down a rather steep incline to four trees, where there must have been 10,000 bats. We tried to throw pebbles to make some fly, but didn't get close enough to be effective. So, we screamed until we disturbed about 500 of them into flying about in the air. It was surreal how they looked like flying people with wings (they are mammals). Their wing span must have been 18 to 24 inches. It was awesome to see several hundred in flight. I asked everyone why do bats hang upside down to roost; no one could answer that question. Finally when I got home I found several articles on Google.com and Discovery Channel clips which answered that: First of all, it puts them in an ideal position for takeoff. Unlike birds, bats can't launch themselves into the air from the ground. Their wings don't produce enough lift to take off from a dead stop; and their hind legs are so small and underdeveloped that they can't run to build up the necessary takeoff speed. Instead, they use their front claws to climb to a high spot, and then fall into flight. By sleeping upside down in a high location, they are all set to launch if they need to escape the roost.

When we got to Kayonza to drop off three of our interpreters, we made a circle holding hands and I told them we may forget their names and the name of the place where we had worked together, but we would never forget the impression they had left on us—for example, working and loving the people we were with in the clinics. I noticed one of our team members with a tear in her eye because our relationships were now over; but inwardly, I had a big smile because it happened. Then we had prayer together and left to return to Kigali.

On the way home from Kayonza, our van got stopped once; the other medical-team van was stopped three times. One of the interpreters was asked to step out of the van so his ID could be checked closely. The team noted that several men had been detained in a small building on the third stop. Some of our team was worried that they might be detained since they didn't have their passports with them. The police were checking to make sure none of the Rwandan troublemakers were trying to sneak back into Kigali; these are the Rwandans that reside in the Congo, but who were run out after the last genocide. The ladies on the evangelical team, who are roommates to our medical team ladies, felt the Holy Spirit telling them to pray for the medical team about the time all this was happening. As soon as the medical team walked into the mission house, they asked what was happening one hour earlier. What a comfort knowing that they were praying for us.

 I had Cindy call Pastor Charles Friday evening when we got back from clinic and ask when I could interview him for my next book. He said he was due to go to the Friday night prayer meeting which usually lasted all night, but he had a while to come by and talk with me then. Talk about a friendly and cordial person, you would just have to meet Pastor Charles to comprehend what a sincere and personable man he is. He came in and we went upstairs to talk. After a few questions, he stated that he had a personal autobiography that he would email me, but he volunteered for the questions anyway.

Pastor Charles said his life started when he was born as a refugee in Uganda; his parents were Rwandan citizens who had to escape the 1959 genocide. He was reared as a Roman Catholic, but he struggled with the Catholic beliefs secondary to the confession of sins to a priest. Charles said while he was growing up he got tired of telling the priest his problems. He realized it was more church and not being a Christian (like Jesus Christ). He often had prayer alone without the priest.

One day he wanted to tell the Lord what was on his heart, so he threw down his Roman Catholic prayer book and cried out to God. This was the turning point of his need for God.

In Uganda there were no missionaries at the time, but there were lots of Muslims with mosques. There was no one to help with his spirituality; he was searching for Jesus Christ. Charles ended up going across town to work with Pastor Francis Bukenya to teach young children how to read and write. One Sunday the pastor's wife asked Charles to accompany her to their church; at first he refused, but after a struggle within himself, he decided to follow her into the church. Charles said his response was not right away, but within a week he realized he was going to give his life to Jesus Christ. There was no altar call at the church then, but he wrote a letter in March 1984 to the pastor and told him he was going to give his life to Jesus Christ.

Charles said he loved evangelism and became a street preacher within a few months. He went with a team around the city preaching, but the people were very hard hearted; they did not know about being born again. People there were overshadowed by Islam and Roman Catholicism. However, he got a lot of training with the street ministry. Then the street ministry led to crusades.

During this time, he was able to go to Bible studies in Kampala. He was attending a church in Gaba serving as a minister of youth. The church was not growing and he found out that many of the people there were very superstitious; they believed in evil spirits controlling the area. The spiritual warfare persisted so they started all night Friday night prayer meetings and finally their witches became weaker and weaker. The witches finally moved out of town when the World Bank bought their houses to build a new water pumping station. In a very short time, all their homes were destroyed and they were paid to leave. After the witches left, the heavens opened up in the community and people started receiving Christ as their Savior and coming to church. Charles said the all-night Friday night prayer meetings were so effective that they still have them now in Rwanda.

Charles was in England in 1994 to learn to be a missionary, when the Rwandan genocide took place. He came back to Uganda in 1995 when many of the families were returning to Rwanda. His father was very brave and wanted to take his family back to Rwanda in 1995. Charles was very moved by what had happened in the genocide of 1994. Charles went to Rwanda to do crusades in 1995,

1996, and 1997. While in Rwanda he started to want to help the children. He began this by sponsoring nine children in a school.

In 2000 while packing to go to Rwanda to start a new ministry, the Lord spoke to him and said, *"Don't go"*. That very next day he met a professor at his church, Dr. Tim Robnett from Multnomah Biblical Seminary in Portland, OR, with his friend from France, Dr. Bill Thomas. God eventually brought Charles to Multnomah through miraculous means. While attending Multnomah, they founded Africa New Life Ministries, with a vision to help orphaned and poor children of Rwanda, train Christian leaders, and conduct evangelistic missions.

After six months in America, Charles felt he had to go back to Rwanda. He moved to Kaonza in the summer of 2001, but later returned to America to finish seminary while raising a family. God started opening doors and many people helped with the formation of Africa New Life Ministries.

In 2003, Charles and his family moved to Rwanda to start the Africa New Life Bible Church. Planting a church was not all he wanted; he did not want a building with four walls, but a whole community, where there was a place to pray, teach the Bible, teach a vocation, and teach and train pastors and future leaders of the community and country. Pastor Charles said, "Every day people come to the Dream Center, and they are won to Jesus Christ."

Rwanda wants orphanages to come to an end, but now AIDS is happening more and more; so, they are helping with the orphanages in hopes that people with skill and heart will come from them.

Pastor Charles says that genocide points to the past; the Dream Center points to the future. In about five years, the Dream Center will be complete; it is a building, but it holds a lot for the people: evangelism, discipleship, and leadership. It is developing leaders to go out and plant churches. Charles says he has been in Kigali for four years, but the best things are yet to happen. God is raising up leaders and the best is yet to be.

Pastor Charles Mugisha Buregeya's autobiography is in APPENDIX B. This was emailed to me with full permission to use it in my book. Charles told me that one day he would write his complete autobiography in the form of a book. I encourage you to read it now in the back section of this book.

We were to go to the Dream Center the next morning to hand out multiple vitamins and worm meds to all the street children. This is another ministry of Pastor Charles and the Dream Center; he allows all the street children to come in twice weekly to have a good meal if they will listen to the Gospel. However, this was the last Saturday in the month and it was a national holiday: UMUGANDA According to Google research under Rwanda holidays: Umuganda is a nationwide community work program implemented by the local government ministry, to keep the capital Kigali, and vicinity, clean. The community work is mandatory for everyone, every last Saturday of the month from 7 a.m. to noon. During Umuganda time, businesses close and no public transport operates in Rwanda. Actually, no one is allowed to leave his or her neighborhood until noon; defying this rule without an official authorization can lead to immediate arrest. Umuganda time is preformed countrywide and involves the participation of all, including the president, top government ministers, and the high-ranking government officials who put aside their formal attire to clean up the country.

We decided this was a nice time for us to just rest!

After 12 noon, the city became alive again; we loaded up in the vans and all went to the mall for lunch and then to a nearby souvenir shop. I loaded up on gorilla and giraffe statues to give to those who had helped sponsor our trip. It was a neat time for all to look at the crafts made by local Rwandans.

From there we got to go tour the DREAM CENTER. It is situated on one of the hillsides. My, what a difference 1½ years makes. The finished auditorium has the capacity of seating at least 700 people for worship or church activities. We went inside and several teenagers were practicing songs for Sunday morning services. They were passionately practicing the HALLELUJAH chorus. From the aura of a worshipful attitude, genuine love for the Lord, and beautiful sounds, several of our team members who were watching and listening had tears rolling down their cheeks; it was a touching and special moment.

We toured some of the other parts of the complex also. One part had a large room, where ladies were sewing clothes; they are taught to sew for a vocation. Several dresses and other clothes were for sale in the room. Other parts are planned soon. Pastor Charles wants the complex to be a community, where you can pray, teach the Bible, train ministers and future leaders of the country, continue ministering to the street children, and be a place, where people can be won to Jesus as Savior. Pastor Charles hopes the complex will be finished within five years, as the Lord is willing.

The following day was GORILLA DAY for eight of our medical team. I had a tough time getting permits for us, but thanks to missionary Kelly Sager, I got the money wired and the permits confirmed. We arose at 3:45 a.m. to get ready; I made sure everyone was up and about. After a quick breakfast, the Primate Safari SUV came at 4:30 a.m. as promised. It was routine stop after routine stop in Kigali; the police were making sure no troublemakers from the Congo were sneaking into the capital. We passed many people bringing their crop produce to town well before dawn. Our driver told us that these folks do this every day. Finally, we got to the Primate Safari's headquarters a few miles from the mountain base and rain forest. After sunrise about 6 a.m., we sure passed some beautiful country on the way. We saw multiple fields of sweet potatoes, corn, Irish potatoes, and many groves of banana trees.

As we approached the Primate Safari headquarters near the base of the mountains, we could see five large mountains (dormant volcanoes); one is in the Congo, three are in Rwanda, and the other in Uganda. At the headquarters, we met our guide that would take us up into the rain forest; his English name was Patience. Patience took our group of eight off to the side and gave us a lecture on the safety features, what to do, what to expect, and what not to do. He proceeded to tell us a lot about the gorillas; he had been doing this for about 15 years.

There are several groups of gorillas in the Rwanda rain forest and our group would be visiting the Kwitonda group; there is one large silverback (about 500 pounds), 2 blackbacks (younger males), 5 females, and 4 babies. Patience was almost comical telling us about the habits of the gorillas; especially, that the silverbacks never have enough females. They often arrange to fight so the winner can have more of the loser's females.

Our driver then took us to the edge of a large field of Irish potatoes just below the edge of the rain forest. As we trekked through, we saw many harvesting the potatoes and placing them in large white sacks to be sold as a cash crop. Patience told us that Primate Safaris pays the owners of this land for the groups to trek through every day on the way to the rain forest.

Then we crossed a stone fence demarcating the edge of the rain forest and the crops. This keeps out a lot of the forest animals, but not the gorillas; they rarely bother the crops. Suddenly we were in a thick green forest with only a trail up into the area of the gorillas. After about 1½ miles we were told to be quiet and stick together; the gorillas had been spotted about 50 yards away. By then, the forest was so thick and crowded with trees, bushes, and vines, you could hardly see more than 100 feet. Suddenly, there they were—

in their natural habitat, moving along at a leisurely rate eating leaves off trees and vines. One medium-sized female and a smaller gorilla were noticed up in a tree eating leaves. They sure made a lot of noise climbing and moving from tree to tree in the air. They came directly over us knocking all manner of dried leaves, small limbs, and dried bark onto us. Then the silverback was seen pulling vines from a tree and rapidly eating the leaves. One of the blackbacks climbed a relatively small tree and a limb broke, but he just fell to the next limb and kept eating leaves. The silverback completely ignored us, not feeling intimidated at all by us, but the females and blackbacks seemed to be irritated by our presence and walked on down the way searching for more food.

What an amazing treat as we got to follow along for almost an hour, seeing these unusual primates in their natural surroundings. At the end of the tour, we were given certificates of having successfully toured the gorillas.

The next day we all got ready and were taken to the airport for the long trip home.

Pastor Emma went to the airport with us and sincerely thanked us so much for our coming to Rwanda and working with the people in Kagayo. It was a real pleasure working with the Africa New Life Ministries. We all give glory to God for the souls saved and helping with the ministries run by Pastor Charles and his wonderful staff. The Africa New Life Ministries are greatly appreciated also; what an effort they are doing for their people—leading them to the saving knowledge of Jesus and helping the community and nation any way they can. No doubt some of us will be returning there again to help.

We had long layovers in almost all our major airports, but it was so nice to be back home again. I want to thank Rev. John Crocker for inviting me and asking me to get a team to work with his group. I greatly appreciate all my team members for their hard work.

Our group in Rwanda, 2008
Medical team

Bill McConathy evangelizing in Kagayo, Rwanda

Gorilla safari at end of trip 2008

Chapter 15

"Put Me in the Middle Seat"

While flying from Nairobi, Kenya, to Kigali, Rwanda, I heard the woman sitting next to me say she was going gorilla watching in Rwanda while there. Eight of my group going to Rwanda were going on a similar trip, so I started a conversation with her about the gorillas. Not long into the conversation I found out she was on holiday from Sydney, Australia, with her just-retired cardiologist dad; her mom was also a physician but did not come on the trip. I then asked her what her vocation was, and she replied that she was a lawyer.

Soon I changed the subject and asked her where she went to church. She said she didn't go anywhere to church; her parents once went to church, but they had not been for years. So, she said she didn't go and didn't feel obligated to go. I asked her if she was a Christian and she said no. I then asked her if she believed in heaven and hell. She said, "Not really." I asked her if she was interested in going to heaven and she said it didn't really matter. I asked her if she knew of Jesus and what He did for all people. She said she knew of faith and salvation, but had never pursued it. I then asked her if I could tell her the plan of salvation so she could accept Jesus to become a Christian, and I got a resounding <u>NO</u>!

With the tone of her answer being so definite, I had been warned not to pursue the matter. Feeling partially defeated, I suddenly became quiet. But at least I had tried, and this seemed like such an intelligent lady.

This reminded me of a trip my wife and I took with some of my relatives to Zurich, Switzerland, a few years ago. My brother-in-law had to be in business meetings all day every day while his wife, my wife, and I went out touring to see all the tourist attractions and beautiful sites in and about Zurich. While touring through the downtown area of Zurich, our guide kept pointing out the beautiful churches and cathedrals; almost all of them were Anglican churches or Catholic churches. He told us that the government mandatorily took out 10 to 12 percent of your earned wages and sends it to the church of your choice. Then I realized why there were such beautiful edifices. I asked him how large the crowds were and he replied that not many went to church. I asked him how often he went and he said he just called and got a copy of the priest's message to read. I decided that the priests and ministers had no incentive to go out and invite a crowd because they were paid regardless.

Later that evening I caught our guide alone and asked him if he believed in Jesus; he said he did. Then I asked if he were to die tonight, would he go to heaven? That question seemed to put a stake into his heart. Suddenly, he took great offense and if looks would kill, I would be dead; pure evil came from his eyes. I proceeded to tell him that he needed to accept Jesus as his personal Savior and not just believe in the church. At this point, he was almost hissing with each breath. The further I pursued the matter, the further tangent he went off on. We had to go at that time, but I was determined to finish our conversation on the bus. While difficult to believe, I upset him so badly, he got on another bus.

On our way home from the medical mission in Rwanda in 2008, I got into a conversation with a chap from London. I first talked with him about London and even showed him my pictures on my digital camera I had taken in London on our day tour nine days earlier. He stated that we got to see a lot in a short period of time. He further stated that he had never been to the London Tower to see the Crown Jewels, and he had never been on the London Eye.

Gradually I got into a religious conversation by asking him where he went to church in London. He stated that he grew up in a Christian home, but never pursued it when he left home. I asked him if he was a Christian and he said no. I asked why and he replied that there was just too much suffering in the world.

I told him a brief summary of our medical mission trip to Rwanda and asked him if I could show him something. I had to get out of the <u>middle seat</u> and get my carry-on luggage to get my keychain Evangecube, but I was happy to have the opportunity to show it to a person who needed its message. I carefully went through the pictures on the cube explaining the message of each step by step; then I asked him if he would like to pray to receive Jesus as his Savior. Again, he replied that there was just too much suffering in the world. I tried to explain to him that the suffering was mostly from a result of sin. I reminded him that he could ask Jesus to forgive all his sins and to ask Him to come into his heart. Repetitiously, he said there was just too much suffering in the world and that he could not believe in a God that allowed that.

I had tried, but he had made up his mind on the subject. Hopefully, he will remember the message the Evangecube gave him and someday apply it to his life.

I don't get negative answers frequently; but, next time I get on an airplane I am likely to say, "Be sure and give me a <u>middle seat</u> (so I can witness to the person on each side of me)."

This brings me to the conclusion that not only do we need a revival in America, but we definitely need revivals for what Jesus has done for mankind in Australia and Europe—and really for the entire world.

Chapter 16

Loss of My Buddy
Eulogy for Mr. George Louis Chandler

*The steps of a good man are ordered by the Lord;
and he delighteth in His way.
Psalm 37:23*

George Chandler was a very good man. Of all the things I have heard about him in the last few days was that he indeed was a good man.

I first met Mr. Chandler at his home in 1971. I had met his beautiful daughter at work (Confederate Memorial Medical Center, where I was training to be a general surgeon) and had asked her out on a date; but, our first date was on a Wednesday night—and you probably guessed it—Vickie couldn't go out until she got home from church. I instantly liked Mr. Chandler. Soon I was coming out to his home to help with odd chores. He and I were just alike; we had only two gears in our transmission: full speed ahead and stop.

We weren't always working; we both loved to go fishing. After Vickie and I married, Mr. Chandler and I would go fishing from the inconvenience of the public pier. Later we bought a house on Cypress Lake, where we could have a close place to fish whenever we wanted. Over the next 16 weekends we built a private pier and boathouse and fixed up the incomplete house so we could live in it.

The Chandlers loved to spend the weekend there with us. You know Cypress Lake may never recover; Mr. Chandler and I put a major dent in the population of the fish in that lake; because of us they made everyone stop yoyo-fishing.

Mr. Chandler was a good religious man; he believed in going to every church service when he could. He taught Sunday School for many years.

He was a prodigy of a peacemaker and I never heard him complain or talk bad about anyone. He was such a positive man. He was always helping repair things at his church. He also taught me several things about life and carpentry. He taught me several valuable lessons in life; for example: always treat people equally and fairly, no matter what. Also, he taught me several things about carpentry; for example: there are six sides to a square and not just four.

My dad died in 1986, so Mr. Chandler became like my dad. He was never but a phone call away when I needed something done. He helped me repair an old house to be used as a doctor's office so I could start private practice in it in 1975; he helped me fix up our lake house, and build an outside garage. He was always there when I needed him; I always seemed to be in his debt. Maybe I tried to pay him back by being good to his daughter.

The last several years of his life we did not fish often any more: I had become a fisherman of men. However, we still remained very close friends. He always encouraged my mission trips; he and Mrs. Chandler would come over to our home and count out thousands of tablets and pills to be used on various mission trips; he even contributed financially to the expenses of all the travel.

On Mr. Chandler's tombstone is the date 1924-2009. I may not remember the dates, but I will always remember the dash between 1924 and 2009. That dash to me represents the 38 years that I knew and loved Mr. Chandler. Anyone who knew and loved Mr. Chandler will know what that little line is worth. It did not matter how much he owned: the cars, his home, or cash. What mattered was how he lived and loved. His death should remind us that we don't know how long our dash will be, but I hope I can make my dash as successful, appreciated, and delightful as that of our Mr. George Chandler.

In my opinion Mr. Chandler got out of life what he wanted: by doing for others.

I may be sad about his passing, but I am glad I will see his smiling face one day soon in heaven; yes, he was a good man and we all loved him.

Of all the relationships I have had in life, this was an extraordinary special one. Mr. George Chandler was <u>MY BUDDY</u>! He was such a special friend; one that may never be replaced. Many people will walk in and out of your life, but only true friends like Mr. Chandler will leave footprints in your heart.

(Most of this was stated by me at his funeral on February 11, 2009. At that time I found out I was not so tough; I had a very difficult time speaking these words without emotional moments.)

Chapter 17

Baguio City, Philippines
City of Pines
2009

Rev. Alan J. Guevarra and I discussed our next visit to the Philippines in early March 2008, when we were still in Coron. We did not determine a definite site until we kept corresponding via email in October. He said we could work in the Pampanga area, where we had worked in 2005, 2006, and 2007. He further stated that there were plenty of pastors and churches that we could work with. Then he offered going to Baguio City, a city about 150 miles north of Manila. Alan stated that Baguio City was well up into the mountains in northern Luzon (the main Philippine Island), and it was very beautiful there. Also in February, the temperature is cool. I asked him if he had a mission church there. He told me he didn't, but he had several pastor friends who would love to have us come and hold medical clinics there. He further stated that our main objective was seeing souls saved. Alan seemed to be encouraging me to take a medical team there, so I agreed.

According to *Wikipedia*, the city is known for its mild climate, its Denver-like nearly one-mile elevation (5,000 feet), and its moist tropical pine forest conducive to the growth of mossy plants and orchids. Its main industry is tourism. It is called the summer capital of the Philippines. It is also a university city. Baguio City was established by Americans in 1900 at the site of an Ibaloi village known as Kafagway. Baguio City is well known as the site of the surrender

Baguio City, Philippines

of General Tomoyuki Yamushita and Vice Admiral Okochi. Here they gave up the entire Imperial Japanese Armed Forces to American authorities at the High Commissioner's Residence in Camp John Hay on September 3, 1945, marking the end of World War II.

According to the 2000 census, Baguio City had a population of 252,386 in 52,302 households. (Take my word for it, since 2000 there are many more people there now.)

Now that the site was set and our usual time of the last week in February scheduled, it was time to start recruiting. Thank God for some of my regulars; Rev. Harrell Shelton and Glen Carter, R.N., had already planned on going from the previous year. Rev. Scotty Teague was almost easy to recruit; this would be his fourth straight year. Billy Weatherall had enjoyed his first mission trip to Rwanda so much he wanted to make all my mission trips if he had the time; his wife, Julie, could not take off the time from her job.

Harrell had suggested I try to get more of our Airline Baptist Church members to go; he asked me to recruit a pharmacist that was a member, but I basically got a "no" answer from the beginning. I then turned to my most reliable friend who has been with me on many trips: Don Salyer, RPh. of Mabank, TX. He was delighted to go and wanted his wife, Lorene, to go also; they were "hired" immediately.

Dr. Lattier, DDS., called me and asked me if he could go on a mission trip with me soon, so I "hired" him immediately for this trip. Unfortunately he called back four days later stating that there were conflicts in his schedule and he could not go after all. Then I tried another dentist who "owes" me for going on two medical mission trips with him; he thought he could go too, but he called back and said he couldn't go. Then I tried a dentist in Bossier City who was on our trip to Mexico several years ago; he couldn't go either. Then I tried my next-door neighbor who wanted to go if his daughter could go. He didn't call back, so I took that as a "no".

157

Next came the task of finding or getting a physician to go on our trip; often this can be most difficult. Physicians are "married" to their practice and it is very difficult to get away. I know; I was there for 25 years. Harrell told me that Dr. Kirk Cofran was a member of our church and to offer the trip to him. First I called, then I met Kirk at church and he seemed willing if he could manage the time off. He prayed about it and finally agreed to go. Kirk is a family practitioner in Shreveport; he had never been on a medical mission trip before. During the trip Kirk and I became good friends and were roommates. I learned to admire Kirk more and more as I found out about him. You will understand when you read the next several paragraphs that I asked him to write so I could feature him in this chapter. Read on and you will see what I mean.

MISSION ROOKIE

The wide world of sports entertainment permeates our society, and from its hierarchy down to the players on a team, the majority of people who are spectators have an understanding of how each part is related to the other. I have chosen this model to describe the fabric of our mission trip to the Philippines from 2/20/09 to 3/2/09 and give insight into my observations, my role in the adventure, and the impact it left on me.

Every team has a General Manager/CEO who sits at the top; this would be God, our Heavenly Father. He sets the goal for the team: to glorify His Son, Jesus Christ, and to bring the message of how He loves us all. The free gift of eternal life is waiting for all who confess they are sinners, in desperate need of a Savior, and surrender their lives to His son, Jesus.

Every team has a coach who assumes responsibility for the teams' organization, operation, and designation of individual roles. Our coach was Dr. Bill Bailey, whose reputation for winning lives for Jesus, showing compassion for team members and the participants, and leadership make him a champion of unequaled stature.

Our team consisted of two Godly preachers (Scotty and Harrell), a pharmacist (Don) and eyeglasses experts (Lorene, Don's wife) and her partner (Billy Weatherall; oil and gas expert and member of America's finest fighting force). The newest member was me (Dr. Kirk Cofran): the Rookie. [The dictionary defines "rookie" as a "raw recruit" or novice.)

I was born into a Christian family, but it was not until the age of 50, after living a life of poor decisions, ungodly behavior, and failed relationships, that I surrendered my life to Jesus as my Lord and Savior in October 1994 and was baptized two weeks later at the First Baptist Church of Carrollton, TX. This historic event was witnessed by my daughter, Valerie, who was subsequently saved and baptized in Birmingham, AL. I expected great changes in my life, but those changes occurred slowly as I sought a relationship with God. I experienced resistance and opposition from my wife in my walk with the Lord but persisted in my goal to be obedient to God's Word and direction for my life. My faith was tested time and again as I experienced four major life changing events with the Lord at my side.

The first event was a near-drowning experience in the waters off Gulf Shores, AL. I was swept out in a matter of seconds 100 feet from the shore in water over my head facing the open angry gulf waters threatening to take my life. I cried out to the Lord to save me, but surrendered to the Lord's divine direction for my life if I was allowed to survive. In a glorious moment, I found myself standing in calm water 6 inches deep and ran for shore. I have never been the same person since then.

The second event was the development of a neuromuscular disorder called idiopathic dystonia. This is a disorder where abnormal impulses from the brain cause uncomfortable muscle contractions in my lower back resulting in an abnormal gait. While driving home from church one Sunday, I prayed fervently to the Great Physician to give me a clue as to what the problem was and He replied, "**DYSTONIA**". I went home and got on my computer and my search revealed the exact symptoms I was experiencing. This journey led to an extensive neurological workup and consultations with three different neurologists (including Dr. Joseph Jankovic at Baylor College of Medicine in Houston, who has written over 700 articles on movement disorders). I was tried on various medications and two sets of Botox injections into my back muscles without response.

At the end of 2004, I concluded that a physical conditioning program and Clonazepam at bedtime was the best approach until my symptoms worsened. My wife and I discussed and came to the decision to pursue surgical intervention as a last resort to maintain my mobility. In April, 2006, I underwent a nine-hour operation (while awake) to place two electrodes in a deep portion of my brain called the globus pallidus. One week later, under general anesthesia, two separate batteries were implanted in my upper chest wall on both sides to power these implanted electrodes. I attended Easter sunrise services at the

Hillcrest Funeral Home site the following Sunday. My post-op recovery was complicated by a subdural hematoma, which was drained surgically and a one week hospitalization for an event, where I was unable to speak. Subsequently, I was treated for a wound infection and completed a two week course in physical therapy to regain my strength. I returned to work full time in June 2006 and have been in full practice since.

The third event occurred in January 2007, when my wife and I separated while she was engaged in an intensive nursing program to obtain her R.N. degree. In April 2007, she advised me that she wanted to formalize a separation agreement with plans to complete a divorce agreement in late 2007 or January 2008. God's grace sustained me during this period of time and that is the only reason I survived.

The fourth event occurred in July 2007, when my lab work revealed an elevated PSA (prostate cancer screening test). I saw an urologist and had a prostate biopsy which revealed prostate cancer. After consultations with physicians, and prayerful deliberation with God, I went through 42 radiation treatments at the Willis-Knighton Cancer Center with encouraging expectations of cure. My treatments were punctuated by brief encounters with other patients going through radiation and chemotherapy, as we discussed God's divine guidance through our individual adventures. I completed my therapy in September 2007 and prepared for the finalization of my divorce in January 2008.

Currently I live alone in a humble apartment surrounded by my Bibles and spiritual books authored by such great preachers as Dr. David Jeremiah, Dr. Charles

Stanley, and many others. God and I meet every morning over coffee and spend 90 minutes together meditating on Bible verses and devotionals which draw us closer together. Sunday after church I devote time to experience the Bible teaching of Dr. Chuck Pourcieu, Joel Osteen, Jack Graham, Kerry Shook, Dr. Robert Jeffress, John Hagge, and Dr. Jeremiah before I return to evening services at Airline Baptist Church.

Dr. Bailey "hired" me to go to the Philippines and after intense conviction by Matthew 28:19, 20 and the above preachers I have mentioned, I agreed to go. What a privilege it was to go and serve God's people on the other side of the world. Being part of the team provided a taste of what Heaven will be like in the presence of other Christians. The trip was similar to my "miracle trip" to Israel in April 2008 with Dr. Jeremiah and 400 other people, but that's another story for another time.

My life has been blessed by a trip to the Holy Land of Israel in April, 2008, and this trip to the Philippines. God has continued to challenge me to a deeper relationship with Him, and His Grace and Mercy are preparing me for the purpose and plans He has for me in the future (Jer 29:11-13). But I can say with certainty that my rookie season in missions was a successful start to further opportunities to serve our Great God and Creator.

I have no idea what God has in store for me next, but I am certain His grace will more than equip me for His purposes. I end this story with some of the Bible verses which have been the pillars of my strength in serving my Great God and Creator:

John 3:16   2 Cor 12:7-10
Phil 4:19   1 Cor 1-13

Prov 3: 5,6   Heb 13:5
Jer 29: 11-13   Matt 6:25-34

Kirk Cofran, M.D.

Rev. Alan Gueverra had taken two trips to Baguio City, the final one lasting four days so he could be sure all the churches were ready for our clinics. We depend on a missionary to prepare the way each time we go on a mission trip.

I personally counted out nearly 48,000 tablets and capsules so I could see how much work goes into the work of the pharmacist. Vickie, my wife, counted some, but mostly labeled the counted tabs/capsules. It took me the better part of 4½ days. Now, I can fully appreciate how much work she does on each of my mission trips for which I procure the meds and pack them for the mission trip. Our church is now helping pay for these meds which is a real help, especially when I personally was footing the bill for most of that cost.

Alcon Labs is so gracious in giving us eye drops/meds in the amount that I request for each mission trip; otherwise, we would not be able to afford all the eye drops/meds we need. Kingsway Charities gives us meds that we order from their list that they have available, at the time. Blessings International is gracious in the meds I need in bulk; I pay wholesale prices for these. Without these, the medical trips just couldn't take place.

Don and Lorene drove to Bossier City and spent the night with us, so they could take the flight from Shreveport; then they, Harrell, Glen, Kirk, Billy, and I took off from Shreveport to Memphis, where Scotty joined us. We flew to Los Angles, Nagoya, Japan, and then on to Manila. Alan and his group picked us up at nearly midnight (local Manila time); we drove 70 miles to Guagua, Pampanga, where we stayed at a local hotel. We ate breakfast early so we could make church at Faith Baptist Church (Alan's church). We were met by Alan's wife and his family at the church. Elnora, Alan's wife, was laden with her sixth pregnancy and due in less than a month. Their children have grown so much in the past year. Soon the church was partially full with church members. Scotty gave a great message which was equivalent to the Sunday School hour for the adults;

Harrell had the younger people for Sunday School in the back of the church. The choir sang and then Alan's oldest daughter sang a solo. Then Harrell gave an inspiring regular church-service message.

After the service we all loaded up in the SUV's and van and headed for Baguio City; the first leg of the journey was on a road like an interstate, but soon we were going through town after crowded town before we finally got to the mountains. We were witnessing the beauty of mountainous terrain with a central gorge with a river at the bottom, as we wound around and around the mountain passes. Finally, we got to the edge of Baguio City and stopped at the large Lion's Head, a large rock shaped in the head of a big lion; it had been further carved and painted to look exactly like a big lion's head. Souvenirs here were abundant; we made plans to stop on the way back.

We soon were in a crowded city with traffic just like Manila—burdened with too much traffic and with atrocious drivers. We made it on to our hotel in La Trinidad out in the edge of the urban area, where fields of strawberries and other vegetables abounded. We were a bit discouraged by the crowded rooms, no hot water, and the non-working showers. Then the full blast of a disco and karaoke were just down the hall. Earplugs would not drown out the sounds. Billy was greeted by one of the feminine men, "Where are you from big boy?" That was further accentuated the next morning by one of the guys saying, "ummmm, ummMM, UMMMM as Billy passed by. We had decided to get another hotel, already. So Alan and group took us to the Golden Pines Hotel which was very nice and quiet.

The traffic was worse in the daytime, but the weather was just gorgeous with temperatures running from 65 in the morning to 75 in the afternoon. We made our way through the maze of traffic to our first work site. As we traveled I found out why they call it the City of Pines. There were pine trees on every hill, valley, and in between; they looked much like our loblolly pines we have in Louisiana.

The first day of work (2/23/09) was at High Crest Baptist Church, where Pastor Jessie Lubiano met us in front of the church and led us up a steep incline (hill) to a covered basketball court. We quickly got the registration line going and soon people began to flock in. Dr. Kirk and Glen, the R.N., would run the medical station; I was going to see medical patients too, but it rapidly became apparent that there were going to be a lot of dental caries that needed extractions, so I went on the opposite side of the basketball court and set up shop. Don soon got busy in pharmacy, and Harrell had to help him as Lorene was busy helping Billy in the eyeglass station. Harrell turned out to be our most flexible member as he had to work in the pharmacy often and be a gopher for everything else. Scotty did most of the spiritual station using the big teaching Evangecube. I could hear him giving the Gospel with the aid of the Evangecube; I never tired of the message that he gave, especially the saving grace of God through his Son, Jesus Christ. Harrell occasionally would relieve him at the spiritual station. Billy and Lorene ran the eyeglass station and there were many smiles as patients came away from the station with a new pair of glasses or sunglasses.

Kirk and Glen saw a lot of patients with the universal complaints of pain, many of the usual complaints at any outpatient setting, but also there was a fair amount of hypertension (some of which was fairly significantly elevated). They treated a lot of children especially with colds and coughing. I saw a lot of dental caries, mostly from lack of proper dental hygiene. I would love to be able to teach dental hygiene so all these dental caries would not happen so frequently.

At lunch the church people fed us fried chicken that had been cooked in a wok; I believe that was some of the best fried chicken I have ever eaten. Gemma and Bernadette (Alan's younger sisters) entertained us by singing AMAZING GRACE acappella. The rest of the day continued smoothly and we saw 247 very appreciative people, and 217 of these accepted Jesus as Savior in the spiritual station.

On 2/24/09 we went to Springhills Bible Baptist Church and worked with Pastor Vergus. The church was situated on a rather steep hillside (mountain), but looking out over the valley below was just beautiful. What ideal weather we had that day! It was 70 degrees with a gentle mountain breeze. Everyone got their station in or around the church, but I got my favorite spot: out under a mango tree. Soon I had 4 assistants; I had someone cleaning and scrubbing the instruments, followed by boiling them; I had a church lady (Rebecca) holding the patient's head, one holding the light for me, and one doing the paperwork for me. With Rebecca's calming voice and nature, I had only one in all the children (as young as four years of age) who wasn't manageable, with the local anesthetic and extraction. If I would have had my dental chair I would have been in complete paradise. But when my back began hurting, obviously from bending over constantly, I always got a massage from the helpers to keep me going. Again, we had the most sumptuous meal with fried chicken (fried in a wok) and numerous fresh vegetables. The day went well with 256 patients being seen and 215 people accepting Jesus as Savior. We finished fairly early and went to the Philippines Police Academy, but we were denied entrance as it was too near closing time for the public.

We had to go to the drugstore in the mall and order more pediatric cough syrup, liquid Tylenol, and cold medicines; the medical team was seeing many more children than we expected. It is just impossible to bring everything you need; your team can't have a complete pharmacy. Also, the liquid is so heavy when it comes to bringing it on the airlines; they have cut us back to 50 pounds per trunk or suitcase instead of 70. Luckily we had funds available, because we expected this could happen.

On 2/25/09, we went back to La Trinidad close to where our first hotel was situated. The fields of vegetables set against the nearby mountains were so picturesque; the clouds were so close to the ground, they seemed to be touching; we were near the top of the mountainous range. People were out in the fields everywhere cultivating and harvesting the many crops. Nearby, vegetable and fruit stands were plentiful; the climate was quite favorable for many crops here.

We were greeted by Pastor Habilling, Jr., and his staff. It was a rather small church and that made it crowded for our group. Don and the pharmacy were out in front of the church, where a tarp had been stretched for protection from the sunlight which had begun to shine as more and more of the clouds dissipated. It was rather crowded in the building with the medical and eyeglass station. The spiritual station was on the back porch and I was out in the backyard next to a chicken and dog coup. No matter to me, I kept busy extracting teeth. A Dalmatian and pit bull were in some of the coups and were for sale—to eat. For lunch—you guessed it—again, we had fried chicken from a wok. Over the day we saw 305 patients with 251 people accepting Jesus as Savior. Again, it was a great day!

On 2/26/09, we went to the Landmark Bible Baptist Church in La Trinidad. It is a much larger structure with three complete floors and a fourth to be developed. The auditorium on the third floor looked like it could hold at least 300 to 400 people in movable chairs. We were greeted by Pastor Carlos Bailitoc and his staff. We had long lines of patients before we knew it. We saw 300 patients and had 255 accept Jesus as Savior. It was another great day!

That evening (Thursday), after a great meal at a restaurant across from our hotel we decided to go down to the local market to shop. There were vendors everywhere along the street. At one spot, there was a significantly larger crowd; so, we ventured over to see what was going on. Then I saw it…the tallest man I have ever seen; he was towering 3 or 4 feet above everyone else. Before anyone could say anything, I had already taken a picture. This **was** the tallest man in the world; I had seen in the morning paper that day that this man from India was visiting; it showed a picture of him in the S&M Mall; the article said he was 27-years old. I did not know that the group with him was charging to have pictures taken with him, but I already had my picture. The man was 8-feet-3-inches tall; he had fingers half the length of my arm; he had scoliosis and had an elevated shoe of about 5 inches on his right foot from disparity in the length of his legs. He was quite a spectacle, but to me he seemed rather sad.

We went on down the street where several in our group, including me, bought jewelry for our folks back home. Alan said there were so many people in town because the annual flower festival was on Saturday. It is a beautiful event; I had looked forward to viewing it, but Alan said it was an all-day event and the downtown area was blocked off for hours; he suggested we might leave Friday right after clinic and head back to Guagua.

On Friday, 2/27/09, we went to a much smaller urban church, the Whitefields Bible Baptist Church. We were greeted there by Pastor Lorenzo Lolensan and staff. We were slightly crowded in the rooms, so I went out on the porch to extract teeth. The eyeglasses team was on the roof with a large parachute type cloth for protection from the sun. We saw 152 patients and had 90 accept Jesus as Savior.

We knew all the pastors would have their work cut out for them. For follow up they took each card that had the name and address, and whether the person had accepted Jesus. The new believers were encouraged to visit and join the churches' services and become members. [THAT IS HOW WE HELP BUILD CHURCHES.]

Having our clothes already in the SUV's and van we took off straightway toward Guagua, but we did stop at the Lion's Head area and buy several souvenirs. I even paid 20 pesos to have my picture taken on a saddled horse. That was one way to show off my newly acquired cowboy hat!

It was going to get dark before the long six-hour journey back to Guagua, so we did not stop at any of the very picturesque and beautiful sites as we went back through the mountains.

At 4 a.m. the next day Christian David (Alan's oldest son) who had vomited several times earlier in the night, came over to Alan's bed. He was burning up with fever, so Alan took him to Mother Teresa of Calcutta Hospital nearby. Alan told us of this, and we volunteered to stay in Guagua instead of going to Manila and shop like we had planned. We all went to see Christian at the hospital and laid hands on him and prayed for him. I was told he could possibly have an appendicitis. You don't know how tempted I was, as an old surgeon, to lay my hands on his abdomen—but I was not asked. Alan was satisfied with his improvement, so we proceeded to go to Manila. (After we arrived home, I got an email from Alan that Christian had been successfully treated for a urinary tract infection and was going home that day—much improved.)

We went to our usual hotel in Manila, the Copacabana, which is not far from the airport; then we went to the Mall of Asia, the largest mall in the eastern hemisphere—and it is still expanding. We went to bed early as we had to rise at 2:30 a.m. to be at the airport at 3:30 a.m. to leave for the long flight home to the U.S.

What an incredible journey; we admire Alan and his co-workers who thirst for the salvation of people for Jesus Christ. We sincerely thank him and the people with whom we worked for the revival setting. I thank all my team members who worked so diligently and without complaint. We saw 1,261 patients and had 1,020 people accept Jesus as Savior. To God be the glory!

We began immediately making plans to return the next year and work with Alan and his pastor friends in the Pampanga region.

Baguio City, Philippines

Baguio City, Philippines
2009

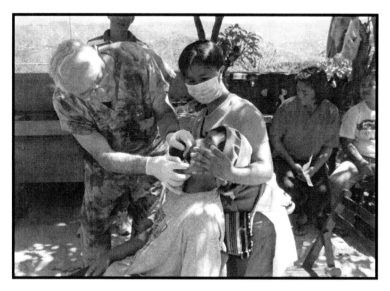

My usual job—extracting teeth

Chapter 18

Togo
The Pearl of West Africa
March 2009

Togo and Benin in West Africa were the home of John and Suzanne Crocker for 10 years; they were assigned to Togo as IMB missionaries in 1995. I met the Crockers in June 2001 when Suzanne was in the hospital in Cotonou, Benin, with lower abdominal pain. I was on a mission trip with the Singermans in Benin when I was asked as a favor to evaluate Suzanne. As circumstances would have it, I ended up helping perform an appendectomy on her. They were so appreciative they asked me to come back to Togo and serve with them in Kara (northern Togo). I brought a medical team when I came with Dr. Richard Thomassian of T.I.M.E. Ministries in November 2002; we worked in Natitingou, north Benin. It was a real joy working with them.

In January 2005 I returned to north Benin with Dr. Thomassian and his evangelical team and brought a medical team. We worked with Suzanne in and around Natitingou while the evangelical team worked separately. We worked in the church that Whitesburg Baptist Church and T.I.M.E. Ministries had helped pay for; later in another site we came within a mile of Togo while in Boukombe. Since that time, I have served with John in Rwanda three times (2007, 2008, and 2009) and Ukraine in 2007.

Togo

I asked John and Suzanne Crocker to write a brief biography about themselves to share with everyone else. First, I will share John's biography:

"God called me to serve Him as a missionary while a student at Samford University in Birmingham, AL. I had been preparing to serve as a pastor when an opportunity to serve as an Alabama Baptist Student Union summer missionary to Israel opened up in 1987. After that summer serving in Israel, God confirmed in my heart that He was calling me to serve Him in global missions.

I met Suzanne at Samford University in Birmingham, AL. After the summer mission in Israel, I returned to Samford with a change in preparations. Instead of preparing for the pastorate, I began to prepare to serve in global missions. Suzanne had been called into missions as well, so we began spending time together and just hanging out. After a while it grew into love; we married and continued our training to follow God's call into career mission service.

We were trained for missions at Mid-America Baptist Theological Seminary and the International Mission Board of the Southern Baptist Convention. Mid America's focus is getting the Gospel to a lost world following God's plan set forth in Acts 1:8, Jerusalem, Judea, Samaria, and the ends of the earth. Upon graduation, we served through the International Mission Board. Before following God's call to West Africa, we received training in everything from language, cross-culture ministry, living in a Third World nation, church planting, evangelism, discipleship, and other practical aspects of global mission service at the International Learning Center of the SBC in Virginia.

Our decision to go to Togo was made after prayer and research on unreached peoples in Africa. Before we began service in Togo, we discovered that Togo, Benin, and Mozambique had the largest number of unreached people who were following African Traditional Religions on the continent of Africa, where God called us to work. God led us to Togo and later to Benin; we spent a little over 10 years serving with the IMB in two nations.

Our main goal while serving in Togo, and later Benin, was to share the Gospel through starting Baptist churches. To accomplish this goal, we worked with training of pastors and leaders in theological education, medical ministry, and church planting through chronological Bible storying, producing radio broadcasts of chronological Bible stories in the Kabiye and Ditamari languages, literacy, and evangelistic outreach, using creative arts and sports ministries.

We were able to join God in the planting of 17 small Baptist churches, produce two series of chronological Bible stories in the Kabiye and Ditamari languages for radio outreach, train pastors and leaders in theological education, do medical ministry, lead children in an orphanage through a Bible Correspondence course, share the Gospel with over 9,000 people through creative arts, sports, medical and chronological Bible storying, and serve in several orphanages and villages in construction of campus buildings and the digging of wells.

Our decision to return to the United States was based upon seeing our ministry established to the point that it would be better for the national believers to lead the ministry instead of us, the missionaries. When a mission ministry is owned by a national ministry, it is at this point that things begin to take off in terms of a church-planting movement. We began to see this happening. At this point, Whitesburg Baptist Church in Huntsville, AL, contacted us to begin praying about coming on staff and serving in the Global Mission's office as the Minister of Missions. After much prayer, we believed this to be God's will for us. I was first exposed to global missions through the leadership of Whitesburg's first Minister of Missions, Dr. Dick Thomassian. After the church called us, we began serving at Whitesburg and now are able to share Christ literally all over the world.

God's vision for Whitesburg Baptist Church in Alabama and beyond is found at www.whitesburgbaptist.org, then click global missions, and finally then click 20/20 vision.

Suzanne Crocker shared the following with me (her biography):
When she was 3-years old Suzanne felt a calling to missions when she was in Mission Friends in her church. When she was about 8, she decided that being a missionary in Africa was her calling. But, at age 14, Suzanne became a believer in Jesus Christ; this confirmed her wanting to be a missionary.

Suzanne began her training to be a nurse after high school. At age 19 she went to Zimbabwe and worked in the Sanyanti Hospital for 8 months. (John was on his Israel mission trip at that same period of time.)

Suzanne and John met at Samford University while students there. They had known each other for a while when they were invited to Atlanta, GA, to attend an Inner City Mission Seminar. Their friends knew that both were interested in becoming missionaries and going to Africa one day, so all the other friends packed into one car and left John and Suzanne alone to go in one car. That was the spark that was needed to get them together; they started dating and love grew, in about one year they were married.

In 1989 the Crockers went to Togo, Africa, as sponsored by the Ministry of Jesus group. They were there eight months but returned to Mid-America Baptist Theological Seminary so John could get his master's degree. When they finished, they went straight back to Togo to serve the Lord as they had wanted for many years. They served there another 9 years before being called back to work in the Global Missions office of Whitesburg Baptist Church.

While I was in Rwanda in 2008 with John, he invited me to bring a medical group to Kara, Togo, when he went in March 2009. I told him I would gather a group and go; Dr. Ron Collins, John's bother-in-law, was to come with us. However, the date had to be changed when it became a necessity because the Baptist Convention would be held the second week in April and that spoiled Ron's participation.

John had put me in contact with Tony Darnell, the IMB missionary to Togo; we exchanged a few emails in preparation for the trip. I arranged to get the meds and supplies and bring them as second suitcases. I was fortunate in recruiting Rev. Sonny De Prang and his wife, Jackie; also Libby Horton volunteered to come do the eye station. Jan Massey, who had been with me to Rwanda the year before, volunteered to be on the medical team. Jeff Patterson, a home builder and contractor, who just happened to be my daughter's employer, found out about our mission trip and wanted to go; he had just returned from Iraq a few months earlier on a mission trip.

Having purchased the meds and supplies from Blessings International, Kingsway Charities, Alcon Labs, and MAP International, I proceeded to do most of the dose packing and labeling of the medicines. I quickly found out how many hours my sweet wife had spent, in my previous trips, meticulously doing all that work. Now,

I can really appreciate her endeavors; that is a real labor of love for the Lord. I could take only four trunks of meds as four people were going from the Shreveport airport; that was a real effort of trying to choose the right meds and the quantity of each. I had a strong hunch we would not have enough of some of the commonly used meds.

Togo, West Africa, is a finger of land slipped between Ghana and Benin; it is bordered to the north by Burkina Faso and the south by the Atlantic Ocean. It has a population of about 6.3 million, according to *Wikipedia*; it has a mostly tropical, sub-Sahara climate. Situated on the Atlantic Ocean, Lome is the capital and borders Ghana (the only capital in the world that borders another country directly). Togo is heavily dependent on both commercial and subsistence agriculture. Kara lies in the north, where the land is mostly a rolling savanna. There are at least 40 ethnic groups in Togo; nearly one million people in and around Kara are Kabiya, 22 percent of the total of the nation.

Our medical team left Shreveport and arrived in Atlanta to meet the evangelical team; then we all flew through Paris to Lome. Tony Darnell and helpers met us at the airport and took us directly to the Baptist Mission House, where we spent the night. I had looked on the Internet and looked at the temperatures and weather, but nothing can truly ready you for the very warm or hot tropical climate when you are used to temperate weather at home. Luckily, we had air conditioning at the mission house. March and early April is the hottest period in Togo; it is one month before the main rainy season and tends to be quite dry. We were fortunate that we caught just the tail end of the harmattan while we were there, but there is enough fine dust for everyone when it is dry and the wind blows.

After breakfast at the mission house the next morning, we got money exchanged, bought a few supplies, packed our vans, and headed north to Kara. Just prior to leaving for Kara we went by

Tony's home and met his wife, Marlene, and their children. I was in the van with Tony and I got to converse with him a lot. I found out he was teaching pastors at the seminary. He and Marlene were the only IMB missionaries in Togo, but we met JJ and Melissa that morning; they were independent Baptist missionaries who were going to help us during the coming week in Kara.

The land was flat and fairly green in the south, but as we moved further north, we began seeing the rolling savannas with less greenery. In the distance, smog was present most of the time; this was a combination of the residual harmattan and smoke from burning the fields in preparation for planting soon. In one area, we went through the edge of the mountains; the traffic was slowed significantly here by the very large 18-wheelers carrying huge loads and traveling at a snail's pace. Teak trees lined the highway on both sides, frequently; the larger trees are used for wood carvings. The weather turned warmer rapidly as the day progressed. We had to cut off the air conditioner in our van so we could have enough power to keep up with the two other vans. Several small villages were scattered along the way. Frequently we saw sacks of charcoal stacked high for sale as well as to be used as firewood by the owners. In the villages were frequent food stands selling wares and food. The road grew worse the further north we went; at that point we were constantly dodging potholes.

Finally about dark we arrived in Kara; the city is typical of many Third World countries with people everywhere along the road. There were people walking, riding, or selling food along the streets. We drove into the Linguistic Center, where we were to stay for the week. We had rooms like dormitories, but there was no air conditioning; however, a ceiling fan was present. Many of us found it difficult to sleep with temperatures in the 90's.

The next morning was Saturday; we had an excellent breakfast in the cafeteria in the Linguistic Center. The pineapple and mango were some of the best I have ever eaten. Then, we drove a few miles in the city to Tomde Baptist Church while the evangelical team headed out to Koujoukadah, Bebede, and St. Margarite. At Tomde Baptist Church we were greeted by Pastor Tchangi Franklin and his staff; he had promised we would have a big crowd that day. JJ had been able to locate a R.N. that was working with their group to help us in the clinic. Lisa Lewis was a welcome sight, as I was the only doctor on our medical team; I gave her the job as nurse practitioner. She said she had never done this, but she fit right in seeing patients. I did manage to pull a few necrotic teeth. The eye team, run by Libby, just happened to be very popular and may have been the busiest station for much of the day. The pharmacy was run by Jan and Jackie with intermittent help from Sonny and Jeff, when they were not doing the spiritual station. Large groups of people were gathered and were given the Gospel and offered a time to respond before they went through the clinic. Most of these were church members or friends of church members, but several still accepted Jesus as Savior in the spiritual presentation. Sonny used the teaching Evangecube to help in his spiritual presentation.

Sonny and Jeff went down the street door to door witnessing, after the spiritual station presentation. About three doors down from the church entrance, Sonny perchance went by a small shop, where a man was working on bicycle tires. When he approached him about Jesus, the man spoke good English and listened closely as Sonny presented the Gospel to him. Wayne, the tire repairman's English name, ended up accepting Jesus as Savior and followed Sonny back to the clinic at the church. We needed more interpreters and Wayne agreed to work with us the remainder of the week; he even came back with us and ate supper with us at the Linguistic Center every night. Wayne turned out to be a real blessing, as he interpreted for Sonny and Jeff almost every day for the rest of the week; he was very effective as an interpreter, and he was very interested in helping explain the saving knowledge of Jesus Christ. What a serendipity!

Koffi was my interpreter for the week; he was a student at the Linguistic Center and spoke excellent English. He endured the entire week with me and was so faithful in his interpreting efforts. He told me one day that his goal was to be a pastor of a big church.

There was a steady crowd of people all day at the church, even as the temperature soared to a moderate 100 degrees F. The crowd was fairly manageable until near the end of the day when they figured out that they might not be seen before the clinic ended. Libby found it very difficult to fit glasses with so many people crowding around. Despite some crowd disorderliness, we saw 232 people as patients, and they were very appreciative. That night, I discussed the crowd control with John and he stated that he would hire two policemen to control the crowd the rest of the week.

On Sunday morning we went back to Tomde Baptist Church to attend and participate in the services. We got to see the church people sing, play their instruments, and occasionally dance. The evangelical team put on a drama act and puppet show that was well received by the crowd. John gave an excellent message in French that was translated to Kabaye for the sake of some of the church members and guests. Afterwards we went to a nearby restaurant for lunch; it is an event when you eat out in Africa; it takes sometimes nearly two hours for preparation and consuming the meal.

That afternoon, the evangelical team went out for more evangelizing, while the medical team got to go to the city market, where food and ordinary wares are sold by the local people for customers. We saw all sorts of local vegetables and food items, as well as some wares used in ordinary life. We even saw one section where fetish things such as dried frogs and snakes, and other animal parts, are sold for use in Voodoo worship; you can imagine the smell.

Early Monday morning, we headed out to Bebeda, where John had formed a church while he was serving as a missionary in Togo. The city roads soon led to rough dirt roads as we left Kara; it was over an hour's drive out into the country. Occasionally, we saw herds of cattle out in the fields. We could tell it was the dry season; there were several people out preparing the fields for planting, anticipating the rainy season soon. Our team was greeted by Pastor Ossido Etche and a large crowd which had gathered, out under the trees in front of the public school there. We were allowed to use two of the classrooms with very ample room inside, but there was little air movement in the rooms; I wish we could have been out under the shade trees. In the classrooms, we had very adequate crowd control with our "big" policemen that John had hired. At least, with this arrangement it was a very peaceful environment. Jeff gave the Gospel presentation to an estimated crowd of well over 200 people; they were very receptive and many accepted Jesus as Savior.

I had several people who wanted me to look at their teeth but infrequently wanted them extracted. I found the people there to have much better than average dental hygiene; they chew on small sticks to get a rough soft edge, then they brush their teeth with the stick. Compared to the city out in the country, where they have a much simpler diet and work harder, I found few people with hypertension. In the city, the diets are just terrible and obesity is not uncommon, according to Tony. We saw several people with the signs and symptoms of malaria, so we empirically treated them for it. Skin infections were not uncommon either. There were plenty of the universal complaints of pain in one part of the body or the other. Probably, the most common complaint was eye irritation from all the ubiquitous dust and pollens. Thanks to Alcon Labs and Kingsway Charities we had plenty of eye drops.

One of the policemen was told that he was to protect me. Anyway, we had NO problems with the crowd that day. (John and I have decided to hire policemen from now on, in all the African countries where we work.) We saw 208 patients and had 125 salvation decisions; it was another good day.

At the end of the work day, several of our medical group went to the Internet café. It was an exercise in futility. I could not get to my email or email anyone back home. I was able to get onto two or three sites in 30 minutes. Other team members found the same frustration. So, I called home a couple of times. Vickie was out during the day, so I called her at 2 a.m (CST) when I knew I could find her; despite the hour, she was still happy to hear from me.

Tuesday we went further out into the country past Bebede to Koukjoudadah, which is really "out in the sticks". We were greeted by Pastor Pokonah Assiki and even a larger crowd than the previous days. We set up in front of a small church; the cover was expanded by placing palm leaves over a makeshift shed, but it turned out to be so much more comfortable being outdoors. Jeff preached to a large crowd gathered out under a big shade tree.

Soon the crowd started through the clinic line; the chief was near the front. He informed me that he wanted us to build a bridge near the village, as it was washed out every year, during the heavy part of the rainy season, and they were stranded from the market and the city. I did not know what to say other than I knew better than to make him a promise I could not keep. Out in the open like we were, it was just invaluable having the security police there. We saw 210 patients and had over 20 decisions for Jesus. Koffi, my interpreter, told me that one of the policemen admired us for working non-stop and so diligently to see all the people that we possibly could. Our team was given a live chicken at the end of the day, and we gladly accepted it. (This was like the widow's mite, a significant and meaningful gift from the grateful person.)

Wednesday morning, we returned to Tomde Baptist Church; we were promised that most of the crowd would not be church members as we had the first clinic day. We were very busy again. It was good to have Lisa back to help with the medical clinic. I did a field circumcision on a young male that had severe phimosis; he would cry every time with urination because of the stricture. It was hot again; even the people who live there were sweating. We saw well over 200 people as patients and had over 200 people accept Jesus. (This was because the crowd was composed of non-members of the church). Libby ran out of eyeglasses as this continued to be a very popular station, particularly because of giving out sunglasses. The crowd got rowdy near the end of the day; some were even climbing over the fence—but remember we had help: our faithful policemen.

Thursday, we went just outside Kara to Lassa Bas, where Pastor Abissi Abalo and his group welcomed us to a large waiting crowd. It was a small church, so Lisa and I worked out in front of the church in a makeshift tent. We were working with an ever diminishing supply of medicines and supplies despite buying more meds at the local pharmacy two days earlier. We finally had to stop as all the common meds like multiple vitamins, worm meds, and pain meds were depleted. The pharmacy had worked tirelessly all week giving out an average of over four prescriptions per person. We were able to see 179 patients and had over 50 salvation decisions. Although shorter, it had been another good day.

Friday morning we had breakfast with several of the pastors we had worked with during the week. John thanked them kindly for their efforts and hard work. I challenged them with the Great Commission. I told them we had come to help them make disciples in their churches; now, it was their responsibility to do the second part of the Great Commission: *"Teaching them whatsoever I have commanded you."* (That is the hard part!) I reminded them that they should go and get those people who had come to the clinics and work with them to make them responsible Christians. I further reminded them that this was what we do as a team; and now we were turning it over to their efforts.

For the week, the medical team had seen 1,033 patients and had nearly 400 people accept Jesus as Savior during the spiritual presentations. Some 400 pairs of eyeglasses and 175 pairs of sunglasses had been given out. Clothes, toothbrushes, and toothpaste had been given to the orphanage. Between the medical and evangelical team, over 4,000 evangelical tracts had been handed out. With the evangelical team's effort, 1,477 people had responded by accepting Jesus as Savior. Hallelujah! To God be the glory! What a great week we had experienced.

We then loaded up the vans and started the long trip back to Lome. The weather grew warmer and warmer as the day progressed. Stopping for a bag lunch at noon was a treat. Along the mountainous regions, we saw at least three large trucks that had just turned over. They obviously were going too fast with a top heavy load. After reaching Lome, we quickly unloaded and went SHOPPING for souvenirs; we would have to put the items in our suitcases that we would have to check early the next morning at the airport. We went down to the artisan village and had a ball purchasing wood carvings, cloth, and many other wares.

The next morning we took our suitcases to the airport; that really saved time just before the flight out. We then drove about town viewing the numerous motorcycles, bicycles, and many automobiles in the crowded capital city. In the center of the city was a large statue of the dove of peace carrying an olive branch in its mouth. We then had a good African-cooked lunch and went to do more shopping at Pirates' Alley. After supper at the mission house, we headed to the airport to fly to Paris overnight.

I asked the team to "fly with the butterfly" (Lunesta), so we would be rested when we got to Paris the next morning. We got there at 6 a.m. and went to our hotel and prepared for a day tour of Paris. John had hired two vans to take us to the middle of Paris, where we would spend the day touring mostly on foot. We walked along the Seine River viewing many of the city's main tourist attractions. At one point we saw at least 500 people in an apparent marathon running along the river. Frequently, we passed small coffee shops and quaint places to eat along the street front.

We stopped at one of the money exchange places to get money exchanged to buy souvenirs and eat. We got duped about 30 percent on the exchange rate.

Soon, we walked on to the Notre Dame Cathedral; it is a pretty site, but the gargoyles on the side of the church reminded me of demonic statues. Inside it was a beautiful monument, however, it was more like a museum than an actual church. Being Palm Sunday, the cathedral was overcrowded inside, so we stayed for a just a few minutes. The service was given in French, English, and German. The singing was very good, especially with the organ music. We strolled through the gardens behind the church and admired the beauty of early spring flowers. The church sits adjacent to the Seine River; the whole area is a visitor's paradise.

As we walked on down the river, we got to view several of the river boats; some had people sitting at tables eating. There were numerous shops along the river to buy souvenirs. Then, we walked on to the Louvre (the French museum equivalent to our Smithsonian in Washington, DC). There was a long line; we found out that the first Sunday of every month the entrance fee is waived. We had to contend with the large crowd, but it was interesting as we strolled through the Richelieu, Sully, and Denon portions of the museum viewing the many Roman, Greek, and Oriental antiquities. We then ventured into the Egyptian antiquities and on to the area of French, German, Flemish, Dutch, Belgian, Russian, Swiss and Scandinavian paintings. Yes, we went by the MONA LISA, but it was so crowded we could not get close. Also, the glass cage about the picture made it hard to adequately view the painting. (There has been a lot of security since someone tried to steal the picture years ago.) Just like the Smithsonian Institutes, there was just no way we would be able to see all the exhibits in such a short time.

From there we went to a restaurant, had a cold drink, and called our vans to pick us up to take us to the Eiffel Tower; it was a couple more miles to that main tourist attraction. The vans finally showed up, and we took off. Shortly thereafter, the lead van got stopped by police; it had one too many passengers. The driver did not have a driver's license, and he was arrested. John and the group proceeded to return to the hotel by the Metro. Meanwhile, our group proceeded to the Eiffel Tower, but the lines were very long, so we just strolled about the front base. (I had the privilege of going up the Eiffel Tower on a previous trip; it has a magnificent view of a very large city.)

We went back to our hotel and had a good night's rest before taking off for the airport early the next morning. Then we flew back to the U.S. to our various places called home. It had been a very good trip!

Togo

Togo, West Africa
March 2009

Lisa Lewis, Jeff Patterson, and missionary Tony Darnell

Chapter 19

Rwanda

Compassion Rwanda
July 2009

Compassion Rwanda unites brothers and sisters from two continents to serve people affected by the 1994 genocide in Kigali, Rwanda. This medical dental clinic event created by Compassion Connect brings volunteer professionals to some of the most urgent needs in this Capital City.

Compassion Connect worked closely with the Luis Palau Association during the Season of Service 2008 in Portland, OR, to provide assistance to five clinics around the area. Following that event, doors were opened to meet with church and civic leaders in Rwanda. After a visit in November 2008, leadership accepted the challenge to form Compassion Rwanda, July 2009.

While still in Kigali, Rwanda, in September 2008, John Crocker heard of the plan and asked me if I would gather a medical team to bring back there in July 2009. I told him I would make it a priority. He told me that the Luis Palau Association and Compassion Connect would be partnering with Africa New Life to do a revival and hold medical and dental clinics in Kigali; it was going to be a **big event.** The initial plan was to do a week long revival, mostly in the soccer stadium every night, but there would be several events and teams supporting the overall program. I was to help lead a medical team.

Rwanda

Compassion Connect is an organization established in the Portland, OR, area with the vision of many churches working together to transform their neighborhoods. They are a proactive resource that supports collaborative efforts between the church, civic, and social service sectors of a community. They are focused in the areas of health, housing, and Compassion Helps (Compassion Helps is an initiative to help churches collaborate to serve schools, social services, and attack local human trafficking.) The Compassion Clinic Events are the most readily available tool for communities to work together in providing free medical/dental care to their neighbors.

John Crocker gave my communication information to Africa New Ministries, then I was called by Alan Hotchkiss about the project. He told me more details about Compassion Connect. We discussed the clinics, sites, and obtaining the meds/supplies for clinics. I told him I had ordered meds/supplies from Sun Enterprises in Kigali the previous year. We discussed payment for this; funds were made available from different resources. He also recommended bringing in as much meds/supplies as I could. I took an instant liking to Alan; we talked on and on about things.

Not long after that Gary Tribbet of Compassion Connect called and we discussed the clinics, sites, logistics and personnel. Gary was much like Alan; he was such an easy person to talk to. We had a few more discussions before our final departure.

I was fortunate in recruiting Dr. Jan Soapes again; she had been to Kigali with me the previous September. She even went trekking up into the rain forest to see the gorillas with us. My wife, Vickie, got her uncle (Sherman French) and his daughter (Tina Sheffield) to volunteer to go with me; also, I had another young couple walk up to me at church one Sunday night and ask to go on my next mission trip Tara Goodwin, R.N., was welcomed on the team. Then I heavily recruited Rev. Scotty Teague who had been with me many times; I needed him to do our spiritual station at the medical clinic.

Medicines and supplies were ordered over the Internet in Kigali through Sunjay with Sun Enterprises; I had ordered meds from him via the Internet the previous year. Naturally it is hard to determine how much meds to order, so we had to order more meds after our clinic started the previous year.

Phyllis Forsyth, R.N. of Compassion Connect, called to chat with me, about the clinic setup and details. I told her that I was ordering the meds from a pharmacy in Kigali like I had the year before. During the conversation I found out we could not use thin plastic bags of any type to dosepak the meds. I went out and cleaned out two Dollar General stores of mail envelopes. I had to go by our church on an errand and mentioned that I needed 6,000 paper envelopes; one of the secretaries mentioned that the staff was throwing away two carts of offering/tithe envelopes and asked me if I wanted them. I took them home and counted them; yes, you guessed it right: there were 6,000 envelopes.

The Compassion Connect group came to Kigali a couple of days prior to us and started clinic at the Dream Center (Pastor Charles Buregeya's church). We came in their second day of clinic. We had arrived at midnight to the Baptist Mission House; we arose early the next morning to take our tour to the Kigali Memorial Center (1994 genocide).

The Kigali Memorial Center is near the center of town located on one of the seven hills of Kigali. It looks more or less like a modern home. Out near the entrance a flame was burning in a disc over a pond of water. I thought this might be an "eternal burning flame", but quickly found out it burned only for the 100 days—from April to July—to denote when the actual genocide was going on in 1994. Down below the building was a large gravesite; we could visit it after paying the entrance fee. A recorder was available for hire at the sites of interest. A guide was assigned to our group; we then proceeded down to the large concrete gravesite. Our guide said that this was the 10th anniversary of the center and over 255,000 had been buried in the site with more being added weekly from mass graves found in the urban areas and countryside. He said these graves are a clear reminder of the cost of ignorance. The center is a permanent memorial to those who fell victim to the genocide and serves as a place for people to grieve those they lost. At the front of the gravesite was a large granite wall like at the Vietnam Memorial in Washington, DC, that named many of the families that were in the gravesite. On down the way, were fresh flowers over three caskets of recently found remains that would soon be buried in the gravesite.

We then entered the center and went counter clockwise, along the walls, which explained the steps of the beginning, the actual, and the post-events of the genocide. Whoa! How cruel men can be to each other. It was so sad to see pictures of thousands of the victims. There were videos of survivors telling of the genocide, the trials afterward, and future of the country to help prevent such a tragedy again. Upstairs, the other genocides of modern history were briefly displayed to let people know that there were other such genocides in the world. The memorial was well put together and should remind humankind that no such event(s) should ever take place again. [On the way home from Rwanda at the airport I noticed a book entitled: **CONSPIRACY TO MURDER, THE RWANDAN GENOCIDE** by Linda Melvern. I purchased this book, and with much effort I read it over a period of time. It is very full of facts about the events leading up to, the actual events, and some of the follow up on the events. Basically the book tells that the massacres perpetrated in Rwanda in 1994 were the result of a strategy; that strategy was adopted and elaborated by political, civil, and military authorities. It was a plan that had been organized at the highest level, and its object was the extermination of the Tutsis. Then there was little or no reprimand for those doing all the atrocities. From those events I know now that the country is trying to reconciliate.

After lunch we went out to the soccer stadium to make sure our site for work was secured for the next morning. Then we went out to the Dream Center to work—or so I thought; the team there was ending up the day as they were very efficient at seeing a large number of people rapidly.

We saw Pastor Charles at the mission house; it was so good to see him again. He told us that groups that come in offering community service have a much easier time gaining access to the country and its people. A medical team is always welcomed as well as groups organizing community activities. The Whitesburg Church group had been requested by the City of Kigali to assist in painting the city's crosswalks. While the team was painting the crosswalks in downtown Kigali, traffic almost came to a standstill. This resulted in the team being able to distribute thousands of invitations to the Hope Festival at the soccer stadium and thousands of Gospel tracts.

The next morning we loaded up our group and headed to the soccer stadium. A large crowd was already gathering; tents had been set up to handle part of the crowd, but the line extended well past that. Scotty got his first chance to witness, with the aid of his teaching Evangecube to a tent full of people through his interpreter. This was what Scotty had come to do; he was in his element. Meanwhile inside work was started. Immediately, the eye clinic was swamped with people wanting exams and eyeglasses. The pharmacy was run by Tara and Rachael (Huntsville, AL). Triage was run by Dana (Huntsville, AL) and Sherman guided the patients to each doctor, and back to the pharmacy.

Jan, a native Rwandan, was my gifted interpreter. At least 16 times she had discerned that the person I was treating needed prayer for salvation. I used my Evangecube each time to explain the

Gospel, then with each person I prayed the Sinner's Prayer for forgiveness and salvation.

We saw many of the universal problems like pain, GI complaints, upper respiratory infections, allergies, and a LOT of eye symptoms. (Initially the governmental agencies allowed us only to do an eye clinic and dental clinic. Later, a medical clinic was added.) We had one native Rwandan doctor to help us the first day; others joined the next two days, and by Saturday we had five medical doctors. That day the dentist, the Compassion Connect team, and five Rwandan doctors saw almost 1,000 patients.

Gary Tribbet (Compassion Connect) bought me a 9-year-old young lady to examine Saturday morning; it was obvious from her gait that she had some form of palsy. She had been a normal child, doing well in school, when she had suddenly been stricken with an acute illness two or three years earlier and left with a significant palsy, deafness, and speech impediment. She had been to the hospital and multiple doctors to no avail; her malady continued. The child and her mother had traveled four hours to get to our clinic. The mother said she did not come for pills; she came for a miracle. I examined her and confirmed a palsy of some type, but could offer her little in the way of treatment; I got a second opinion from one of the Rwandan doctors. He sent her to the referral service we had set up if people needed specialty care or hospitalization. In about an hour Gary brought her back to our room and asked all the pastors and doctors to circle around and lay hands on her for prayer of healing. A pastor from Kampala, Uganda, led the prayer; it was powerful. This was an emotional and stirring event; many tears were shed during the prayers. At the end of the prayers, the little girl very plainly said in Kinyarwandan and interpreted, "That was a nice prayer, Pastor." Then she motioned her hand at all of us and said, "Thank you for praying for me; continue to pray for me, I have the faith I will be OK." Then Gary tearfully said in a joyful praise, "That girl is more whole than any of us."

During clinic time, Andrew Palau and several of his staff came through the clinic thanking us for participating in the overall project. The "famous guitar player" Enric Sifa who had won RWANDA HAS TALENT also came through the clinic, so we got to take pictures with him.

Outside the stadium a large platform had been erected; David Lubben, Enric Sifa, and Nicole C. Mullen were singing, performing, or preaching from it to large crowds. John got to preach for close to 45 minutes each day at the stadium and had great results with people wanting to accept Jesus. Friday and Saturday night at 6:45 p.m. Andrew Palau, son of Evangelist Luis Palau, preached to a crowd estimated to be 15,000 to 17,000 people. The stadium was just not large enough for the platform and the large crowds, so the parking lot and adjacent areas were utilized. Andrew Palau gave a passionate message and over 5,000 cards to accept Jesus were accepted by the crowd, and later turned in by the recipients.

After the message Scotty, Tara, and I got to meet Andrew. Scotty told Andrew that he had heard his dad, Luis, preach and tell how the 3 G's (GOLD, GIRLS, and GLORY) could ruin any ministry; Andrew smiled and asked us to help keep him humble.

Sunday morning we went to a REAL praise service at the Dream Center. The song service was very stirring; most everyone had his hands and arms raised, many were dancing in the aisles. Every one was lifted up praising our Savior. Pastor Charles' friend and "classmate" during their growing up years gave the sermon: "God's vision in your life". It was a powerful and stirring message—one of the best I have ever heard.

While at the Dream Center, we saw Kelly and Laura Sager attending the morning service we attended. Kelly and Laura are IMB missionaries to Rwanda; we worked with them the first time we were in Rwanda. It was so pleasant to see them. I asked about the children and they told us we would see them at the mall when we got pizza later that day.

Sunday afternoon was a down day (rest time), but we chose to go shopping in the downtown area at one of the main souvenir shops. Everyone that went purchased a few or several souvenirs for the folks back home. I got several fuzzy gorilla dolls for those who had supported my efforts for this particular mission trip.

Later that afternoon, our medical team met up with the evangelical team at the downtown mall, and John bought us all pizza. The Sagers came in shortly after we arrived. My, how all six of their children had grown since we were there in 2007. I got to talk with Tegan and Brick; they told me about their furlough for several months in Oregon, but they seemed perfectly happy to be back **home** in Rawanda.

Early Monday morning the Compassion Connect group went back home. Some members of Andrew Palau's team were on an airplane going to Chicago from Amsterdam that got some smoke in the cabin and lost cabin pressure. They initially thought that their pilots were going to ditch the plane in the cold Atlantic, but instead they were able to make it on to Iceland. Two days later the team caught a flight on to Portland.

Our medical team went to the Dream Center for two days of clinic there. We just about ran out of eyeglasses; the sunglasses had long ago been selected by the patients. Tina Sheffield had been a real trooper during the week. She worked the eyeglasses station mostly alone with an interpreter. In the pharmacy, some types of meds were getting scarce. Scotty had evangelized to near the end, even when no patients were left. However, several people came over and wanted to share with him about their memories and the hardships of the past genocide. Some of this became very emotional.

Jan, my interpreter, had been asking me to pray for several people to receive Jesus as Savior. When we were in the process of the salvation prayer for one older lady and I said in the prayer that Jesus had died on the cross for her, she threw up her arms and stood up praising God. When we prayed and told her that Jesus would now live in her heart forever, I thought the lady was going to be raptured immediately. She was so excited to have Jesus in her heart. That event made the highlight of my week!

I told Jan there were two parts to the Great Commission: the first was to make disciples; the second was to teach, whatsoever, the Lord had commanded. I told her that she had watched me for three days using the Evangecube for salvation purposes; now, it was time for her to apply that principle. I had Jan practice on me with the Evangecube; then, the next two days Jan led six more people to Jesus with the Evangecube and prayer. At the end of the clinic I gave her my Evangecube to use on other people that she discerned needed Jesus.

Jan was recommended to Pastor Emma, Pastor Fred, and later I presented her case to Pastor Charles. She was given an appointment to see Pastor Charles and I hope he hired her for the New Africa Life Ministries.

For the week, 1,715 patients had been seen in the medical clinics. John Crocker's group and the medical team had 4,067 professions of faith in Jesus Christ. About 6,000 Gospel tracts had been distributed. The Andrew Palau group had several thousand profess Jesus as Savior. Hallelujah, praise the Lord! What a week of work for the Kingdom!

At the end of the last work day we packed all the meds we had left over and we decided to take them to Kageyo to give to the refugee village for use.

I always like to reward my "troops" who work so diligently all week. When I heard we could go by the Akagera National Park adjacent to Kageyo (where we were delivering the supplies), I jumped at the opportunity to go there first. Deborah, of New Africa Life Ministries, and our driver agreed to take us there.

We had to get up at 3:30 a.m. and be ready by 4:00 a.m. so we could make the four-hour drive to the Akagera National Park. We packed three suitcases of left-over meds and two large boxes of supplies to take to Kageyo. Not long after sunrise we got to see the beautiful countryside; the rolling hills had fog and low clouds hovering over the valleys and covering several of the hillsides. Along with the light of day came a bustling of activity along the highway of people traveling to and fro, or simply going to work another day in the field. The fields were green with crops, or being readied for a new planting soon. The pre-dawn coolness warmed as the sun came over the hills; it was going to be another beautiful day in Rwanda.

Finally, as we approached Akagera the hills had given way to a more or less flat savannah with grass and tangled acacia woodlands; it is quite different from the breezy cultivated hills that characterize much of Rwanda. This portion borders Tanzania. We all went into the admission house to sign up and pay our fees. One of the guides then rode with us in our van to venture out into the park. It was not long before we saw several zebras, then bushbucks, and then the most gorgeous giraffes I have ever witnessed. We also witnessed several species of antelope and a flock of guinea fowl. All the animals were very well nourished. Most of the animals did not want us close so they would flee, but it seemed that this was an ordinary day for homo sapiens to come and gawk at them and their natural habitat. What a magnificent Creator we have; His creations are just beyond description of beauty. The male giraffes had to be over 15 feet tall; one seemed to stand and watch us admire him.

We then drove by one of the rangers' houses to look at the Lake Ihema; on the other side is Tanzania. One of the rangers was cleaning fish he had recently caught from the lake. Then we drove on around the lake to where the hippopotami live; we initially saw at least five. They must have felt threatened and quickly went out into the lake, where they feel more secure. Again, all the animals were well nourished.

We came out of the reserve and went to the nearby hotel, where we had a sack lunch on the pavilion. As we approached our van on exiting, we saw several baboons. One was strutting across the parking lot like he was the Number One (don't you bother me) baboon. We proceeded over to where they were and gave the male a cereal bar. When he bit into it, he rapidly discarded it. That was not what he was wanting.

Only a few miles away was Kageyo; we proceeded there while viewing the marked changes that had taken place just a few months ago in September 2008 when we worked five days in the refugee village. There were more cows at the watering hole; young boys and men were attending them. They were placing water from the pond into watering troughs so the cows would not muddy the water. Further into the village were more houses and more concrete buildings with tin roofs; vegetables and fruit trees were planted almost everywhere now. Before, the people had almost seemed hopeless with little activity. Our group had witnessed to several hundred of the people there in our previous clinics; many had accepted Jesus as Savior. Now they had a church in the village. Hallelujah! The Lord is so good. I am sure many of the converts our spiritual team had led to the Lord last year were now worshiping our King.

We went by the clinic first to deliver the remaining meds and supplies. One of the nurse practitioners and the pharmacist were there and very happily accepted the meds and supplies. They just could not believe we would give them all these supplies. I told them, "We are giving this freely; you be sure you give it freely to the people in this village." Both expressed such smiles of gratitude.

We proceeded on to the school building, where I gave the schoolmaster three soccer balls (with a pump) to use for the school. There we met Dr. Soapes' sponsored child, David, and his mother. Judy Corcoran, N.P. from Huntsville, AL, also met one of her two sponsored children there. What an emotional meeting it was for everyone. We then proceeded to David's home to take a large sack of millet flour and several other groceries that Dr. Soapes had bought for the family. We found the three-room house very simple with minimal furniture (one small table, two small benches, and a straw mat on the floor; this mat also served as their bed). The family was elated at the friendship and groceries. David had recently been in the hospital for seizures and malnutrition. Earlier, Dr. Soapes had been by the hospital in Kigali and gotten the CT scan of David's head and medical records; she gave them to David's mom to keep.

We then went to Judy's other sponsored-child's home and gave her a bunch of goodies. One of the Huntsville sponsors could not make the trip, so John Crocker asked Dr. Soapes to take her a big sack of things to the sponsored child. We all witnessed several Alabama t-shirts and jerseys being put on the child; being that I was taking photos to send to the sponsor, I could not resist putting my **LSU** hat on the child with her Alabama Tide jersey.

I had met Mike Tracy of Living Water International at the mission house shortly after our arrival. He told me that while he was there he was arranging to dig several water wells in Rwanda. I was so gratified to find out later that he was going to dig another water well at Kageyo; the first one was non-functional. That was why the people were taking large containers of water for personal consumption when we were there in September 2008 and at the present.

I am so thankful for the hard work put in by the African New Life Ministries, Compassion Connect group, Whitesburg Baptist Church evangelical team, and all those on my team that helped. I am thankful for Cindy and Jerry Prouty at the Baptist Mission

House, all the interpreters, and personnel who helped the whole week. It was a BIG THING! Praise God for His blessings and grace on this event. His name was proclaimed mightily.

John Crocker told me that his evangelical team and our medical team were invited to come back to Rwanda the next year; he said they may go to Uganda for a few days, in the same trip. As for me, I was off to India next.

Our medical team
Rwanda, 2009

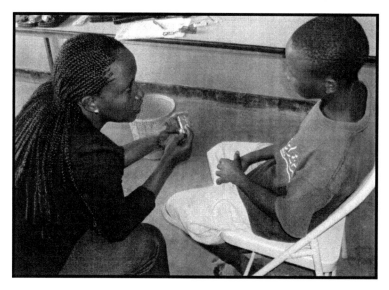

I taught my interpreter to successfully use the Evangecube

Scotty and me with evanglist Andrew Palau

The crowd gathering for the Andrew Palau team

Chapter 20

When One Door Closes, Another Opens

I thoroughly enjoyed the two previous trips to China. I was asked to return immediately, after the earthquake in April 2008, as a general surgeon, with a crew ready to operate. We were invited to the earthquake area 200 miles south of Beijing, but logistically and time wise I just couldn't go then. Later, we were invited to come back to China by MMR (Medical Mission Response) to go work in the earthquake area in small medical teams. I volunteered for this and had made my reservation to MMR for the trip by April 2009.

When the word was broadcast over the Internet and world news that there was a new flu in Mexico City, I thought little of this affecting the whole world. Not long afterwards, the flu had spread to several other countries, including the United States.

According to *Wikipedia*, the 2009 flu pandemic is an A(H1N1) pandemic and global outbreak of influenza A virus subtype H1N1, identified in April 2009, commonly referred to as the "swine flu", which is transmitted between humans. The new strain spread widely beyond North America with confirmed cases in 98 countries.

On June 11, 2009, the WHO (World Health Organization) declared the outbreak had become a pandemic. The WHO declared a Pandemic Alert Level of six out of a maximum of six, which described the degree to which the virus had been able to spread among humans. WHO had hesitated to raise the alert level and declare a phase 6 pandemic because the virus to date had caused generally mild symptoms, even though the pandemic level describes spread of the virus rather than its severity. Having raised the threat to a level of 6 caused many countries to adopt a variety of plans, such as shutting borders, barring events, and curtailing travel. A move to phase 6 meant that "emergency plans are instantly triggered around the globe."

We were notified, by telephone and email, that our trip to China had been cancelled. A professor was going to lecture to a group of workers in Hong Kong; he was quarantined for seven days, because he was an American and the level 6 pandemic alert was in effect. MMR said it could not take the chance that we would be quarantined also.

I was more than a little bit disappointed; I was looking forward to the trip and experience. But, within 2 weeks, I got a telephone call and email from MMR inviting me and a couple of others to Lebanon or India. I did not give an immediate answer. I told Dan Bivins that I wanted to pray and think about it for a few days. Meanwhile, I called and talked with Sonny De Prang and he said he would pray and think about it.

Over the weekend I could not get a clear answer until I talked with Dan Bivins again and also with Sonny. Because we could openly evangelize in India, we chose to go to India. So, one door had been closed, but two more opened and we chose the one where we could openly talk about Jesus and His love.

Chapter 21

Uttar Pradesh, India
The Never-Ending Line
2009

 After settling what country we would go to instead of China, Sonny De Prang and I prepared for India. We talked with Dan Bivins several times and obtained very helpful information. Dan got visas for us and ordered our airplane tickets. About a week before we left we had a conference call with the field representatives with whom we would be working; this was very helpful. I was able to obtain a few supplies that were not available in Uttar Pradesh.

 With the aid of Google, I did a little research and found out that Uttar Pradesh was one of the most populated areas on Earth. If the state of Uttar Pradesh was a country, it would be the seventh most populated area in the world. It is located in the north central part of India just south of Nepal. The main language there is Hindi, the most used language in India. The main religion there is Hindu, but many Christians are there, too.

 We found out through communication with the field worker that the climate this time of year would be rather warm and humid. There had been a fairly prolonged drought in the immediate area. The field workers had very close work relationships with some of the local pastors with whom we would be working.

 Sonny and I met up with Diann Harris, a retired R.N., in the Dallas-Fort Worth airport and together we continued on our flight through Amsterdam to Delhi. We were met at the airport by a local field worker who took us to our hotel in Delhi. When we got off the airplane, we stepped into a very warm humid surrounding that would become very familiar over the next two weeks. It was so nice to lie down and sleep after 20 hours of flight.

The next morning we took a taxi to the domestic airport and flew one hour northeast to Lucknow, where we were met by one of our field workers with whom we would be working. It was so nice to have someone meet us at the airport. We immediately went to the person's home and picked up the spouse and rest of the team that would be traveling with us. I was asked to ride in the vehicle with the minister who would be my interpreter for the next nine working days. We then drove six hours in the direction of Nepal. The traffic was very busy and crowded; there were automobiles, big trucks, motorcycles, bicycles, and people everywhere. The landscape was mainly people, but we passed many fields of rice, sugar cane, and occasionally a few vegetable patches. The topography was rather flat. Brahma bulls or cows were frequently along the highway—and too often in the median of the highway; there seemed to be no governing force as to where these bulls could be or where they wanted to be. The traffic did not seem to bother them at all. As darkness approached, travel became very dangerous. Large trucks had stopped on the road with no lights and no reflectors. More than once, we had a narrow miss by some of these trucks or other stopped vehicles. It seemed our driver enjoyed the very challenging job of narrow misses and the marked congestion. Finally, we made it to our hotel which would be our home for the next four nights. The food that night was very tasty and scrumptious.

The next morning we had to have room service bring our food to the room because the restaurant did not open until 10 a.m. As we stepped out onto the front of the hotel it was a most interesting and intriguing panorama of new sites, sounds, and smells. There were multiple bicycles, motorcycles, rickshaws, and many ambulating. Many of these were school children headed to school. Of course, the honking of horns, screeching of tires, and other typical sounds went with this scenario. We were as much an attraction to the town folks as these new sites and sounds were to us. If we were to wave at any of these folks, they very cordially waved back. Across the street was a vendor cooking his breakfast foods; many stopped by for a purchase. It was a rather busy scene as we departed and got on the road to our first clinic site. In no time, we were in the midst of the mainstream of traffic; it was amazing how the people driving would bob in and out of traffic in a hurry to get on their way.

Soon, we turned off the main road to a one-lane road; this road was for two-way traffic and care was needed to pass an oncoming vehicle. We went further into the countryside passing large fields of sugar cane and rice fields. There were few trees; all the land was covered with crops or dwellings for people. Water buffalo and cattle were observed frequently. We finally arrived at a public school for what appeared to be grades 1 through 6. Initially there were few people other than the school children; two classes quickly came outside in the shade of the building onto blankets to give us prearranged space. The workers in our group proceeded to put up a rather large cloth tent called a *shamiana* for shade with blankets on the ground for sitting space. It did not take long until the local people found out we had arrived; the crowd began to gather quickly. Meanwhile, we set up our clinic in the two school rooms.

With the aid of an interpreter, Sonny gave a very good sermon to the crowd that had gathered. They seemed very attentive and listened closely. Many raised their hands at the end of the sermon to accept Jesus as Savior.

A national physician soon showed up as prearranged. He did not speak a lot of English but seemed to understand it pretty well. He was very polite and seemed happy to be working with us. Soon, I was seeing patients—a lot of patients, as the crowd grew quickly. I began to see the most wide array of illnesses and conditions I have seen anywhere in the world. Many came in stating that they had tuberculosis and wanted meds for it; they had run out of the free meds the governmental hospital had given them. Skin problems were numerous, especially impetigo from mosquito bites. There were the ubiquitous and multiple types of pain that can be found anywhere in the world. Other frequent findings were cataracts and opacified corneas from infection or trauma. The pharmacy, in the next school room, kept very busy with all our requests for meds for these people. I saw several neurological cases, like cerebral palsy or post-meningitis palsy that no doctor could do anything about. I guess they thought an American doctor could do something. A few had dental caries or even a tooth abscess, but no one that day wanted a tooth pulled. One said it was Ramadan and she could not take pain meds because of the fasting rules until sunset.

One man was sent to me from triage with a low blood pressure; his reading was 80/60. Further history revealed he had been sick several days with fever and coughing. On examination I found him quite warm and sweating. When I listened to his lungs, it was obvious he had pneumonia. I told him he needed to go to the hospital, but he did not want to go. I put two grams of Rocephin in a bottle of Ringer's Lactate and gave it to him over 30 minutes; his BP rose to 90/60 and he seemed a little better. I gave him oral antibiotics to take at home, but I insisted he go to the hospital if he didn't improve very soon. In about two hours, he returned stating he felt worse; I insisted he go to the hospital immediately.

By noon, the heat and humidity began to take their toll; I felt somewhat drained of energy. By the end of the evening, the national doctor and I had seen over 300 patients in about 6½ hours, which meant everyone was quite busy. Sonny got to preach a couple more times, but he frequently helped Diann in the pharmacy. It was a good day; the people were friendly and very receptive. About the time we thought we were through, more people would show up; there just seemed to be a never-ending line of people.

The next day, we went out further into the countryside to another public building like a school. We set up shop quickly and as the crowd gathered I got to witness to them about the Gospel using the Evangecube as a visual aid. A few were responsive to this. As the crowd filtered in, I noticed again how the women wore very bright and colorful dresses; the Moslems wore their typical attire, including burkhas. The crowd grew larger much faster this day; crowd control became a little more difficult. Again, we saw a very wide array of illnesses and conditions. Occasionally I took advantage of the knowledge of the national doctor because I had not seen certain types of rashes or illnesses before. By the end of the day, we were running short of the more common meds and would have to go to a local pharmacy to replenish them for the next day. During the day Sonny and the field worker got to preach to the crowd; they were very responsive to the Gospel; many accepted Jesus. Again, there was just a never-ending line of people waiting to be seen. There was one thing that was constant that day: the deafening noise that the people would make; this was mainly from fussing at one another in line. The field workers had to go to several pharmacies to get the supplies we needed. This got to be an everyday occurrence as we saw a lot of people and gave away a lot of medicine.

The third day, we went out into the country to another public school. Soon after we arrived, the children, ranging in age from 6 to 12, were made to get in lines by the school administrator, so Sonny got to preach to them; several other people also listened in. As the morning wore on, the heat index seemed to rise to 110 degrees F. I felt like I was going to **melt;** Diann experienced heat exhaustion. I moved out from the classroom onto the porch, where there was a slight breeze; it was 10 degrees cooler there. The others stayed in the building; by the end of the day they were almost exhausted. Again, we saw a broad array of diseases; the national doctor helped out when I was unfamiliar with the disease processes. Again, Sonny had good response to the Gospel. Near the end of the day, <u>the line just never ended</u>; my interpreter told me we were now seeing people who just wanted something, so we called it a day.

After spending another night at our hotel, we left early and headed back toward Lucknow. We went to a village, where the field workers know and work frequently with one of the pastors. After arrival we went out to another school site, where a clinic had been set up for us. First, we had a ribbon cutting event. One of our field workers got to cut a red ribbon symbolically opening the first medical clinic of this type in the village. Sonny got to preach the opening and had a good message for the folks. Another national doctor was to help me again, but a "city doctor" showed up; he was not familiar with our meds and could not use my examining tools. He only gave out meds to folks in the village for their chief complaint; I found out he was not a licensed doctor. After a while, he just left. Nevertheless, I kept real busy but was cooled by a fan. For the first time, I felt energized. We saw over 300 patients again; the wide array of illnesses continued. The crowd control was a little better because of the arrangements of the building where we were working. I thought for a change I had seen all the patients, but the line just never ended; finally, it was getting late and we called it a day.

As we sat in the open living room area, warm and tired from the day, the pastor's children came over to Sonny and me and gave us a most helpful massage of the scalp, arms, and back. What a relaxing event for the end of a hard working day. Our meal had been prepared for us by the pastor's wife and other relatives. We had a very good authentic Indian meal cooked for us; it was delicious. The pastor and his wife wanted Sonny and me to take their bed that night, but we asked for an empty room, where we could use our air mattresses we brought with us. We did just fine with that, as we had a ceiling fan and it turned cooler after 10 p.m.

The next morning we had a good breakfast including puri (fried Indian wheat flatbread); it was better than pancakes. Then we went much further out into the countryside. The area was just beautiful with all the sugar cane fields alternating with the rice fields. There were a few corn patches or vegetables. The only trees we saw were in the reserve forests, where thousands of monkeys live, mostly Rhesus monkeys. The monkeys would just stay in the highway until our vehicle bluffed them off the road. We saw several brick factories along the roads; there is little wood, so some building material has to be manufactured.

After a somewhat lengthy drive out into the countryside, we made it to a public school building, where we were to work for the day. A cloth tent had been erected and several people were already waiting for us. As more gathered, Sonny got to preach again about salvation through Jesus Christ; several accepted Jesus. Again a "city doctor" showed up, but he did not seem to want to see any patients; he seemed too uncomfortable with the situation and soon left. That left me alone again as the physician, but the crowd was not quite as big as previous clinics.

While we were waiting for the evening meal, the local pharmacist, who was a friend of the pastor, asked us to come over to his home. He had been at the clinic helping us out the first day. When we arrived, it was very noticeable that this was also his place of business, a pharmacy. I have never seen such precision of lined bottles and supplies in the room that was part of his home. We were introduced to his wife, two daughters, his mother, and his dad. Then he very cordially proceeded to give us water to drink, nuts, and small pastries. He seemed very proud of his place of business and wanted us to take several pictures of everyone. I was asked by one of our field workers to give a three-minute testimony through an interpreter. I knew these folks were Hindu by the statues and pictures in the room, so as best as I could in three minutes I carefully tried to explain what it took to be a Christian. Soon, it was time to go back to the pastor's home for a good cooked Indian meal.

After a good breakfast with Indian baturi and chole, before 8 a.m. we went to set up clinic in the church of the pastor with whom we had been working; we were going to see people medically instead of having church services. I expected we would have a large crowd, and soon that was very evident. The national doctor joined me again; he helped out as the line of people grew rapidly. Crowd control soon became a problem. On two occasions the crowd burst past the door keepers, into the church, only to stand dumbfounded as if to say *what do we do now that we are in here?* With a little help from the pastor, control was reinstituted, but the line was unending; we had seen all the church members, then we started seeing everyone else in the village. Again, we saw a wide array on illnesses. I was not surprised at all the respiratory difficulties because of all the dust, pollen, humidity, and heat. We saw several with asthma.

Outside Sonny, the pastor, and field worker were having a large harvest of people listening to the Gospel. Sonny later told me they had a good response. Inside, we continued to see the masses. Our medical slip would give the pastor the name of the patient or family; this was a definite way to get in their door later to visit and present the Gospel to the individual. This is an excellent way to help build the membership of the local church.

We were running out of meds again, so we closed shop early so we could get on the road and try to make it to Lucknow before dark. Again, the traffic was horrific.

We saw the end result of one fatal accident (it was in the local newspaper the next morning). We arrived at the field workers' home and had a quick supper, before going to our five-star hotel for the next four days. It was nice.

The next day was our day off! What a break, after working so hard for six straight days. I got to use a computer downstairs in the business office and caught up with part of the world again. Also, I had some trades to do; so, I could sway the stock market again. We had a TV in our room, but only an occasional English subtitle to tell us what was going on. I did watch about an hour of TV of the locals giving a dance and music concert. The Indian attire was so colorful. The field workers had to go buy more meds, as we had three more days of clinics. That night we went to Barbecue Nation for an appetizing meal; some of the food was quite different from what I thought barbecue was, but it was very good.

On Tuesday, we drove from Lucknow to a village almost two hours away. We got to see some pretty countryside again on the way out. The road seemed to be narrower and less traveled as we finally approached the brick church, where we would be working for the day. There were several people already assembled at the cloth tent, and as more arrived, Sonny gave the Gospel message to this group; the folks were very receptive. Inside the church was no electricity, so no fans today—and it was going to be a scorcher of a day. The heat index was high, and I seemed to move in slow motion all day. Again, a "city doctor" showed up, but he did not seem to want to see any patients; or, he was too uncomfortable with the situation and left soon. That left me as the lone physician again, but the crowd was not nearly as large as the previous clinics.

After a couple of hours of clinic, I was asked to come outside to see a man who was on an ox cart; they said he was having trouble breathing and could not come inside the church to be seen. On approaching the ox cart, I saw what appeared to be a healthy 50-year-old man. He was supine on the bed of the ox cart and could not seem to sit up. I quickly listened to his chest and other than a mild tachycardia, it seemed fine. I asked what the problem was and I was told that he had a hydrocoele, so I pulled the cloth back and pulled his underwear down. I was initially dumbfounded by what I saw; there was marked swelling of his genitalia and large groin nodes with areas of granulation over these. There was a piece of cotton over the left mid groin which had a small amount of blood present, so I went back into the church to get a pair of gloves. When I came back and lifted the cotton off: swish, swish, swish poured the blood from an arterial bleeder directly over the femoral artery. I quickly put the cotton back on and waited until it was not actively bleeding, then I went back into the church and got a surgical kit and suture to stop the bleeding.

After anesthetizing the area the best I could, I proceeded to put a figure of eight chromic suture into stop the bleeding. My field worker had gotten a bit pale and dizzy and had to sit under the tree for a moment. He recovered from the vertigo soon, and I asked to question the man a bit more. We found out that he had been to a hospital and sent home to die from terminal cancer, as there was nothing they could do. I asked the field worker to ask the man about his salvation. The man told us that he had things settled with God. I got our nurse to give him some pain pills so that he could go home.

As the afternoon passed, the heat index climbed. I was fortunate to have a man who was frequently twirling a fan over me—if not for him I know I would have melted. The array of disease continued, but they seemed to be worse in this village, probably because it was miles from any medical facility. Many of the people did not even know what a hospital was. We ran out of inhalers for asthma patients. as this was a frequent complaint. The mayor of the village limited the number that came as we were limited by not having a national doctor to help us that day. Sonny got to preach at least twice more that day and continued to have good results from the crowd for salvation to Jesus. I know that Sonny was gratified by

Uttar Pradesh, India

having the privilege to present the Gospel to these people, but he was more satisfied by the good results.

The following two days, we went to a school building in a village much closer to our main city. We were fortunate in having a different national doctor who helped us out. Each afternoon I was brought hot tea, and it was quite good. Also I was brought a vegetarian somosa (spiced potato) which was piping hot and very good; I was not afraid to eat it because it was so hot (physically). We were able to see over 350 patients the first day and over 425 the last day. The last day of clinic we finally saw just about everyone that had been in the never-ending lines. We were seriously running out of meds by the end of the clinics. During those two days, Sonny was able to preach at least three or four times each day and had excellent results with response from the people. These pastors would have their homework cut out for them after we left, but they now had an open door to go visit them and invite them to their local churches. My interpreter was one of those who would start the next day following up on the large number of people we had seen.

During the nine days of clinics, we saw well over 3,300 people and had several hundred give indications that they wanted to accept Jesus as Savior. To God be the glory!

The last day in Lucknow we went to the mall, which is much like one of the typical malls we have in the U.S. We were on a mission to buy my interpreter a baby carrier; his wife was 3½ months pregnant. It was my suggestion as I wanted to reward my interpreter for his valiant work with me for nine days. Naturally, we had to have lunch at McDonalds before leaving the mall. We had to go get some money exchanged at a local bank; then, we went to a very nice souvenir shop. There I bought several nice gifts for the folks back home who had helped support me on these mission trips.

We went out to a local orphanage, where the field workers have friends who own and manage it. We saw 30 children. Almost all the boys had ringworms. One of our field workers left and went to a local pharmacy to buy antifungal medicine; we were out of this from all the clinics we had run. A few of the children had external otitis, and I irrigated their ears clear. All the girls were normal. After the physicals, the children were gathered and they sang a couple of songs for us, then Sonny prayed for them. What a sweet bunch of children; many of them were partially Oriental in origin. They had been brought in from villages near Tibet and or China. This turned out to be a real serendipity for our overall trip.

We proceeded to my interpreter's home and were cordially greeted by him, his wife, and his mother. His wife was very polite and courteous and seemed honored that we would visit them in their home. His mother told us that she felt much better since I had pulled her three symptomatic dental caries a few days earlier. We were given hot tea and a couple of fried Indian snacks that were very delicious. When we presented the baby carrier, you should have seen the sincere thanks and glow in their eyes as a sign of appreciation. We had to leave after a brief visit and headed back to the field workers' home to do a bit of last-minute packing and rearranging, since we had bought the souvenirs.

I want to sincerely thank the field workers, Dan at MMR, the pastors, interpreters, drivers, and our small team for doing a fabulous job attending to the illnesses we saw as best we could, and especially the opportunities of presenting the Gospel to the thousands with whom we came into contact.

We then headed to the airport, flew to Delhi, on to Amsterdam, and finally back to the U.S. It was a long, but fruitful trip of making friends, sharing the Gospel, and having many to accept Jesus as Savior.

Uttar Pradesh, India

Our team in Uttar Predesh, India
2009

Typical crowd for clinic

Ready to plow the field

Typical jewelry

Chapter 22

Kampong Cham, Cambodia
2009

This was our fourth trip to Cambodia to work with Tony and Trish Pitaniello. We missed the trip when their fourth daughter, Adelaide, was born in 2006; they had to go to Bangkok, Thailand for Trish's C-section birth. In 2008 the family was on leave in the Dallas, TX, area until late July 2009. On communication with Tony during that time, Tony said he was bringing in medical teams again. He had been bringing in large surgical teams, but the government shut that down. I agreed to recruit a group and come the third week in November, the week that we usually go. Tony asked that I bring a group of 13; this would be the largest team he could logistically handle.

I began recruiting immediately. In less than a month I had my 13 chosen from volunteers, many who had been before and loved working with the Pitaniellos. As time progressed, I told one of the members not to come, as his wife was to have a baby less than two weeks after we got back from Cambodia. Then I had another who decided he did not have enough financing to go. Two days before we left, another developed frostbite of his feet. On the morning before we left early that afternoon, I got a call from Don and Lorene Salyers' neighbor stating that Lorene had just had a stroke and had to be rushed to a hospital. **So, the rest of us were led by our dreams, and not pushed by our problems.**

That meant I would have to carry an extra suitcase that I would have to pay for. I had ordered medicines and supplies, and many of these had been dose packed by Vickie and me. Also, Tony had me order a lot of meds in Cambodia as he was not sure customs would let us bring meds into the country. This was accomplished over the Internet with Jessica, the pharmacist that worked with Tony. I wanted to take my dental chair, as there are always a lot of necrotic teeth to extract in Cambodia. My back just kills me if I do the extractions in a straight back chair as I have done many times. The lady at American Airlines counter let me take the extra suitcase without charge because so many had dropped out recently. But, when I got to Los Angeles with another airline, then I was charged.

That left eight of us: Dr. Kirk Cofran, Rosemary Andrews, R.N., Vickie, my wife, Rev. Harrell Shelton, associate pastor of Airline Baptist Church, Billy Weatherall, and I were the group from Airline Baptist Church. I was blessed with the addition of Rev. Sonny De Prang and his wife, Jackie, from the First Baptist Church of Bossier City. We left Shreveport before 2 p.m. Friday, to Dallas/Fort Worth, on to Los Angeles; we crossed the international date line to get to Taipei by Sunday morning; we then flew on to Phnom Penh arriving just before noon. We had flown for well over 20 hours and despite the "flying with the butterfly" (Lunesta), we were almost exhausted.

We were so lucky to get our visas, collect all our suitcases, and then get through customs without one hassle. Outside, we met Tony and Abass (Tony's right-hand man and helper), Jessica Lemm (pharmacist that works with Tony), and two recently assigned missionaries to Cambodia, and Tim and Laura (they are taking language school and will be transferred to Kampong Cham to work with the Pitaniellos) were also there with their van to transport us to the Asian Hotel in downtown Phnom Penh. We immediately placed our suitcases in our rooms and hurried back downstairs to go shopping for groceries for the week; we would have cereal, fruit, and snacks for breakfast and peanut butter and jelly sandwiches for lunch. We were going to the Russian Market, but it would be closed in less than an hour, so we decided to take a tour of the city and shop when we came back to Phnom Penh after the clinics.

As we drove through the streets of Phnom Penh you could still see some of the old French buildings. Soon we arrived at the Independence Monument; this was built in 1958 to celebrate independence from France. It was built in the shape of the temples that one sees at the Angkor Wat ruins. (Angkor Wat is on the national flag of Cambodia.) The American Embassy was not too far down the street.

Then we drove on down to the Royal Palace (King's Palace); this is where the king lives (Kingdom of Cambodia). The gold pagodas adorn the complex, but you can see the Silver Pagoda within the complex. Across from the Royal palace is the riverfront, where the Sisowath Quay lies; it has several national flags aligning the river's edge. This is where the Bassac, Mekong, and Tonle Rivers converge. We could see a lot of hyacinth plants floating down the rivers from the recent tropical storm that flooded some of the waters upstream. We did not go to the Tuol Sleng Genocide Museum (Killing Fields) as Tony really dislikes what occurred to the Cambodian citizens. After the tour, we had supper at the KFC (Kentucky Fried Chicken) place in the Asian hotel, a new addition since we were there in 2007.

The following morning, we ate breakfast at the hotel and proceeded to go to the CSI Mercy Medical Center in Phnom Penh; we went to pick up the meds I had Jessica get for me, but they were on the way across town when we arrived. Meanwhile, one of the doctors wanted me to see a couple of surgical problems, since I was a general surgeon. The first was a 19-year-old male who had been in a motorcycle wreck several weeks earlier and the trauma ruptured his jejunum; the repair leaked and formed an abscess, which had to be drained. A proximal jejunostomy had to be preformed; now the patient was in difficulty with nutrition as there was such a large output from the proximal jejunostomy. The tube in the distal jejunostomy was not able to keep up with the output from the proximal one. I was asked about my recommendations for the problem. This certainly was not easy; the jejunum needed to be reanastomosed soon, but this would be such a risky task at this point. (What a "Catch 22" situation this was.) All I could do was to recommend to limit the oral intake to lower the losses in the proximal jejunostomy and increase input through the distal (tube) jejunostomy.

The next case was a young female with a left liver lobe abscess which had been drained. This lady looked good, and she should not have had a real problem with the drainage they had provided and the proper antibiotics. I just recommended not pulling the drains for 10 days.

Soon our meds arrived and we were on the way to Kampong Cham, which was a drive three hours to the northeast. Tony has relocated his home after his last missionary tour to where the Western Cham reside. Along the way we could see many rice fields, brick factories, Buddhist temples, many Cambodian homes built on stilts along the road side, occasional banana groves, and yet more rice fields. Soon, we arrived at Kampong Cham, which resides on the bank of the Mekong River. This year Tony had reserved us rooms in a new hotel, the Kampong Pros Hotel. We unloaded our suitcases and immediately left for the distant village, where Tony and Abass had chosen for us to work this year. We got to view some more pretty countryside before arriving at a maze of rubber tree farms. These trees had been planted there many years before; there were many plots with different ages of the trees. Many trees had white latex sap dripping into collection pans near the bottom of the tree.

Finally, we arrived at the house where our clinic would be set up for the week. The house was slightly larger than usual-size home, but it was on stilts like many of the homes there. Several people were already crowded about the place as word had gotten out that we would be there for the week. We unloaded and immediately began to set up our stations. Jackie would have triage at the entrance room to the house; off to the corner would be the pharmacy, where Jessica and Harrell began to unload all the meds. Vickie and Billy set up a table where the eyeglasses station would be. Dr. Cofran and Rosemary settled into two more tables, where the medical station would be. I placed my dental chair and supplies just past the eyeglasses station. At the end of the house, Sonny and Abass set up the spiritual station. Within a few minutes, Jackie was already triaging patients to be seen. The flow was slightly slow to start with, but soon we got into a groove and the pace quickened. Within the next three hours, we had seen several patients, but stopped early as we wanted to get back to town before dark; this time of year, dark arrives at about 6:30 p.m.

The weather all week was clear and warm, but the tropical humidity had to be accounted for; Tony had fans for each station powered by a generator at the back of the house.

Almost every night, we got to eat at one of the local Asian restaurants, where we had a wide selection of local cuisine; everyone seemed to enjoy the food. Trish and the Pitaniello children were able to join us a couple of nights for supper.

For the next four days, we held all-day clinics. We had plenty of meds between what I had brought and the meds Jessica had gotten for me in Cambodia. The reading glasses were given out in three days, as the eye station is always the most popular station. Vickie and Billy were diligent in getting the best eyeglasses for each patient. Dr. Cofran and Rosemary saw a wide variety of illnesses and pathology. I helped seeing medical patients when I was not extracting necrotic teeth. We found several surgical problems like large goiters, many with thyrotoxicosis. Several hernias and surgical problems were referred to Phnom Penh for evaluation. Some of these would have to be referred on to Bangkok, Thailand, for specialty surgery. Tony had a special form and it was stamped with a seal to make it authentic for presentation to the CSI Mercy Medical Center in Phnom Penh.

We found many of the common maladies seen universally. There were many complaints of pain of one type or the other, from the hard-working people. Several of the children had colds. A variety of skin conditions were discovered. Dr. Cofran had me excise a basal cell carcinoma from an older gentleman's anterior chest wall that measured about 2 x 3 cm. As you would expect, I had a big audience for this procedure.

Billy and Vickie sure could have used the other suitcase of prescription eyeglasses, but circumstances make cases: Lorene had had a cerebral aneurysm rupture, and that could not be foretold. (We got several emails from Libby Horton about Lorene's progress in the hospital in Tyler, TX. She had to be medivaced from the first hospital to Tyler for a burr hole to relieve the cerebral pressure from the bleeding; then, she had to have embolization of the bleeding vessel by radiological intervention. She was still in the ICU when we left Cambodia.)

I pulled necrotic teeth almost all day every day. I finally have come to the conclusion that dental hygiene and prevention are a necessity; I plan on implementing this on my next mission trip. There is no dental education in many of the countries we go to.

The spiritual station had several people at each presentation; many of these people listened very intently, but Tony asked us not to ask for any decisions at present. Tony and Abass will go back to the village soon to ask for any decisions that the people may be willing to make. Most of the people in the clinic went through the spiritual station.

Kampong Cham, Cambodia

In the past Tony has told us that the Christians are taking over the nation; when the need was so great, during the period of the killing fields—who helped? Not the Buddhists nor the Muslims, but the Christians. Now the people are learning who to turn to. The monks go but to beg from the poor; the Muslims are of no help, but the Christians are there to really care for the people's needs. Tony said he may not have built a lot of churches, but a network of Christians has become so strong in the Cham people to whom he is ministering that it will prevail.

Sonny did most of the presentations, but had Harrell do several also. Jessica and Billy also made a presentation at the spiritual station using the "spiritual towel" Tony had on the wall for us. I am sure when Tony and Abass return to the village for spiritual decisions that they will have a very favorable response.

Trish came and helped at the medical station on Thursday; she is a R.N. That meant Tony had to attend the home schooling, cooking, and home chores while Trish worked. She was in her own element seeing patients at the clinic. She and Jessica occasionally go out into the village to do wound care and treat what illnesses that they can.

Over the 4½ days, we saw 733 patients; I am convinced the people are very appreciative. I am sure when any of the villages in the area are asked if they would like free medical evaluation and advice, eyeglasses, dental care, and free medicines, they will jump at the opportunity.

On the way back from the village, I admired the multitude of straight lines of rubber trees; these were obviously planted many years ago. According to research on Google (from an article in LEARN NC by Margery H. Freeman) about 90 percent of the rubber trees in the world are in south Asia, many being transplanted there from other nations. After looking up the information, I can explain many of the things I saw during the trips through the maze of trees. I saw many hammocks in the groves of trees, some with people in them; they rest there at night between chores in working on the trees. Each night small incisions (injuries) are cut into the trees' bark so the milky sap (latex) will drip down into the bowls before drying out in the tropical sun. Workers collect the tapped latex from the bowls the following morning and place it in large cans. I saw one group of people with six five-gallon buckets of latex. Progressively lower cuts are made in the rubber trees, allowing them to be tapped for many years.

After sufficient amounts are collected, basins of latex are processed with an acid to coagulate it, making the latex more solid. The acid is then removed by rolling the latex under pressure into thin sheets, which are smoked over a fire to stabilize the rubber. In that form rubber can be exported. Rubber is elastic latex from the **Hevea braziliensis**—a tree that is coagulated or turned from liquid to semi-solid form. Waterproof and elastic, rubber is used for sports balls, vehicle tires, and many other practical items manufactured around the world. This is one of Cambodia's main exports.

Friday night we were invited over to Trish and Tony's house for supper, where we enjoyed some great company and very good food. Trish and her national cook had taken most of the day to prepare some curry stew and some French bread; it was scrumptious.

Tony and Trish have four adorable and well-mannered children. They were a delight to be around, especially when Harrell got out "Grandpa" and put on a spectacular show for everyone. Most of the children were afraid of Grandpa, but when Harrell allowed Tony to try out the puppet, the children soon were hugging and loving on him. What a pleasure to enjoy good company and good food.

The next morning, we reloaded and headed back to Phnom Penh. On the way, Tony stopped and got some fried tarantulas, but only Tony's sons would eat some of the legs off the tarantulas. On the way back, the van carrying the luggage had a flat, then our van carrying most of the group had a flat, also. Fortunately, we had a man come along who had a jack that would work; two of those in the vans would not work; we found out later that he was a Christian. We gave him at least two days wages to help; we had a need and I am sure he had a need.

We returned to the Asian Hotel, placed our luggage in the rooms, had lunch at the KFC Restaurant downstairs, and then we headed out to the Russian Market. There are bargains galore; we got souvenirs for family and friends. I got souvenirs to show appreciation to some of those who helped sponsor this trip: Alcon Labs, Kingsway Charities, and Blessings International. These companies are so important or we would not be able to treat so many with such valuable medicines and supplies.

We rested that night, and got up early to go to the New Market down the street from our hotel. We wanted to get a few more souvenirs before going back to the hotel, eat, load up, and head to the airport for the long journey back home.

It was a most satisfying trip; I had my wife, Vickie, and the other folks who were fantastic help in the clinics and company on the trip. We appreciate the Pitaniellos and hope to repeat the trip next year; by then Tim and Laura will be there working along side us.

We were saddened by receiving the news of Lorene Salyer's death almost one month after her stroke; she had been in the ICU for almost 3 weeks after her surgery and radiological embolization of the bleeding aneurysm. What a privilege it has been to have Lorene and Don with me on so many trips; they were always wanting to go serve the Lord the very best they could. I am sure God has a very special place for one of His faithful servants.

On the Go for the Lord

Cambodia, November 2009
(Left to Right) Dr. Kirk Cofran, Rev. Harrell Shelton,
RoseMary Andrews, Vickie Bailey, Dr. Bill Bailey, Sonny DePrang,
Billy Weatherall (behind Sonny), Jackie DePrang, Jessica Lemm

Chapter 23

Is There a Santa Claus?

December 2009 seemed to be rocking along as usual; I had already recruited my team for the Philippines and had tickets ordered for the group. Medicines and supplies had been ordered. Half of my team was new recruits; they were so excited about getting to go on a medical mission trip.

T'was the week before Christmas in our Sunday School department. Joyce Vardeman had asked our pastor's daughter, Cecilia, to call one of the local high schools and see if there was a student in real need. Cecilia, who works at a local high school, asked the principal about this. She found out about many needy students, but one really stood out. There was this one student who occasionally missed school because he did not have enough clothes to wear that day. Joyce asked for donations for the young man; several dollars were collected from our department. Someone had already bought him a pair of shoes because the ones he had were so worn.

I called Joyce and got his mom's telephone number. Joyce told us that they were down on their luck; they were staying in a downtown motel and were paying, by the week, to stay there. The mom had been able to hire on at a local restaurant. I had Vickie, my wife, call the mom at the motel. She was very cordial, but she was worried about her son; he had very few clothes to wear. She further stated that he was such a good boy; he had never given her any problems. And his birthday was the next day.

Vickie set up an appointment for us to pick up the son (Jeremy) at 10:30 a.m. the next morning; we were taking him to J.C. Penney to go clothes shopping. Immediately after the phone call, Vickie went to the store and got cake mix to make him a birthday cake.

When we went to the motel, we met Jeremy who politely welcomed us. On the distant bed was a lady sleeping. We asked if that was his mom, but he said it was his mom's roommate. She had a similar story of hard luck. She was working at the same restaurant his mom was, and the mom had invited her to share their room until she could get on her feet. Jeremy was so pleased to get a birthday cake.

We arrived at J.C. Penney and Jeremy said he had never been there before. We proceeded to tell him to get some pants, shirts, etc. Vickie told him to get what was popular now; we had no idea what teenagers really wanted to wear nowadays. With a little encouragement, he got two pairs of blue jeans, two long sleeve shirts, a warm jacket, a belt, three sets of socks, and three men's briefs. I asked him if he had any dress clothes. You can imagine the answer to that. Jeremy did not even know his neck size; so, we had the sales lady measure him. We insisted he get a dress shirt, dress pants, and a matching tie. Jeremy was quite shy, so I did not go into the dressing room with him to make sure the clothes fit properly. It was evident that he kept texting someone on his telephone.

We were surprised at the low cost of the clothes, but we knew J.C.Penney had very good clothes at reasonable cost. By the end of the shopping spree, it was lunch time. I told Jeremy that we were all going to the food court for lunch. I asked him if he had ever had a Chic-Fils-A sandwich, and he indicated that he had not. I told him that he was going to have one now. While eating, we had a little more conversation about himself. He was interested in art and drawing; he indicated that this was what he had in mind for the future when he finished high school. He had managed to obtain a few supplies from an art school, and he had been practicing on his skills.

I asked what he was getting his mom for Christmas. He related that he had been given a $25 scholarship for Christmas from his high school and was going to buy her something with that. I later found out that someone from our church gave $200 to the school where Jeremy goes, and he got one portion of it.

On the way back to the car, we went back through J.C. Penney and I bought him a $100 gift certificate to give his mom for Christmas. Besides being very appreciative, now his eyes were glowing with happiness.

On the way back to his motel room, we agreed that he (and his mom, if possible) would be ready to go church with us the upcoming Sunday. We would pick him (or them) up 30 minutes before church started. He could sit with me in the early morning service, while Vickie taught her Sunday School class. Then he could go with me to my Sunday School class that I taught, and the next Sunday I would take him to his age group.

As I got out of my car I handed Jeremy a Bible (King James Version) I had for some time, but it was in excellent condition. It was from James Robinson, a TV evangelist that I once supported quite heavily. He had told me he was not a speed reader, but I encouraged him to take his time and read this slowly and absorb it.

I found out later that he had been texting his mom; he was amazed that some couple he had never met, wanted to buy him all those clothes. Later, when his mom got back to the motel room, he had laid out all his presents (clothes) on the bed for her to see. His mom cried when she saw his birthday cake and all the clothes.

Vickie and I felt some of the real meaning of Christmas that day; what a real joy it was to give to someone who really needed it.

Yes, this is the Christmas season, and YES, THERE IS A SANTA CLAUS!!

As a follow up on this story, the following Sunday I went to pick up Laurie and Jeremy after failing to reach them on the telephone. I went to their motel room and left a layer or two of epithelium from my right knuckles on the door. No answer. I even went to the desk at the front of the motel and had housekeeping go check for me. No answer. Needless to say I was a little disappointed.

Two weeks later Joyce brought them to church. I met Laurie for the first time personally in the early morning church service; Jeremy was taken to his appropriate age group by Joyce's grandson. Jeremy was to be invited to the Wednesday night service by the Vardemans also.

Later Joyce told me that Laurie had enjoyed church so much and met some very friendly people; Laurie is going to try to make Sunday her off day at work, so she can attend church regularly. Perhaps there will be a good ending to this story. All we can do is to plant the seeds. The rest is up to God.

Chapter 24

Are You Going to Haiti?

On January 12, 2010, a massive earthquake jolted Haiti; it was the magnitude of 7.0 (moment magnitude; this causes serious damage over an area greater than 100 miles in populated areas), but the epicenter was fairly close to the surface and only ten miles from Port-au-Prince, the capital of Haiti. Not long after the event, there was news on CNN and Fox News about the devastation; many were hurt or killed. Initially the airport was so damaged that traffic was very limited in and out of Haiti.

In the next 24 hours, it was very evident that a very catastrophic event had occurred; the toll in and around the capital was estimated to be in the tens of thousands. Within another 24 hours, it was estimated that there may have been over 100,000 killed. Most of the buildings in Port-au-Prince were devastated. (Eventually, the estimated killed was said to be close to 200,000.)

A cry for help arose from many sources. Many volunteered from all over the world, but getting into the capital was a real problem. It became evident that the very infrastructure of the nation was lacking; what had been there was in shambles.

I got several emails and calls to see if I was going to Haiti. (I had never been to Haiti before.) I watched the world news and looked at much of the material on the Internet, but I was convinced that this situation was not what my group would specialize in. Yes, I am a general surgeon and could operate, but with what group? My groups specialize basically in evangelism. Our medical team goes to churches, schools, out patient facilities, or even homes set up for a medical clinic. We do general medicine, eyeglasses, and extraction of teeth, all to attract the people so <u>evangelism</u> can be presented. In Haiti, the initial needs were food, water, and shelter as well as the rescue and treatment of all those hurt.

In my heart, I wanted so much to help, but with all the chaos, lack of infrastructure, and other logistical things—like being scheduled to work my shifts in the ER—I just could not go. Yes, I did make a donation to a medical supply group that supplies such needs.

The Lord always has good things to come out of such bad happenings. The extreme poverty, corruption, and all the other bad things should call for change in this land. I hope that our nation will be a very good neighbor and help as much as possible. I pray that God will finally be seen as the real underlying need for Haiti.

Chapter 25
Pampanga, Philippines
2010

Somehow recruiting for medical missions seems to be getting tougher; especially recently, after the passing of one of my regular workers. Lorene Salyer had been to the Philippines and Cambodia with Don to help in the pharmacy and eye station on several occasions. She will be missed.

Recruiting doctors for these trips has also been more difficult. Times have gotten harder in taking time off for trips like these; the doctors seem to be married to their practices. Occasionally, I am fortunate to get a retired doctor to go with me; otherwise, I have to recruit months ahead for a mission trip.

This was my sixth straight year to go to the Philippines and work with Missionary Pastor Alan Gueverra. We were fortunate in getting our regular ministers, Rev. Harrell Shelton and Rev. Scotty Teague to go again; both are always a joy to work with. This will be their fifth straight year. Rev. Chad Grayson just left Airline Baptist Church for the First Baptist Church in Tupelo, MS; he will be remembered for helping start these trips to the Philippines. Chad introduced me to Rev. Alan Guevarra via the Internet in 2004. He and Lenora were staying at my home while looking for a place to live as he had just been chosen as our new pastor at Airline Baptist Church in Bossier City, Louisiana. Our church and teams plan to make the Philippines and Alan a yearly event (mission).

New recruits from Airline Baptist Church were Stacy Humphrey, R.N., Cynthia Waldrop, R.N., and Cynthia's daughter, Leslie. Leslie is a college student and wanted to come along. They were all excited about going on the trip.

The female cashiers at Dollar Tree know Vickie, my wife, and me at first glance; we have been there to get reading and sun glasses for the last three of four of our trips. We have more than a full suitcase of glasses ready for the trip. This seems to be our most popular station; everyone wants their eyes checked and a pair of glasses, even if it is just a pair of sunglasses. We cannot seem to take enough eyeglasses for the whole trip. By the week before we left, Vickie and I had dose-packed all the meds and I had five suitcases packed for the trip plus my dental chair. Rev. Billy Pierce had us come down in front of the church the Sunday night before we left for prayer, laying on of hands, and dedication for our mission to the Philippines. (What a compliment from our church!)

On February 19, 2010, the Airline Baptist folks met at the airport in Shreveport by 5 a.m. We met Scotty in Memphis and proceeded on to Detroit before boarding and leaving for Nagoya, Japan, on the way to Manila. Pastor Alan Guevarra and several of his missionary pastor friends met us at the airport, and we proceeded northeast about 70 miles to the King's Royal Hotel near Guagua. Alan told us to rest until noon; he said he would pick us up for lunch.

After lunch at the large SM Mall in San Fernando, we went to Alan's church (Faith Baptist Church). Alan's oldest daughter, age 9, sang a very beautiful number during the service. While preaching, Scotty had to demonstrate a little of his visual aids to the crowd. I got to give a brief testimony of why I do medical missions. Then Harrell got to preach and demonstrate "Grandpa" to the children. It was a good service; many young people were present. According to Alan, there were many more adults in the regular Sunday morning service.

While there, we got to see Elnora, Alan's wife, and all the children. The children are just precious and favor the parents very closely. Elnora is five months pregnant with number seven. (I told Alan that we needed to operate on him while we were there, but he said number seven would be the last.)

On the front wall of the church is a collection of pictures of the pastors who are local missionaries and many who are in foreign places like Thailand, Vietnam, and Guam. Talking about being mission minded; these folks live it.

While walking in front of his church, Alan showed us the construction of the road that is going on. The government is raising the level of the road 1.2 meters because of the frequent flooding, especially with all the tropical storms this past year. Alan said he would have to build up the property two meters and relocate the concrete slab over where there is a small lagoon now; that means hauling in more soil to fill that in and then raising it two meters about the ground level now. Also, he says they have had to treat the church building for termites recently. Harrell and I told Alan that perhaps our church can help with some of these expenses. Airline Baptist Church has helped pay for a lot of the additions to his church and help purchase two large vans to carry people to and from church on Sunday.

After a hearty breakfast at the hotel Monday morning, Alan arrived in the van, and we headed west. Along the way there was a moderate amount of traffic; we saw several buses, motorcycles, and a few jeepneys (most of the jeepneys are used as taxis in the cities). It was going to be a beautiful day despite some of the haze in the sky in the distance. Several rice fields were at different stages of maturation. We went to Wenceslao Village and set up clinic in the Wenceslao Elementary School. Stacy and Cynthia were my nurse practitioners; I had them close by for any questions. Almost immediately they were busy seeing patients. Harrell had the pharmacy set up next door; Leslie worked in the same room with the glasses station. I had to limit Leslie to giving away only 110 pairs of eyeglasses per day as there was no way we could have brought enough glasses for everyone that wanted them. Each day after the allotment of glasses was given out, I had Leslie go help Harrell in the pharmacy; Elnora (Alan's wife) also came to interpret and help with the medications.

Scotty was in the next room with two other missionary pastors. After a room full had been gathered, the Gospel was given by Scotty and interpreted by the Filipino pastors. Meanwhile, I started out seeing medical patients; that did not last long. The word got out that tooth extractions were being offered. Immediately, I began extracting teeth with Joshua as my interpreter and light holder. He was very good at both. Our team jelled rapidly and ran smoothly for the rest of the week.

On Tuesday we went to Morning Sun Village and worked at the Morning Sun Health Clinic. The Health Clinic director came by and welcomed us there. At noon Alan brought us chicken sandwiches. Every one stayed busy all day. At the end of each day we went to the SM Mall for supper and to get further supplies and water for the next day. I tried to bring most of the things we needed, but I had no idea we would be seeing so many children patients. We had already started running out of liquid Tylenol and children's decongestants.

On Wednesday we went to Concepcion, Lubao, Pampanga, to the elementary school. Again there were many to see. Stacy and Cynthia stayed very busy seeing the medical patients; I had more teeth to extract than there should have been; there is little or no dental hygiene taught there. For lunch, we were invited into a private home and had a fantastic meal of egg rolls and chicken. What a treat! By the end of the very warm day, I was getting hot and worn out. Harrell came by and relieved me; he helped extract nine upper teeth in one older lady. Again, we had to get more meds and supplies at the mall when we went to supper. We shopped briefly for a few things for the folks back home; the mall is almost westernized. I loved to walk alongside Harrell and watch the people stare at him as he walks by; he is at least 12 to 18 inches taller than the average Filipino.

We found out Thursday's schedule had to be changed; there was an emergency meeting at the Sta. Barbara Elementary School, so we decided to take our R & R day and go to Mount Samat and then go souvenir shopping.

Alan took our group to Mount Samat which is a mountain in the Town of Pilar in the Province of Bataan. It is the site of the **Dambana ng Kagitingan** or "Shrine of Valor". According to *Wikipedia*, along with the island fortress of Corregidor, Mt. Samat was the site of the most vicious battle against the Japanese Imperial Army in 1942 during the Battle of Bataan. Suffering heavy losses against the Japanese all over Luzon (the main north island) Filipino and American soldiers retreated to Baatan Peninsula to regroup for a last valiant, but futile stand. This retreat to Bataan is part of a United States strategy known as War Plan Orange.

After the fierce battle lasting three days, 78,000 exhausted, sick, and starving men under Major General Edward P. King surrendered to the Japanese on April 9, 1942. It was, and still is, the single largest surrender of U.S. and Philippine forces ever. These forces were led on the Bataan Death March. There was no way to accurately count the casualties, but it is believed that up to 25 percent of the men died.

The mountain is now a war memorial. A huge white cross stands as a mute but eloquent reminder of the men who died there. It also acts as a tourist attraction with a war museum nearby that has a wide array of displays from paintings of the Philippine heroes to armaments used by the American, Filipino, and Japanese forces during the heat of the battle.

The Shrine of Valor sits atop Mt. Samat; it was built in 1966 in memory of those soldiers of World War II. It consists of the "Colonade", a marble capped structure with an altar, esplanade, and a museum. Inside the museum, you can learn about the battle of Bataan and the Death March that followed. The captured U.S. and Filipino soldiers were forced to march more than a hundred kilometers (61 miles) from Bataan to Tarlac.

The Memorial Cross is a towering structure of concrete, steel, and marble. It is 92 meters (295 feet) high and the arms' length is 15 meters (46 feet) on each side. An elevator goes up to the arms of the cross, where the viewing galleries are found. The exterior finish of the cross, at the base up to an 11 meter (34 feet) level is capped with "Nabiag Nga Bato" sculptural base relief's depicting significant battles and historical events.

When we were there this year, the elevator was closed. We wanted to walk up the stairs, but these were said to be rusted and unstable. My group that went in 2007 got to go up to the top and view the magnificent beauty of the countryside and nearby ocean.

After visiting the lower monument and reading the inscriptions on the walls, we loaded up in the van and drove the Bataan Road back to San Fernando. We saw kilometer markers all along the Bataan Death March route. We then drove to Angeles to go souvenir shopping.

Friday we went to Sta. Barbara Elementary School, where we found ourselves very busy again. We were running out of supplies rapidly now.

Saturday we went to Sta. Rita Health Center to see patients for about five hours. All the eyeglasses were given out. Needless to say "our small team" worked very hard in warm weather. Thank goodness, Alan had furnished fans for us and we had electricity at each site. For the week, we saw a total of 1,272 patients; eyeglasses were given to 557 people; 340 teeth were extracted while the nurse practitioners saw to the medical needs. The salvation station had a total of 979 people who accepted Jesus as Lord and Savior. To God be the glory! Scotty had told me that Rio and some of the other pastors had brought him to tears with their enthusiasm in preaching the Gospel.

The pastors will have a harvest to follow up on. Hopefully, many of these people will join the church nearby that the other missionary pastors locally have available. (What a way to add to your church!)

After leaving Sta. Rita Health Center, we went to Pastor Rio's church; Rio is married to Gemna (Alan's sister). They have a large one-room church; on the side is a lean-to building that Rio and Gemna live in. Most of the pastors live in part of the church building where the pastor serves.

What an eventful and hard week of work, but look at all the fruit of our labors. We feel so blessed to work with Alan and his missionary pastors every year. As General McArthur once told the Filipino people, "I shall return." Well, we told Alan we would return next year. He and I had already discussed that; next March we plan to go back to Baguio City, in the northern part of Luzon, where we worked in 2009.

I was the first in my row on the airplane going from Manila to Japan. Then a young Filippino came and took her seat next to me, on the inside. She said that she had never flown before and wondered if she might exchange seats. I told her that she would have to wait until all the passengers had loaded; then, she could ask the stewardess if another seat was available. The airplane was filled to capacity when everyone got on.

After a while I got into a conversation about where she was from and where she was headed. She told me that she lived in Manila, and that she was headed to Dallas to a business meeting about running franchise businesses. Then I asked her where she went to church. She responded by saying that she was Catholic. My next question was, "What do you think it takes for a person to go to heaven?"

She replied with a works answer by saying; "I think you have to do good works and be a good person."

I then asked her if she minded if I explained the Gospel in the Evangecube. I reached up and got my card Evangecube and very carefully explained it to her. When I got to the part where she needs to know Jesus as a personal Savior, she said she would like to pray and receive Jesus.

I just happened to have a copy of my book: *You Will Never Run Out of Jesus*, so I gave it to her. While I was trying to sleep, she read several chapters.

Before we parted from those adjoining seats, I told her that maybe she could join us next year and go to Baguio City and help with our medical/evangelical team. She said she would.

Several days after I got home, I finally found an occasion to sit down and email the address she had given me. The email is as follows:

> Dear Jermaine,
>
> On the way back I found out my mother had just died; the next day, my oldest first cousin died. So, I have been busy going to visitation and funerals most of the week. I had meant to email you earlier.
>
> First of all, CONGRATULATIONS on the most important decision you will ever make: believing in Jesus as your Lord and Savior. Please follow up on that promise to Jesus. Read the Gospel of John in the New Testament and it will plainly tell you what Jesus did for us from His

beloved disciple, John. It is important that you read and study His Word daily.

I hope your classes are going well and that you like the "big D" (Dallas).

We will be coming back to the Philippines next March, and we will be going up to Baguio City. I hope you will be able to go with us for the week that we are in country.

On the go for the Lord,
Dr. Bill Bailey

In a few hours, I received the following email from her:

Hi Dr. Bailey,

Sorry to hear that your mom and your cousin just died. I would like to extend my sincerest condolences. I am sure that they are peacefully at rest right now in heaven together with the Lord. Also, sorry, I wasn't able to send an email last Monday. I've been very busy learning the new process in the office. I don't go to class anymore Dr. Bailey, I've already graduated, and I'm going to Dallas to attend some business meetings and undergo some comprehensive trainings as well. I'm gonna fly back to Manila on April 17.

More so, I would like to extend my deepest gratitude for all the kindness and spiritual guidance that you've given to me. You are rest assured that I will never forget the vow that I've made with the Lord. I'm gonna fulfill my mission and assure that I will continue preaching His words, just like what you've been doing. Thank you so much for the book that you gave me.

I am looking forward on joining with you on proclaiming the words of Jesus and evangelizing the Filipino people. There are lots of indigent Pinoys who need your help. You are a blessing to all the people in the world. You are the living proof of God. May you never get tired of doing what you have already started. I am on the process of following your path Dr. Bailey. May the Good Lord be with you always.

Best regards,
Maine

Pampanga, Philippines

Philippines
February 2010

Philippines
February 2010

Chapter 26

61st Angola Day

> I was in prison and you came to me.
> Matthew 25: 36c

Several weeks prior to the 61st Angola Day in Louisiana, an invitation came via Internet through the state Gideon's International network to any Gideon that would like to make the annual visitation day. I had started to go to the Hunt State Prison for its annual Gideon's prison visitation, but when I found out that someone from the Bossier Gideon's camp was going to Angola, I sent my information in for the Angola State Prison Gideon's visit. That person just happened to be our camp president, Ivory Youngblood. After talking with him, I made arrangements to get a nearby hotel room; we had to be there at 7 a.m. at the prison gate for orientation. It is a five-hour drive from Bossier City to Angola. I got some information from some of our camp members who had been before.

According to *Wikipedia*, the Louisiana State Penitentiary (also know as **Angola** and **The Farm**) is the largest maximum security prison in the United States with over 5,000 inmates and 1,800 staff members. Angola is still run as a working farm like it was back in the 1800's when slaves did all the work. Angola is the only penitentiary in the U.S. to be issued a FCC license to operate a radio station, KLSP (Louisiana State Penitentiary); it is a 100-watt radio station that operates from inside the prison to approximately 6,000 potential listeners, including the prisoners and staff. There is a museum which features among its exhibits, Louisiana's old electric chair called, "Old Sparky", last used in 1991. The prison hosts a rodeo every April and October, and its inmates produce the award-winning magazine, **The Angolite,** which is available to the general public and is relatively uncensored.

Ivory and I stayed in north Baton Rouge and got up at 4:45 a.m. to eat breakfast and drive on to Tunica; Angola is an 18,000-acre complex immediately adjacent, in an oxbow of the Mississippi River, in eastern Louisiana. Due to daylight savings time, it was dark, and we missed our Angola State Prison sign. I was already upset because I had not been informed to wear a sport coat and tie; Ivory was upset because he had not gotten federal clearance through the state Gideons. We drove on to the edge of Mississippi before we noted our error. Now, we would be late for the 7 a.m. orientation, not properly dressed (me), and Ivory not authorized. We had prayed about this the night before. Oh, we of little faith! We were 20 minutes late, but everyone was just arriving. Ivory was on the list as we went through the entrance gate; he had been approved after a call to our state Gideon president, that we had made the night before, from our hotel. Apparently, he had interceded for Ivory.

We immediately were asked to go into a building near the entrance gate, where we were put in a small room with fan ventilation to be checked for narcotics. Then we drove for about three miles to the Orientation Center. Many old observation towers still stood at almost every corner; most of these are no longer used. On the way, we noticed no less than five different church buildings or chapels, all of different religious orientations. As we looked out over the large open fields, we could see several of the fields being plowed for early crops. A gentle cool wind was blowing in from the west; it was the first day of spring and what a beautiful day it was turning out to be. In the distance, we could see cows and horses in different fields. There were few trees except along the tree lines at the edge of the prison grounds. We soon were enveloped in a vast farm that was just surreal.

On our entrance to the orientation, breakfast was being served; we had gone to great effort to have breakfast before we came. Soon everyone was asked to sit; the service started with prayer by the Gideon state chaplain, Don Price. We all joined in a good Christian song: **WHAT A FRIEND WE HAVE IN JESUS.** Gideon state president John Boesch, then made a welcoming speech, stating that this was the 61st annual meeting of Gideons there to do prison ministry. He commented how Warden Burl Cain had changed Angola from the meanest and most dangerous prison in America to the **safest.** There have been many changes; now religious matters are prominent. A prisoner could now get a seminary degree in the prison, several other college degrees were also available. Warden Cain said it was a God thing, not him.

A roll call of parishes was made; less than half of the parishes were represented by the 75 to 80 Gideons present. Over half of the Gideons present were there for the first time.

Warden Cain could not make the meeting, but one of the assistant wardens made an introductory talk on the Louisiana State Penitentiary, Angola. He gave a list of statistics about Angola. On the list were the escapes from Angola; these have been few. He said Angola was quite a secure place. The last escapes were in 2003, and all three of the escapees were brought back quickly. There have been exceptionally few murders in the last several years. There were also only a few suicides. There have been several assaults on the staff, but these get less and less every year. Where there had been several hundred assaults of inmates on inmates; these continue to decrease every year. Further, he said there were more Christians per capita in Angola than anywhere in the state. (WOW!!)

After several other instructions of DO'S and DON'TS from the assistant warden, we were assigned to groups. Our Bossier camp, Ivory and I, joined with five from the Denham Springs group to go with our liaison, Le Roy. (Le Roy said he had worked there for 20 years.) We introduced ourselves to each other and were told to follow Le Roy to our assignment, the Spruce subdivision. We drove in our own vehicles, for about two miles, to a large complex of prison blocks. We noted a lot of activity in and around the prison yards. Prisoners were going out on details to work in the fields accompanied by a security on horseback; a few were playing basketball; and then some were just sitting out in the sun. On entering the prison blocks, we were placed in a holding room while the in door was locked; then the other door was opened, and we proceeded on into the prison blocks.

I was astonished to see many female security guards; most of these were safely behind locked cage areas doing the jobs of checking prisoners in and out of the prison blocks. All the security people were very cordial and friendly. In fact, most of the prisoners were very friendly and spoke to us or said good morning greetings. We walked, and walked, and walked some more through blocks and blocks of the prison divisions until the last one, Spruce.

Once inside, we were able to walk down between the bunk beds where the prisoners were. It was obvious many were already outside as over half the bunks were empty. The seven of us started going down the aisles and asking if anyone needed a Bible or if they could be engaged in a conversation. The first three told me that they had a Bible. Finally, I found one that did not have a Bible. We engaged in a conversation and he assured me he was a born-again Christian. Then I proceeded to ask if he knew anyone in the room that needed witnessing to. I was pointed to a person a couple of bunks down the aisle, so I proceeded to engage in a conversation with him by offering him a Bible. During our conversation he indicated he was not a Christian, so I asked him if I could show him something. So, I pulled out my Evangecube and told him the basic story of Jesus' love for him. He prayed to receive Jesus as Savior. Joy radiated from his face after the prayer. I then asked him his prison number so I could fill out the form that identified that prisoner's name and location. The chaplain would then follow up with that person.

We made several rooms in the Spruce block; one room was almost empty, so I asked where everyone was. I was told that they were out on the basketball court. I asked Le Roy if we could go out there and he said O.K., but as we headed out there, everyone was starting to return for head count. (Head count is made six times daily; this is apparently a good way to keep up with everyone.) One of the large gates was locked as we were headed out of the Spruce subdivision so the head count could be made. I had another accept Jesus while I was in the Spruce area. The Denham Spring Gideon group had seen me using my Evangecube, and they had me demonstrate its use; they were excited about its use as an evangelistic tool. They said they were anxious to get one soon. As we exited those prison blocks, we called a number that had been given to us and our group was assigned an area (EER) near the administrative department.

We drove about three miles back toward the entrance to this area. After going through a series of electronic controlled gates, we entered an area where there was only one prisoner per cell and we had to communicate through the bars; we were not allowed in the individual room. Immediately, it dawned on me that these guys were more hard-core prisoners. Many let us know that they did not want to talk to us; some by pretending to be asleep, some stating that they did not want to be bothered, or that he was Muslim and not interested in any of our Christian conversation or Bibles. Nevertheless, some were friendly and welcomed conversation or dialogue. One was not sure of his salvation, so I took him through the Evangecube presentation and he prayed to receive Jesus as Savior. We went through several blocks before we finished there. It was noticeable how clean all the hallways and floors were; no adverse smells were detectable. We called for further assignments, but we were told that our assignments had been completed. I doubt that our Gideon groups got to see many of the over 5,200 prisoners there. But, during some of the conversations, I did find out that many groups do come in to witness, and many of the prisoners witness to other prisoners. I also found out that there was a chapel, church, or mosque for every religion represented in the prison.

By now it was 1:30 p.m. and we were asking about lunch. Someone told us that we were so close to finishing that we were not asked to lunch there. I was looking forward to sitting down and eating with the prisoners so I could witness some more to them. As we left to go back to the orientation site, I gave Le Roy a new Evangecube that had instructions inside on how to give a proper presentation. He was very appreciative and promised me he would use it frequently. He said he liked to witness to the prisoners.

Most, if not all, had to be impressed by the atmosphere in the prison. Most of the people there afforded us at least a smile. The grounds were vast horizons of well cared for farm land, livestock, church buildings, observation towers, and of course, the many prison cell blocks. I must compliment the administrative staff there.

On arriving back at the orientation site, we gave our statistics to the Gideon statistician. I do not have the total number, but several had a salvation experience, and many Bibles were handed out. It was a great day! We were all invited back next year, at the same date, in 2011.

Chapter 27

North China
2010

In April 2009 we were unable to go to China because of the H1N1 Virus (Swine flu), but we volunteered again for the next year. Early in the year we began preparing for our trip. Rev. Sonny De-Prang and I volunteered to go where He needed us. It was mentioned that we might go to the site of the earthquake that happened soon after our last trip to China. When we got to Hong Kong, we were assigned to a new area in north China; this was to be the first group there. As several times before in my travels, I was to be with a pioneer group to that site. This was an answer to my prayer anyway; I wanted to go where the Lord could use us.

It was nice to see Don at the airport. After an all-night flight, we had arrived in Hong Kong. We were taken to our hotel near the IHR offices to place our suitcases, eat breakfast, and head to orientation. At breakfast we met Mary Beard, R.N., and her husband, and several others going on another team. It was nice to see Dr. Rollin and Judy Burhans; we had served together in north China on our last trip.

At orientation, it was great to see Nancy and Dr. Bill. The orientation started off with each introducing himself/herself and telling a brief synopsis of themselves. It turned out to be a very personable time and a great way of introduction for each member; this seemed to bond the group immediately. We were to be divided into two

North China

teams. Sonny and I were going with Mary and Bill Beard to north China. (I knew Mary from my first trip to China in 2006.) The other group was larger; they were assigned to northwest China.

That night we all went to a very nice local Chinese restaurant and enjoyed some excellent Chinese cuisine. I got a picture of Mary with the chicken head in her chopsticks, but this was for the photo op. (I had a real fear of having to eat a rooster head or a chicken foot when I was in south China in 2006). It sure was nice to rest in a nice bed that night before we headed north the next morning.

We rode in a bus north to the "border"; mainland China and Hong Kong still have not really incorporated into each other fully. We went through passport control before heading further to the regional airport at Shenshen. Once on the airplane, we were delayed because of the weather nearby, so we got a nice meal on the plane before going to our assigned city.

We found out later that there was a major earthquake, 7.9 on the Richter earthquake scale, in Yushu County. The doctor that was to be assigned to our group applied to work in the earthquake area; after approval by the government, he was accepted. He had been in-country for about four weeks doing clinics elsewhere.

Our field worker, who met us at the airport, had tried to be at orientation in Hong Kong, but due to problems with his visa, he could not come. Mary thought our assigned city was going to be a one-road, one-horse town; she must have been surprised; we were greeted by a bustling, attractive city. Many in the U.S. would have said it was a huge city, but not by Chinese standards. We were taken to a central city hotel that was quite nice by any standards. It had snowed two days earlier in the city, and I was expecting some residual snow, but none was anywhere to be found. It was quite cool, but not like the weather report I had seen on the Internet for the last two weeks; it had been down into the 20s at night for several days.

After a hearty Chinese breakfast buffet in our hotel the next morning, we met with our three field workers who would work with us all week. They took us to a site where we met the regional field workers. These workers told us that our presence was an answer to many prayers; they were very excited about us being there. Many months of preparation had gone on to secure all the aspects of this trip; they were praying that this also would help their assigned tasks there. It was certain to help build bridges with the local people and help support relationships that had already been established. We were greeted with several boxes of purchased medicines, to count into dose packs and to hand out in our clinics. After a brief orientation and a couple hours of counting out meds, we started out on a Chinese cuisine tour (for the whole week) that I will never forget. The food was wholesome, nutritional, and very tasty. I don't think I have ever had Chinese food this good in the U.S.

The next morning we took our equipment and prepared meds, down the street several blocks, to our assigned location. A local physician had volunteered to share his office with us. It was quite crowded after all the workers and English-speaking university students showed up; I was partially surprised at their proficiency in the English language; they were English majors. Apparently, the news had not gotten out; we were slow starting off, but as the day progressed, we saw more and more people. We saw several people with the universal complaints you would see any where in the world, but we also heard some of the weirdest complaints I have ever run across. What really surprised me was the fact that we could proclaim the Good News. Sonny was "floating" with his activities, so he was given more opportunities.

One of the student English majors, who was my interpreter at the time, and I got into a lengthy conversation about being a member of the family. I showed her the **Evangecube** and she was almost persuaded. Later, Sonny also talked with her. The last day she came by with a heavy heart and admitted that she had become a member of the People's Party so she could get a better job. She seemed a little sad about the situation, but under the circumstances she could not proceed with our membership.

At meal time each day we were always treated to the best of China in the local restaurants. So we looked forward to meal time.

Over the three days we were located there, Sonny had the opportunity to see several accept Him as new family members. I had **one**. A young college student came in just to see what was going on. After brief exam, I showed him the **Evangecube** and he saw the Truth. Our lead field worker took him to the back office and was assured of his decision. What a thrill to see people accept our primary goal there. The doctor and his staff were so cordial and friendly; I know we had to be a pain for the days we were there; it was obvious he was family, too.

Apparently, the doctor had enough confidence in me; the last morning he brought his wife to see me. We were not busy yet, so I took over 30 minutes examining and talking with her. I am not sure I really helped, but it sure was a nice visit. The family members seemed real happy about our visit.

Each day after work our field worker, who had never been to this city, took us to a different part of the city to explore, sightsee, shop, and of course enjoy the local cuisine. Late one afternoon we went to town center, where several kites were flying; also many different types of kites were for sale. All of us bought some. Then we proceeded to go to the Muslim quarters. Actually, it was one of the most picturesque parts of the city. Our field worker took us to a "hole in the wall" Moslem restaurant and all seven of us ate for less than $15 (US $ value), with tip, and the food was actually quite good.

The second day after work, we went to the Buddhist temple area, where many shops were also available. The temple had Buddhist monks who were actively working out in one area with a small sawmill. Naturally, we had to seek out another nice restaurant. We went to a Mongolian restaurant, where we actively prepared part of our meal by cooking the meat and vegetables in a boiling pan of milk on our table. Here we saw the famous horsehead violin being played. It sounded quite different than any similar instruments I had heard.

On Sunday, we went to one of the field worker's apartment to study the Book. Naturally, afterwards, we went to a nice local Chinese restaurant for more delectable food. Next we were able to go to the Cultural Center and do some real shopping, but I bought my major gifts in a local shop down the street. I bought a handmade copper kettle, statue of Ghenghis Khan, and a native wedding hat. Also, we went to a person's home nearby and were shown a nice array of homemade silver products. I could not resist buying my wife a nice silver bracelet.

The following two days we went to a restaurant in an apartment complex to hold clinic. We saw more patients than at the first location, but many of these were already in the family. Again we had all the universal complaints you would expect; I had one young man (age 36) who feared he was going to die. I questioned him further; then I examined him as thoroughly as I could. I told him that what he really needed was the answer on the **Evangecube**. He was receptive, but could just not make the final decision. Luckily one of the people there worked with him; he said he would follow up personally with him.

At both work sites the people were so friendly and receptive. We could have not had it any better with the translators, sponsors of our clinics, and our field workers. Our touring, shopping, and cuisine choices could have not been better. The final morning we met briefly with the field worker leaders for debriefing. They exemplified our efforts and the overall work done; this would go a long way in their overall goals. We were invited back. Later that day we went to the regional airport and returned to Shenshen. While there, I saw a lady flying a remote-controlled model helicopter; she flew it over 40 feet into the air, then back into her hand. I just had to get four of those for my grandchildren. (Later, I found out it was difficult even for me to control.) Then we continued on our way back to Hong Kong.

The following morning at debriefing we heard a summary of everyone's experiences. Dr. Bob Patterson, the physician originally assigned to our group, gave his unique experiences at the recent earthquake site. He and a few others were allowed in after governmental approval. He described the devastating effects of the earthquake and what they were able to do at the site. It was cold there; he said he wore the same multiple layers of clothing each day for almost a week. It was not yet time for presenting the Good News there at this time.

The other team told of their many experiences at the previous earthquake site. The people there also sounded very friendly and appreciative. Overall it had been a very good trip for them. Our team then shared our trip. We had the afternoon to shop, rest, or go sightseeing. I chose to catch up on the computer at the office site; I had to sway Wall Street the following day with my trades.

Some of us rested the remainder of the afternoon; then we all went down to the harbor for a great Western-type meal. It was a great time of fellowship and enjoying the food we were more accustomed to.

Mary and Bill Beard and I have agreed to go on future mission trips together; we had a great time working together on our team. Nancy and Don said they would be delighted to help us return to work with the Chinese people

What a wonderful experience! I highly recommend going to China for anyone willing to work with a great group of workers and the very friendly, receptive, appreciative Chinese people. I certainly plan on going again hopefully soon.

North China

North China
2010

North China
2010

Chapter 28

Draganesti, Romania
2010

During the Christmas holidays when Pastor Tim Keith and his wife, Kim, were visiting at my home, Tim asked me if I would consider gathering a medical team to go with his evangelical group to Draganesti-Olt, Romania, in May 2010. He said this would be the third trip his church (Woodland Place Baptist Church) had taken to Romania. I responded by telling him that I would pray about it. Soon I put out an email asking several people who had been on previous trips with me to consider going. The responses were very good. Before I knew it, three other doctors and several nurses had volunteered to go with me.

As time arrived to order the tickets, I began to get some unwanted news; one of the doctors had come down with viral cardiomyopathy and was essentially put to bed rest. That meant his resident would not be going either. Then, the other doctor I was really depending on going told me he could not go as his fiancée did not have the vacation time to go. Naturally, he felt he should not go either. A familiar situation had arisen yet again. At first I was discouraged and called Pastor Tim about this. He said one of the doctors in his church would probably go. That did not pan out either; he was going on another mission at that same time slot. This had happened before, so I recruited some good nurses who could work as nurse practitioners; one of them just happened to be Pastor Tim's mother, Joyce Keith.

Don Salyer, my reliable pharmacist who has been on several trips with me before, decided to go, but his son and daughter had told him that if he went again, one of them would have to go too. As it turned out the son was busy; luckily, Kim his daughter in Tyler, TX, said she would go.

Once while calling a prescription into CVS Pharmacy in Haughton, I asked the pharmacist if she would like to go on a medical mission trip. Amazingly, I got the answer I wanted to hear. So, remembering this, I called Judy Hodgkins; after some family discussions, she decided to go.

My team was taking shape. I asked Billy Weatherall to go with me, and I told him of the two trips I had scheduled soon. He wanted to go on both, but I told him I really needed him on the Romanian trip, so he agreed to go.

Another of my reliable nurses was Rosemary Andrews. When asked, she said she would like to go also. That about completed the team, as I was asked not to bring any evangelical team members; Tim said he would take care of that portion.

I was introduced to Pastor Raul over the Internet, as well as missionaries Kevin and Michelle Weppler and Bob and Diane Wagstaff. Pastor Raul visited the U.S. and was in Houston for a few days. I conversed over the phone with him about the upcoming medical mission trip. He was delighted that we were coming. I offered my dental skills, but he said that I would have to work in the local dentist's office and invite the church's friends in for any service to be rendered. When I told this to one of my dentist friends who had wanted to go, he gave a very sharp negative answer. Pastor Raul described a very socialistic medical environment there. Also, he told me one of the local doctors would come to help us, but that doctor would have to fulfill the government's obligation first.

I would like to interject Pastor Raul Costea's biography at this point. Part of this is from him personally and some from his website. I will put this basically in his words:

> After I was born again, I understood that the greatest thing you could do for Him on this earth is to bring others to Christ. I have spiritually grown in cell groups and began concerning character and the Lord's work as well. Certain verses in the Bible began to powerfully talk to me and I understood the Lord wanted me to dedicate myself entirely to His work. One of these verses is the one in Isaiah 53 where the Scripture says, "He will see the fruit of His work and enliven." I only had one motivation in this missionary work: Jesus to be enlivened by many gained souls. From then on, my heart's desire is that at the end of every day Jesus would be pleased with me and I would hear the words: "Well done good servant."
>
> I attended a Bible college and also followed His guidance to an area where there were only 0.2 percent evangelical (from all the denominations) Christians. Here I started working in the villages around Slatina. Also, after a year, the Lord compelled us to start a work with orphans. Since then we have found a Christian family to take over the work with the orphans.
>
> After a period of several years, the Lord impelled me to move south to the city of Draganesti-Olt. I was sent to Draganesti by the Baptist Church in Alba Iulia. Here in Corabia, another city, and the surrounding villages we wish to plant churches. We know the work is the Lord's, who works through the church, so we thought we could make available a missionary house, where missionaries

from our or other countries can come and work in the area.

My goal is to coordinate ministry in the area, make partnerships, and communicate between local churches, foreign and other Romanian churches. I am ministering to the missionaries and pastors in the churches in Draganesti-Olt. We share the Gospel in various ways; for example, in one village we started the ministry by using the "Jesus" film. In that day, I was very happy because over 100 people came to see the film. But also, about six to eight people wanted to beat me. I wasn't aware of this, and the worst one of them came to me and told me, "You know that in the last days false prophets will come." I thought he wanted to know more about Jesus; in fact, he needed a reason to catch me in a trap. If I would defend myself, then he would say I am the false prophet. I said to him, "Yes, you are right, I will show you what they look like in the Bible." He did not expect this answer, so he said, "No, it is not necessary." He did not have a backup question, so he tried to escape. But, God helped me to find his address the next week. I visited him and he hid, but finally I found him home; however, he was drunk. I asked him to pray with me, and from that moment, God changed him totally. His wife said to me, "What have you done to my husband? I want to be like that." And, in one night she became a Christian also. In their house, we started a house church in that village. Everything the Lord did through us, and everything He will do is to His praise.

Iceland had a major volcano eruption in early May and the ash clouds shut down flights into and out of Europe for over a week. This was about two weeks before our flight was scheduled. Then

British Airways announced a strike for four weeks; that was our carrier from Dallas to Bucharest and back. But we were determined to still go; our flight from Bucharest back to London was canceled, but that flight was luckily rescheduled three hours later.

Our group from Shreveport met Don and Kim in Dallas and we flew on to London; we met Rev. Tim Keith and his group of three (Brent, Connie, and Barbara) from his church at the Heathrow Airport. Then it was on to Bucharest; we arrived there after 4 p.m. We were met there by Florian, a local driver enlisted to assist Pastor Raul's ministry when needed; we were lucky to get all but one suitcase for the entire group. All the meds and eyeglasses made it. We loaded up and made our way very slowly across Bucharest for the next 2½ hours, as it was the Friday afternoon traffic rush. It was after 10:30 p.m. when we finally arrived at our host missionaries' home, our home for the week. Kevin and Michelle Weppler (Canadian missionaries to Romania) had a dormitory addition added to their home for people just like us to host a maximum of 14 people at a time.

Kevin and Michelle Weppler, from Hanover, Ontario, Canada, are full-time missionaries with EMCC (Evangelical Missionary Church of Canada and its mission arm, World Partners Canada; they have been in Romania to serve since an invitation went out to them on a visit there in December 2006. They were in the area as asked by some university students from Arad, to help with some food hampers and Christmas shoeboxes to the town of Draganesti-Olt, this is one of the poorest areas of all southern Romania. What started out to be just a short mission trip to Oltenia soon turned into something more permanent. It seems that Pastor Raul and the missionary team there had been praying for two years for a foreign missionary couple to assist them with the ministry. By the end of that weekend, Pastor Raul was telling them, "You are the ones we have been praying for!" After much prayer (by the Wepplers and their family in Canada) they felt God was calling them to be obedient and move to the Oltenia area of Romania. Kevin and Michelle purchased a house to be used by visiting teams to stay when coming from the U.S., Canada, and UK while in the Draganesti-Olt area. They want to walk in complete obedience to Him; they are excited to see how He uses them as they partner with this ministry.

After a hearty breakfast the next morning (Saturday), Pastor Raul Costea came as scheduled at 8:30 a.m. to pick us up; we loaded up our supplies in two vans and went to Speranta (Hope) Baptist Church to meet with our interpreters. Mihai (Michael) was assigned to me. Among the group was George and Dana; they pastor a house church in their home in Stoenesti, a village of about 2,500 people. Also present was Cristi and Roxana Simion; Cristi was recently ordained and works with Pastor Raul as worship leader within the church and mission work. Pastor Raul's wife, Ana, was also present. Dorothy Reid, a Canadian missionary and the children's worker, would likewise join us. We then went to the town hall at Stoenesti; it is located directly across from a moderate size Orthodox Church.

We were welcomed by the mayor of the village; he wore a sash of Romanian flag colors: yellow, red, and blue and proceeded to welcome us into his office. There he made a brief speech welcoming us to the village and thanking us for coming. He insisted we take a group picture; he wants that posted in newspapers back home. We made the pictures; then we were taken to the auditorium and introduced to the crowd awaiting us. Most of these were older women and a few older men. These folks were dressed like they were living in the 1950s and had several layers of clothes on. We had been told that the unemployment rate was 70 to 80 percent and many of the people appeared very poor.

The pharmacy was set up in the mayor's office; the eye station was set up in a larger room down the hall. Rosemary, Joyce, and I were given a medium-sized room to do our medical clinic—and extract teeth if needed; the Mayor had given permission to me for that. He said he would take the responsibility of that service. Pastor Raul reminded me that this was the only place I had permission to perform extractions all week.

It didn't take long to find out one of the most prevalent problems: HYPERTENSION. It seemed over half of those 50 or over had it. Michelle later told me it was the life style and diet they eat there; everything is fried in oil, and almost everyone uses too much salt. Many of the complaints were universal complaints found anywhere: pain in the back, knees, and shoulders; headaches; congestion, stomach ache, etc. Where the people got the idea that their kidneys, liver, or pancreas were hurting, I am not sure, but it seems that a local doctor told them that.

When I went to pull my first tooth, Mihai said he was not up to that procedure; he left, and Michelle, a former nurse in Canada; had to come translate and assist me the rest of the day. One lady was very finicky about her tooth, and I had a hard time anesthetizing it, so I did a mandibular block. While waiting for the block to work, I went down the hall to get a new pair of readers; my nose piece had broken off. I did not know she was making a big scene; the Mayor had even come in to calm her down. I returned not knowing of this, calmly extracted her tooth, and then she went away happy.

The day went fairly smooth; we saw all the people that had been given a number to be seen; these had the seal of the mayor on them so no one could just sneak in. After we finished, the mayor again wanted us to line up on the front porch of the town hall and make more pictures. It had been a pleasant day at the clinic.

We went back to the Wepplers' (our home for the week) and had supper. Billy and I decided to go for a walk; it does not get dark until almost 9 p.m. there at night. We took off down the straight road for a moderate distance, but decided to take a trek up the hillside; the low area was the old riverbed of the Olt River; it is very fertile with dark loam soil. We could see wheat growing almost as far as the eye could see. Scattered poppies, daisies, and several other colorful wild flowers were seen all along the roadside and some were mixed in with the wheat.

    We ran across a man and woman cutting grass along the roadside with a scythe and placing it in a horse drawn wagon; this must have been for the horse, as the people in Draganesti have little property. The wheat fields are owned by large corporations; many of those are Italian. Billy asked if he could pick up some of the cut grass with the pitch fork and place it in the wagon; they granted him his wish. I just had to take his picture doing this. Further up the road we ran into a young man with his milk cow grazing along the roadside, then along came a large herd of goats mulching on grass and weeds. A dog was calmly walking along with the owner, but I bet if one of those goats had gone astray, he would have heard from that dog quickly. Finally, we came up to the crest of the hill and could see the River Olt in the distant background along with Draganesti in the foreground. The sun was setting so we had to get on back to the Team house.

    Sunday morning, Don had an episode where he became disoriented and confused; we gathered at his side and had prayer. Initially I thought Don may have had a small stroke. Kim started having diarrhea and hematochezia, so I insisted both of them stay at the Team house.

    I asked Billy to do the glasses and Judy to work the pharmacy when we went to the Parieti Baptist Church in Parieti. We were all asked to give testimonies during the service. As we walked in, the pastor of the church was still preaching. It did not take long to tell he was very passionate in his sermon. Pastor Raul later told me that the pastor was a deacon in the Orthodox Church; when he first came there, he had come to the service to see if Pastor Raul was a false prophet or heretic. As it turned out, this man got touched with the Holy Spirit and soon became a member of the church. There were a few others that had come to throw him out of town and ended up members of the church.

After song services, as led by Cristi Simion, Billy, Judy, and I gave our testimonies to the crowd with Pastor Raul as the interpreter. Then, Pastor Tim gave a good message. Afterwards, we got out our supplies and set up clinic for the members of the church who wanted to be seen. We saw well over 40 people over the next 2½ hours.

When we returned to the Wepplers', Don was much better, and Kim's problem was better. What answered prayers! Michelle had me see a couple of neighbors on consultation in the living room. One was about spousal abuse from alcoholism; this is not an infrequent occurrence in Romania.

Sunday night we all went to Speranta Baptist Church for worship services. Billy and I were asked to give our testimonies again after the singing service. Rev. Tim preached again. The church was full; the people had been told that if they wanted to be seen in the medical clinic the next morning, they could get a ticket to be seen. Everyone in the service seemed to have a good time.

Kevin and I got into a conversation later that night about Romania. He said it was a socialistic nation. Most of the young people who had any incentive at all had moved to Bucharest or other large cities to look for a job. That left many of the older folks in the communities or villages, and they were basically very poor. The unemployment rate was between 70 to 80 percent, and you can imagine the hardships of the people.

The Speranta Baptist Church was the site of our clinic for the next two days. Billy had to work the eyeglass station by himself, and Judy had the pharmacy to herself most of the time. Judy is a fast learner; she was able to write the directions on the meds in Romanian by the end of the first day of clinic. We worked almost 10 hours both days and saw over 180 patients each day. We continued to see a lot of hypertension and were almost completely out of anti-hypertension meds by the end of the fourth day.

We got to meet IMB missionaries, Bob and Diane Wagstaff, while in the church; Diane occasionally helped out with interpreting. Bob remained quiet as he was still recovering from major back surgery. They lived about one hour away, but are an active part of the mission work there.

On Wednesday, we went to another nearby village, Radominesti. We were welcomed by the vice-mayor at the Cultural Center; the mayor was in an important business meeting. Again, the sidewalks were lined by many older women and men; few children were to be seen. Horse drawn buggies had brought several of them to the clinic.

There were many sad stories during these clinics. Many of the widows were asked why they were not taking their prescribed medications. They quickly replied that they could not afford these, as they had to eat. Several of the people would take their anti-hypertension meds only when they felt bad. Michelle told me that sometimes when some of the widows went to the pharmacy, they could only buy one pill.

My sphygmomanometer (blood pressure machine) cuff was torn up by the end of the clinics; I had to go up to near 300 mmHg pressure to capture some of the hypertensive values. Billy told me he had given all the reading glasses away (over 420) and nearly 500 prescription glasses were given; only a few were left which no one could use. We did have a fair amount of meds and supplies left, so I gave these to Michelle to give to Dr. Alina Gabor and a nurse in the Speranta Baptist Church. Dr. Gabor was supposed to have helped us in the clinics, after she met her obligations with the government clinic, but she was away with other colleagues doing medical missions for the week several hours away on the Danube River. This region had been severely hit by flooding several years ago. Dr. Gabor was overwhelmed with our generosity for the meds, and she expressed regrets that she could not help us.

For the week, we had seen over 650 patients in the five clinic days; the Gospel had been shared with a host of people that had come through the clinics by Rev. Tim, Brent, Connie, and Barbara. The Gospel was shared with well over 300 people in a one-on-one setting and at least this many more in a corporate setting. Several people accepted Christ into their lives and many doors were opened for the spread of the Gospel in these villages. Pastor Raul and all his mission team were very satisfied by our work. We all know the people were very gracious, kind, and extremely thankful for our presence.

After the last work day, we were all invited to go to George and Dana's home for supper. Dana had prepared us a very delicious fish and vegetable meal. While there we met their two beautiful daughters, age 3 and 5. Before we left I asked Dana to pack their bags; I wanted to take both of them home with me. You can guess the answer to that.

I must commend Michelle, who cooked for us all week; the meals were delicious. Kevin made sure we were comfortable with our accommodations. I enjoyed Michelle and Kevin's answers to the many questions I asked them.

Thursday morning, we left via van and drove back to Bucharest through the beautiful countryside. There were wheat fields everywhere out in the country. Wild poppies, daisies, and other flowers also adorned the hillsides. I thought we were going to a souvenir shop or two, but we were taken to a modern mall near the airport. We got to eat a good meal (KFC for me) and roam through the big mall for almost three hours. Then we headed to the airport. I did manage to buy a few souvenirs at the airport the last morning before boarding for London.

We spent the night in London, but it was after 7 p.m. before we arrived at the hotel; most of us ate supper and went to bed. The next morning we flew from London back home.

Our medical team wants to thank Pastor Tim Keith and his church for sponsoring the trip. We were able to attract large crowds so the Gospel could be presented. Pastor Raul Costea was gratified with our presence and work; the medical clinics are an avenue for his mission team to enter new territories.

Romania, May 2010

Romania, May 2010

Billy Weatherall pitchforking grass in Draganesti

Chapter 29

Ecuador
"The Evangelicals"
2010

While trying to get doctor recruits for the Philippines in late 2009, I called Dr. David Colvin (someone had told me he went on medical missions) and asked him to go to the Philippines with us. He said he could not, but asked me if I would be interested in going to Ecuador in July of 2010. I asked him to email me some information and I would consider it. David said the weather was so nice in Ecuador; that sounded very inviting.

The meeting for the group effort for the Ecuador trip was called in early May 2010. I attended the meeting and was intrigued by the mission work already going on in Ecuador. There would be a construction team, a VBS (Vacation Bible School), and a medical team going. I asked how many I could invite on the medical team.

We had another meeting and most all the team members were invited; this consisted of Ellerbe Road Baptist Church, Airline Baptist Church, and Wedgeworth Baptist Church. I had volunteered to send all my meds that I had accumulated or had left over from the previous mission trip. David had a large suitcase of prescription glasses he had obtained from the Lions' Club. I ordered 425 pair of reading eyeglasses from In Focus. David had to order more meds that I did not have available.

Ellerbe Road Baptist Church kept us fully informed of all the steps to get ready. Our three church groups met at the airport in

Ecuador

Shreveport on July 23; we took off for Houston. From there, we flew to Quito, the capital of Ecuador; it was cool there (in the 50s). That night we spent the night at the Howard Johnson Hotel, but after a good breakfast, we loaded up on our bus and headed south on the Pan American Highway to Camp Chacauco. This delightful retreat was purchased and started by Steve and Carol Thompson, U.S. missionaries to Ecuador.

Steve and Carol Thompson are a picture of lives dedicated to missions and to spreading the Gospel of Jesus Christ. Originally from Texas, the Thompsons moved to Ecuador in 1987 to serve as missionaries with the International Mission Board. Over the years, the Thompsons have been involved in various forms of ministry and outreach in Ecuador, all with a primary focus of evangelism, church planting, and church development. After 23 years of service, Steve and Carol remain at and build up the local church. During the year, Steve and Carol work with local believers and pastors to spread the Gospel through conferences, vacation Bible schools, and youth retreats. They also hold pastor-training classes and worship conferences to help strengthen and build up the local church.

While they served in Ecuador, God began to reveal to Steve and Carol a vision for a strategic location where they could provide theological education, space for church retreats, facilities for summer camps, and retreat cabins for Ecuadorian pastors. They began construction on their first camp in 1996 and quickly saw the benefits to local churches and believers. In 2001, God provided a second location camp in the central mountain region of Ecuador.

UNPES Jungle Camp was the first camp ground and is located on the edges of the Ecuadorian jungle. The Thompsons spend part of the summer hosting children's and youth camps from their jungle location and then move to the mountain camp for the latter part of the summer. Camp Chacauco is a beautiful, hand-built retreat center in the central mountain region of Ecuador. It was originally designed as a retreat center for local pastors and has become a place for students to hear the Gospel of Jesus Christ through youth camps and sports ministry.

Servant Life has been sending groups to Ecuador to serve with the Thompsons since 2006. Groups traveling to Ecuador help to lead and facilitate the youth's and the children's camps alongside Steve and Carol. They may also have opportunities to minister to the local churches. They ask people to join them as they help the people of Ecuador know Christ through His Word.

We toured the camp and facilities. We got to see the future seminary building; it was quite a comfortable place to stay.

Early Sunday morning as we stepped out into the chilled Andean Mountain air, the clouds were still sitting on the mountain tops. In the distance to the south was Tungurahua Volcano. It could not be seen well for the clouds, but smoke could be seen coming from the top. Its activity has been continuous since 1999. It was a gorgeous winter day in mid-Ecuador. After breakfast, we loaded up on the bus and went to Pastor Felix's church in Latacunga, the First Baptist Church of Latacunga. Ellerbe Road Baptist Church has put a lot of work and resources into the building of this church. The construction team would be working all week on the church. We were sincerely welcomed by the very friendly people there. During the main service Rev. Dennis Sims gave a very inspirational sermon. The auditorium was mostly packed by nationals.

After church, we went to our "home" for the week in Salcedo, the Rumipamga Inn. It had once been a large ranch, but had been converted to a very nice inn. No air conditioning was present, but who needs air conditioning in the 40s to 60s? The First Baptist Church of Latacunga sent a chicken lunch to our inn. After lunch we went out to the town hall of Salache/Taniloma to see how to set up for our clinics the next two days. On the way back we stopped at the Salache Baptist Church site, where a fresh slab had been

Ecuador

poured that morning for the future church building. The neighbors feel so threatened by the **evangelicals** building a church there; many of their Catholic neighbors had threatened to have their electricity, water for home use, and water for crop irrigation cut off. We all had prayer at the site; then we went into an add-on to their home, where church was being held at the present. There was room for only about 40, but they had put as many as 77 in the small structure recently. So, they felt compelled to build a larger structure. A town council meeting had been set for Wednesday night to discuss what to do with the new church site and the evangelicals.

Catholicism is considered like a cult in several of the South and Central American countries. I certainly heard a lot of this along the Amazon River area, when I was there. The Catholics do not welcome any competition and are prejudiced against any others, especially the evangelicals. In my opinion, that is why the Muslims are not present in this part of the world; they are not welcome.

The next morning, after an excellent breakfast at the inn, we loaded up and went to work at the Salache/Taniloma town hall; the construction team went to Pastor Felix's church in Latacunga, and the VBS team was assigned to another place. The crowd came in slowly at first, but momentum built later in the day. We had a national dentist, Dr. Fabricio Miranda, who did all the dental work for the week. Several of our medical group rotated through his station; they said he did a fantastic job of repairing teeth, extracting teeth, doing veneers, and cleansing teeth. I gave him a large bag of toothpaste, toothbrushes, and floss to give to the patients. (A member of ABC had given these to me for the clinics). The spiritual station was run by national pastors and helpers; they had good results all week. The eyeglasses station was run by Vickie Bailey and several others as they rotated through. Frequently we saw smiles on many faces as they left the eye station. The medical station had four doctors: Dr. David Colvin, Dr. Tom Arnold, Dr. Kirk Cofran and me.

The doctors saw many of the universal things seen just about anywhere in the world. We saw many sun parched cheeks and/or faces. I was surprised that I did not see any skin cancer or many sun-related skin diseases. The people were very congenial and very appreciative of our presence and help. It was obvious they were a relatively poor people economically, but their spirit was excellent.

In the afternoon, after most of the low-lying clouds had moved on or evaporated, Cotopaxi could be seen toward the north (south of Quito). Cotopaxi is one of the highest active volcanoes in the world; it is situated about 17 miles south of Quito, Ecuador. It reaches to a height of 19,347 feet. The snow-covered top made it a magnificent sight; it looked like a majestic cone in the distance. It has a big glacier from all the accumulated snow on its top. The main danger of a huge eruption of Cotopaxi would be the flow of ice from its glacier. If there were to be a very large explosion, the melting glacier would destroy most of the settlements, because of the valley in the suburban area of Quito. It would almost present danger to Latacunga which is situated in the south valley. Nevertheless, it was a picturesque sight in the distance.

Rev. Harrell Shelton, associate pastor of Airline Baptist Church, spent a lot of time rotating through all the stations helping out where needed; he also spent a lot of time entertaining the crowds with Grandpa (Abuelo), his Basset Hound, Jackson (*perro* Jackson), and a new addition to his puppet collection: "Cha Cha" the frog (Spanish also *Cha Cha*). All seemed to thoroughly enjoy the antics and messages.

We spent the second day of clinic there; the crowd really increased as word had gotten out about the free services. At the end of the work day, we had prayer in the upper room where the town council meeting would take place the next night. We prayed for His will to be done. (The Holy Spirit was present Wednesday night; the meeting went well for the small church. Even some other members of the village vouched for the church.)

Wednesday morning we went up to the Compania Baja community center to hold clinic. Our bus had to climb curving roads, often hairpin curves, up and up until we finally arrived about 10,500 feet. Looking out over the mountainside, the view was just gorgeous; clouds were sitting on the nearby mountains, and the gentle cool breeze was so refreshing. Once again the crowd came in slow the first day, but that afternoon and the next day we saw a fair number of people. It was obvious that these folks were even more economically challenged than those down the mountain. The people here seemed to be more of the Inca (Indian) heritage. I finally saw a case of basal cell carcinoma on the nose; it was fairly advanced. I was told that the person had had it for over two years but had refused to have anything done about it.

From the height of Campania Baja in the Andes Mountains, I noticed in the distant valley what appeared to be a body of water. I asked Dennis what river it was; he said it was a series of hot houses. They were so numerous that they appeared like a large river or lake from where we stood. Dennis stated that cut roses were one of largest exports of the country and most went to the U.S.

When I got home and looked it up on the Internet, I found that cut roses and flowers are the fourth largest export of Ecuador. Approximately 70 percent of these roses and 30 percent of the cut flowers grown in Ecuador go to the U.S. Bananas, oil, and shrimp are the top exports of Ecuador.

For the week we saw 815 people; 480 came to know Jesus as Savior. All of these will be followed up by the church members to get them to church, and hopefully enroll them as members of the church. This is how you grow your church from a mission trip.

The VBS was very successful; a lot of work at the First Baptist Church of Latacunga was accomplished by the construction team.

We ate dinner at the Rumipamba Inn each night; it was always a very good meal. Also breakfast was a delight every morning. Vickie said she could get used to someone cooking her meals every night.

Friday morning we loaded up in the bus and headed for the equator, 10 miles north of Quito. On the way we stopped at Pastor Felix's church and admired all the work that had been done by our construction team and the nationals during the week. They had gone a long way toward constructing two more *banos* (bathrooms); also, they had made and stained over a dozen tables and over two dozen church benches. The walls in the entrance were also painted by the group. The church people were so happy and grateful for all the work that was done that week.

Admiring the countryside, we traveled north for another two hours until we made it to Quito, which is in the midst of the Andes highlands. The valleys and hills were packed with dwellings; no wonder they have over three million people living there. The city is just beautiful; it is in a valley between two mountain ranges running in a north-south direction. Finally, we made it to Ciudad-Mitad del Mundo (the city in the middle of the world). It is a gorgeous tourist site on the equator. Even though the sun was shining, a gentle breeze of cool air made it a very delightful day. We immediately went and had a great lunch at the Yaravi Restaurant; many of us enjoyed some of the fresh fruit they have there. Some of us went up into the Equator Museum. Inside the museum were exhibits of the different tribes and groups of primitive people of Ecuador. One of them was the Huaorani (formerly known as Aucas); this is the group featured in the book **Through the Gates of Splendor** and later the movie **The End of the Spear.**

All ended up going through some of the very interesting souvenir shops; most of us made purchases. I made a few purchases to help pay back the generosity of some of the people who help support our mission work. It was a delightful place to see, dine, and shop.

Next, we went to downtown Quito to a large artisan spot to shop some more; more purchases were made. The place was crowded with tourists; some were children who tended to be on the beggar side. Then we went back to the Howard Johnson Hotel to leave our suitcases, so we would then go to a modern mall for dinner. Early the next morning we headed back to Houston, then on home. What a fantastic trip!!

Rev. Harrell Shelton and I have talked with the Thompsons about setting up a trip next year from Airline Baptist Church to work with them. We prefer working with the missionaries than just one church there. Ellerbe Road Baptist Church was an excellent host on this trip.

Ecuador, July 2010

Ecuador, July 2010

Chapter 30

Cairo, Egypt
The City of 1,000 Minarets
2010

Cairo had been on my "bucket list" for years. My first attempt to go there was in 1987 when I was going to take my family on a Holy Land tour and to Egypt. That did not work out, as we started building a new home about that time.

Then in April 2010 I heard about a trip being planned to Cairo, Egypt, so I asked to be included on that plan from Medical Missions Response. When we were in China, I mentioned the trip to Sonny De Prang; he stated that he would like to go also. Later he asked Jackie, his wife, to go, and she agreed.

While in Ecuador in July 2010 I asked several of the team members of that group if they would like to go to Egypt. I got only one serious response; Marla Armstrong said she wanted to go.

Vickie, my wife, and I went to Houston two weeks before our trip to Egypt to learn how to properly prescribe eyeglasses. We took the In Focus Eye Training Seminar for a couple of days. The retinoscopy part was a bit complicated, but we found out about the I-test Eye Exam from one of the participants, in the course; we then ordered one from Richmond Products in New Mexico. It sure simplifies doing the readers and some of the prescription glasses. The focometer was the other instrument for which instructions were given; we had been using this for a few years.

The members of the team and workers in Egypt had a conference call set up by Dan Bivins. It sure was nice to get several questions answered and some instructions given first hand. Britni, our physician assistant, asked about personal gifts for the workers; it was determined that indigenous gifts from our city, state, or region would be most appropriate. I had over 500 pairs of prescription glasses from the Lion's Club; I also had 450 reading glasses I purchased for the trip.

Rev. Sonny DePrang and his wife, Jackie, Marla Armstrong, and I left Shreveport and met Britni McBryde, the physician assistant from Tucson, AZ, in Atlanta; we then proceeded to JFK Airport in NYC and on to Cairo, Egypt, overnight. It was almost 4 p.m. the next day when we arrived; Cairo is seven hours ahead of CST. We were met by our hosts and taken to our hotel. After placing our suitcases in the hotel, we headed out for a good American meal at a nearby food mall. The weather was warm (91 degrees F.), but the humidity was much lower. (In Louisiana when we left, the temperature was 95 and humid.) On the Internet I had seen where it had been 95 to 105 in Cairo during the day, but thank goodness it was cooling off some.

After a good night's rest, our group was taken by our hosts to the Coptic area of the city. We traveled by SUV past the Citadel. According to an Egyptian tour guide site on the Internet, the Citadel is a very popular tourist attraction; it is situated on a spur of limestone that had been detached from its parent Moqattam Hills by quarrying. It is one of the world's greatest monuments to medieval warfare, as well as a highly visible landmark on Cairo's eastern skyline. It once was used to protect against the **Crusaders.** Originally, it served as both a fortress and a royal city. Within the property you can see the animated silhouette and twin minarets of the Mohammed Ali Mosque; it is the most visible mosque in Cairo.

Cairo, Egypt

Soon we went through Garbage City; this is the place where most of the 13 million tons of trash per week are brought from Cairo, a city of almost 20 million people, to be processed. Originally, it was worse than a pig sty with all the rotten smell, flies, and filth that a huge heap of trash can produce, but today the operators recycle up to 90 percent of all the trash brought to the "city". The city has stores, schools, and churches. This transformation started when the Garbage City people called a pastor to their church in 1974; the transformation started with nine people in their tin building.

The Cave Church Mokattam soon came into view; it is a magnificent crypt in the side of the mountain. Since 1986 Father Samaan and his church developed this from a hollow area in the side of the mountain. It seats over 20,000; one would have to see this structure to appreciate the size of this mammoth church. (You can find out a lot of information about it from the Internet when you look up "Cave Church of Cairo".) It has picturesque, larger than life sized mosaics of Jesus' crucifixion, the open tomb where Jesus came out, Jesus' ascension into heaven, and several others carved into or from the mountain side. Near the front is a large mural painting of the miracle of Mt. Mokattam being moved by prayer. Also, there is a picture of St. Samaan. We were met near the podium by one of the church workers, who explained the history of the church and about St. Samaan (St. Simon, the shoemaker and "the Tanner"). I ended up buying the book: **The Biography of SAINT SAMAAN, the shoemaker and the "Tanner"**. It tells of the miracle of the movement of Mokattam Mountain in A.D. 979 by Simon, the Coptic Pope, and the people's prayer.

Marla, Britni, and I ascended the rows of seats to the top of the church and were quite winded by the exercise. At the top, near one side is a modern church structure with a cross on both steeples.

We walked on down to the Church of Saint Marcus (St. Mark) just down the hill. Inside a cave is a sprawling church with several hundred seats. There are a few stone carvings of the events in Jesus' life. (Mark the Apostle was said to have started this church in A.D. 42 when he was visiting and evangelizing in Egypt. The Coptic Orthodox Church has its origins from then.)

There was yet one more Coptic church down the hill, but I did not remember seeing its name. From there we drove back to a portion of Garbage City, where paper is shredded and made into recycled paper; we witnessed first hand how the recycled paper was made by hand. Also in this complex is a technical school to teach women to make cloth, sew, make quilts, and weave: this sure helps the economy in the city. We went into a retail section and bought some samples of their crafts; I bought a molded Egyptian face made from the recycled paper.

Going across part of the city, we went to the Nile River, got on a sailboat, and took a leisurely and relaxing tour that lasted about one hour. The Nile River is the lifeline of Egypt and especially the city of Cairo; Cairo gets less than two inches of rain per year. As we sailed across and up the river, we could see the cities of Cairo to the east and Giza to the west. The skyline of Cairo showed many more large buildings than Giza. The water in the Nile did not appear as clear as its origin from Lake Victoria in Uganda (I saw that when I was in Uganda in 2008). Many pollutants are dumped into the river. Along the western bank, we could see patches of bulrushes; I could picture baby Moses in his basket along the shore.

We were taken to a Lebanese restaurant for supper that day; our leader said many of the native or national restaurants were not safe for us to eat in, so we did not try any the next couple of weeks. We decided to take the trolley back across the city to near our hotel.

This month was Ramadan; that meant the Muslims were fasting from sunrise to sunset. (Ramadan is the month that Allah gave Mohammed the Quran.) This Muslim holy month affected businesses and scheduling throughout the whole city. However, I was told that the Egyptian people do not really get going until around noon anyway.

The following day our first clinic was scheduled to start about 4 p.m.; we wouldn't leave for the church until 1 p.m. So after a hearty breakfast in our hotel, Marla, Britni, and I decided to explore the area around our hotel. As we walked along the streets, cars were parked everywhere conceivable—often double- or even triple-parked in some areas. Often the sidewalks were used for parking, if a car would fit there. As we ventured out to one of the main highways, it was obvious that traffic was heavy. The noise of a big city was evident. We finally went to a nearby Shell gas station and asked if there was a mall nearby; we were told that the City Stars Mall was several blocks away. We were told we should hire a taxi to take us. Luckily, the cab driver understood enough English to get us to the mall.

Because of Ramadan the mall did not open until 11 a.m., so we sat and people-watched for an hour. It was fascinating to see all the people pass with their custom wear; frequently many were in a hurry. Once in the mall, we explored briefly all six floors of the mall; it was just as modern as any of our malls back home. We had a quick lunch before heading back to the hotel for our scheduled time for pickup to go to the church.

I was called via our cell phone assigned to our group and asked if I would do some minor surgery on one of our company workers who resided in the city; I agreed and we met in my room, where I trimmed an ingrown toenail under digital block. I had several in my room as an audience.

All loaded up, we made our way across the city to the first church. Driving in the city is usually a real experience; traffic was getting heavier. Often what was a two-lane highway turned into three- or four-lanes; road manners were often ignored. As we went along, numerous mosques with their minarets stood out everywhere. Occasionally there was a mosque adjacent to a Christian (Coptic) church, or another mosque at the end of the block. There is no question that this is the city of 1,000 minarets.

Finally we arrived at the church and noted on the sign in front that it had been founded in the 1930s. We were welcomed by the pastor and fellow members who would be helping us in the clinic. Soon I was introduced to my interpreter; he was an Egyptian physician who works some and is still seeking extra training. He spoke very good English; that was a good thing since as mentioned previously I am foreign-language impaired. We all sought our stations and set up things ready to receive patients. We started shortly before 5 p.m.; we were supposed to be finished by 10 p.m, but that didn't happen; we finished at 1 a.m. The reason for this was that it took a long time with some of the people. They would come in with X-Rays, CT scans, MRIs, cardiology or pulmonary consults, and often a long list of meds they were on or had tried in the past. These were their actual records. (My physician interpreter told me that Egyptian doctors keep no records or tests in their offices; the patients keep them. He said the patients are responsible for their own records and tests; if they lose them, the tests have to be repeated.) Going through these records was "OK", except when two or three of the other family members wanted them all explained completely over again. A couple of times even my interpreter was ready to bang his head against the wall because of the frustration this caused. But politeness, kindness, and being concerned were our orders of the day.

We saw some hypertension, diabetes—some out of control—and many of the aches and pains found universally. The people were polite, courteous, very gracious, and appreciative of our help. The eyeglasses station stayed busy; Sonny and Jackie seldom sat down from the constant stream of people. The rooms were not large enough for a 20-foot reading on the Snelling Chart, but they compromised and did the best they could. Sonny told me later that the Lord sure was with them during the week as they felt like real novices doing eyeglasses. The people were very satisfied with the glasses they were given. Britni remained busy as well; occasionally she would come see me about a problem patient.

During the clinic I began to see a pattern of the classic Egyptian look: the olive skin, the slightly longer, gently curved nose, and dark hair. Occasionally I noticed the most beautiful eyes; they were a mixture of blue, brown, and black—and very noticeable. All nations have their good-looking people; we certainly were seeing some of them here.

At 1 a.m. when the last patient was seen, I was requested to make a house call to a member of the church. I agreed and we walked a couple of blocks and ascended a flight of stairs to the fourth floor. There I was introduced to a lady who had back surgery over two years earlier and was not improving. By history and exam of her CT scans, it was obvious she had undergone a decompressive laminectomy through 6 vertebrae for spinal stenosis. She never really improved and was now almost bedridden. After I went through all her records and CT scans, including the postop CTs, I was asked my opinion. Come to find out, she had been to four other physicians. Two were for further surgery, and two were against it. I guessed that would make me the tiebreaker.

About that time the lady started crying and shouting with her arms stretched toward the ceiling. The pastor told me she was crying out, "My God, My God, why have you forsaken me." Soon there was not a dry eye in the room. I asked the pastor if I could pray for her. Over the next few minutes, I gave a fervent prayer for relief of her pain and proper decision as what to do for her recovery. The pastor interpreted my prayer; then, he gave a prayer himself. Then the lady tried to get up on her walker and fell back onto her bed. My decision was that she would probably not improve without further surgery, but she was getting very weak from this situation. Needless to say, I left a little more than sad.

By the time we got back to our hotel, it was after 2:30 a.m. The traffic across the city was busier than in the afternoon. The Muslims were out celebrating by going out, shopping, or eating—after fasting all day for Ramadan. It took us twice as long as the early afternoon.

The next day was a repeat at the same church. Our team had jelled into a very operative team. Marla and one of our company workers did the pharmacy. Evangelism was done by the church or staff. Sonny and Jackie stayed very busy in the eyeglasses station and never got a break. (They are tough!)

The next two days of work were supposed to be in a hospital wing in a suburb of the city, but the night before we were to start the clinic was canceled by the hospital administrator. Our workers then decided to try the clinic in an unapproved church, but they indicated that this was not feasible. Our workers then lined up two orphanages for us to work in the next two days.

When we arrived at the first orphanage the following evening, we heard music coming from one portion of the building. Several of us followed the sound of the music and soon discovered the children celebrating worship in music and song. It was so enthusiastically done that we felt like joining in. It was so neat seeing some of the children bowing on their knees in song and praise. Then we were assigned a large room, where we set up exam stations, the eyeglass station, and the pharmacy. We did wellness exams on all the children; then we saw several adult workers and their relatives as well. Before leaving, we were invited to the arts-and-crafts room, where several of us purchased some of their handiwork. One of mine was a beautiful foil picture of Mary and Joseph bringing baby Jesus to Egypt for safety from Herod's fury.

The next morning we went to the second orphanage not far from our hotel. It was a former hotel made into an orphanage for children. There were nearly 40 boys and girls waiting for us to do wellness exams; the children were very well mannered. They looked well nourished and happy; we found no real illnesses. I had the opportunity to meet the physician who helped take care of the children. I told him how well the children looked and behaved. He was very gracious and appreciative of us coming that day.

Klan Il Khalili is the old world bazaar near the center of the city. It is situated in front of some ancient mosques; one has a twin minaret—said to be the very first one in the country. At last we were where the real shopping was! Soon we were in the gauntlet of souvenirs shops with all the merchants wanting to sell us something. Our workers had their favorite shops, where they take their visiting friends. We went to the alabaster shop and "I went ape"; I bought several items for family and friends back home, including a large vase I knew I would have to take in my carry-on luggage back home to my wife. It weighs almost 11 pounds. In other stores I found a King Tut head mask, a head bust of Queen Nefertiti (biological mother of King Tut), a miniature replica of an ancient Egyptian boat made of camel bone, a silver necklace of the Egyptian goddess Isis, and a silver necklace of the Great Pyramids and the Great Sphinx. In all, I bought nearly 30 items and gifts. Many of my friends, who have been with me on other trips, would have been jealous of all the items available!

The following day we went across the Nile River to Giza. The city comes right up to the pyramid grounds on three sides, the desert is only in the background on the west side. All the pictures and documentary films I have seen of this scene do not picture it as accurately as seeing it for one's self. The Giza Plateau extends to the edge of the Western Desert; it is dominated by the three great pyramids and the Great Sphinx. The Pyramid of Khufu is the largest and oldest of the Giza Necropolis. According to *Wikipedia* on the Internet, it took over 20 years to build and was concluded around 2560 B.C. The Great Pyramid was the tallest structure built by man for the next 3,800 years; it is 482-feet high. It is estimated that there are 2.3 million limestone blocks that were transported by boat to build this pyramid.

The size of the great pyramids is something you have to experience personally. We got to climb up several layers of the huge stones that make the pyramids. To the side of the largest pyramid is a canal that once connected to the Nile River. The river is now several hundred feet away; the huge stones were brought in one by one on boats to build these gigantic monuments. Originally, the great pyramids were covered with smooth limestone that had been polished, but most of this was removed either when attempts were made to dismantle the pyramids or a large earthquake damaged them. Much of the limestone covering has been used in structures in downtown Cairo.

We got to go down one of the narrow passages into the largest pyramid; it was a four-feet by four-feet tunnel. It was hot and stuffy, and grew more so as you went deeper. Near the end of one of the passages was the "door to eternal life"—their idea of eternal life, not mine. Inside one of the passages were statues carved into the huge rocks. We noted hieroglyphics on some of the entrances and passages of the tunnels.

Further along we ran into one of our Egyptian interpreter's friends who had six camels waiting for us to ride. Marla let one of them "kiss" her face. It was quite unique riding the camel for one-half mile around to the Great Sphinx of Giza. This structure is the largest monolith statue in the world; it is a statue of a reclining sphinx (a mythical creature with a lion's body and a human head). The Sphinx lies in front of the second pyramid (Pyramid of Khara). It consists of limestone that has been carved to become the monolith. The face of the Great Sphinx has parts missing, especially the nose. There is a story that Napoleon's men damaged it when they were practice shooting a cannon at it. However, many think that the damage was caused by erosion over time. It was a very unique experience to see all this.

We then proceeded to go out further into the outer limits of the city to Suqqara and the Imhotep Museum. As we traveled about nine miles south, it was obvious we were following one of the many canals that are used to irrigate the farm land, date trees, and other agricultural projects. The area is green only where irrigation is done. There were many groves of date palm trees; many were loaded with differing stages of maturity.

According to *Wikipedia*, Pharaoh Djoser of the Third Dynasty of Egypt commissioned his official, Imhotep, to build the first of the pyramids at Saqqura. The structure is a step pyramid with levels like a step compared to the great pyramids at Giza which are not. The museum is named after Imhotep; it has five halls filled with ancient discoveries like alabaster jars, mummies in sarcophagi, many statues of stone and bronze, etc. We took a walking tour through two of the step pyramids. One of the men there placed his head scarf on Marla; she looked like a real sheik. (Naturally, I have a picture to verify this.) Yes, the man wanted to be paid for his efforts.

When we got back near our hotel, the street was lined with soldiers on both sides at intervals of 10 feet; this meant the president was leaving his home to go somewhere. We did not get close enough to see him though.

To start the next day we went to the Museum of Egyptian Antiquities (known commonly as the **EGYPTIAN MUSEUM,** in downtown Cairo). It opened in 1902 and contains 120,000 items; a representative amount is on display; the remainder is in storerooms. The ground floor has huge statues; the upper floor has many small statues and jewels. King Tut (Tutankhamon) treasures and the mummies are displayed there. My favorite was the famous Gold Mask of the king's face. (I wish the museum had allowed cameras in there; we had to check them in at the front desk or they would have been taken from us if used.) Although centuries earlier King Tut's tomb had been raided a couple of times, it was basically intact when discovered; all the items are now on display at the museum.

Sunday night we went back to the first church for regular weekly services. We saw many of the people we had seen in the clinic earlier in the week. The pastor preached a passionate sermon, Part of the sermon was interpreted for us by a member sitting behind us, who spoke English. Then Sonny and I got to serve the Lord's Supper to the congregation. That was a special moment. After church our group formed a receiving line and were greeted and thanked by most everyone.

The next two days we went to a local church across the city to hold clinic. The church was actually two lower-floot apartments joined together. I was in the pastor's office the first day, then Britni switched with me the next day. Authentic Egyptian food was served both days around 5 p.m. Like others in the group, I had finally contracted the gastro-intestinal blues and had no appetite for both meals, but they sure looked good; the rest of the group said the food tasted great. I lay down on some chairs and went to sleep during the eating hour because I felt so bad.

Basically the same universal problems were found in the clinic over those two days; several had uncontrolled diabetes and hypertension. The pastor and people were so pleased that we came and gave medicine and eyeglasses. Driving back across town, after Ramadan fasting was over, took almost three times as long to get back to our hotel as it did to get to our clinic destination earlier in the day.

The next morning we went to a sewing center, where mothers with cerebral palsy children are brought in to learn sewing and other crafts while the children are taken care of by the staff. We did wellness exams and fitted a few glasses to some of the women. It was a well-organized center; the people were so friendly and appreciative.

We ate a lunch of sandwiches on the way to our next clinic in the northern section of the city. It was obvious we were in the lower economic section of town. The church we worked in the next two days had no church sign, but many people showed up for the clinic. I was told that the pastor had worked for 20 years to build a nice congregation. We certainly saw a number of people during those two afternoons. That night we celebrated at Outback Steakhouse.

Over the week Sonny and Jackie gave out over 300 pair of prescription and reading glasses. The medical team saw over 500 people, and the pharmacy gave out an average of three prescriptions per patient. The team worked tirelessly and for long hours at times. We had a team that was very efficient and showed the love of the Master to the people. The evangelism was handled by the pastors and staff. Our team had done what we were requested to do in the overall scheme of things. I am sure the Master will use our work to further the kingdom.

Friday is Egypt's weekly holiday. It is like our Sunday. It is the big worship day for the Muslims, Many of the Christians honor that schedule, and have church on Friday. Our workers took us to the Heliopolis Community Church; it is an interdenominational and international English-speaking church; it provides Christian nurture through worship, teaching, pastoral care, and fellowship. We entered just as the service had started. I immediately felt right at home. The worshiping in songs was outstanding; it was lead by a song director; several members played musical instruments. The sermon was from the Gospel of John, chapters two and three. It was a very touching message, and eight people came to the front at the end of the message for eternal reasons.

After lunch at Chili's, I am sure you can guess what we did—yes, we went shopping at the old world bazaar of Klan Il Khahili again; we bought more souvenirs and gifts. Then it was back to the hotel to pack all those things we had purchased.

What a great two weeks we had! We toured; we worked; we toured some more, and we worked some more; we shopped and then shopped some more. The workers were well prepared for us, and the whole trip was well organized. It was an enjoyable time. To summarize, it was a great trip. We were invited to return and bring some more personnel and go to Upper Egypt (south Egypt) in the area of Luxor and the Valley of the Kings.

Cairo, Egypt

Our group at the sphinx and pyramids

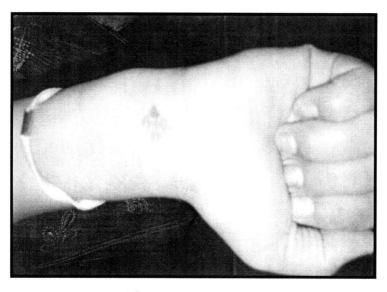

The Coptic cross tattoo

Cairo/Giza, Egypt
2010

Chapter 31

My Word Shall Not Return Unto Me Void

*So shall my word be that goeth forth out of my mouth:
it shall not shall not return unto me void,
but it shall accomplish that which I please,
and it shall prosper in the thing where to I sent it.*
Isaiah 55:11

Over our last few visits to the prisons, it has become obvious that witnessing to the prisoners has had a significant impact. It is much less often that someone accepts the Lord as Savior; they all state that they know Jesus personally. What a feeling to hear this said. It is not just my group, but also several others that witness to the prisoners.

Less and less Bibles are now given out; most of the prisoners have ones that we have given them. It has been my philosophy as a Gideon that anyone that wanted a Bible gets one. The librarian at one of the prisons told me that he had several dozen Bibles in the library that were left there when prisoners went home without them.

There are daily Bible study groups now; they use some of the Bible study material such as the Sunday School books, **Daily Bread, Open Windows,** or other materials we have taken them. More than one of the security guards has told me that there have been minimal riots since the Bibles and witnessing to the prisoners have taken place. Indeed, the Word of God is not returning void.

Frequently I get emails from the missionaries (that we have worked with) stating what an impact our medical work and evangelism has had on their overall plan. The medical team is an excellent way to attract people to the clinics, so the Gospel can be presented. It has been my pleasure to be on several of the pioneer groups to a new place or previously untouched area. Yes, the Word of God is not returning void.

Chapter 32

What is a Soul Worth?

God created each of us in His own image and with great love. He gave us the choice of choosing what we will do with His Son. Jesus sacrificed Himself so our sins could be forgiven, but we must choose if we will accept Him. Jesus also gave us the Great Commission (Matthew 28:19, 20), so it is our duty to go tell others about Jesus.

He gave each of us a soul (the eternal part of a living being) and that is what will go to heaven if we accept Jesus as Savior. I have often wondered, just what is a soul worth? If you apply the Great Commission to that question, then **you** have more to do.

Is it worth trusting Jesus to give you strength to go and tell? Yes, if you have the proper faith, you will want to share the Gospel.

Does that mean you need to know the Word of God to be able to share? Then you need to read and study God's Word and be ready when the opportunity arises.

Does that mean you need to be like Christ? Yes, people watch what you do, so much more than what you say. You may be the only "Bible" some people ever see. You must follow along in Jesus' footprints.

Does it mean you need to go on church visitation? If you don't, then they will not come to your church and hear the Word of God. Programs like F.A.I.T.H. teach you to witness properly. What a thrill it is to lead someone to the saving knowledge of Jesus. Does that mean you give up one, two, or three nights per month for a couple of hours to go? Is that what a soul is worth?

Is it worth a soul for you to prepare, spend your resources, be out of your comfort zone, and give of your time to go on a foreign mission? Is it worth a soul to be away from your home to go to a place where it may be uncomfortable or perhaps hot? Are you willing to spend a little more on medical supplies so you can reach more? Is it worth the effort to lead hundreds or perhaps thousands to Christ?

Is it worth a soul to prepare and do prison ministry? Most people seem turned off by talking, giving Bibles, or sharing with the individual prisoner. I know it is worth the effort. Literally hundreds have been reached and given their lives to Jesus through sharing His word by a group I go to prison with. Also many Bibles have been given to allow them to read and study the Gospel.

Are you prepared to be able to share with your neighbor or someone on the job?

Will you pray the **Jabez Prayer** and ask God to expand your borders?

How much time do you have left to witness to someone?

I Samuel 20:3 (KJV) says ...*but truly as the Lord liveth, and as thy soul liveth, there is but a step between me and death.*

Yes, what is a soul worth? In Ecclesiastes 12:13 the summary of God's word is written: *Fear (reverence) God, for this is the entire duty of man.*

What will you do to present God's Word to save a soul?

Epilogue

Will this be the last writing or book that I do? Good question!

I certainly plan on continuing my short-term medical missions until the Lord sees fit that I don't. I have been so blessed to have made my passion the commission that Jesus requests of each of us. It has been an honor to have written these three books about the local, regional, and foreign trips I have been part of. I just hope I have proclaimed the glory and majesty of my Savior to the utmost of my ability.

Appendix A
Email from Barbara and Jeff Singerman

12/19/2005

Dear Ayizo Prayer Warriors,

We praise God for your prayers concerning the job proposal that was handed to us some weeks by Randy Arnett, our new West Africa Area Director.

Let me preface the general job description of what we were invited to do with information about what is happening in West Africa, so you'll better understand the setting.

Missionaries have been in Burkina Faso, Cote d'Ivoire, Togo, and Benin for about 25 years or so. Benin is the least evangelized of these nations for it was under a communist dictator until 1990. There was no freedom in Benin, up until it became a democracy in 1991, to do the work. Most of these four country's people groups, which total 295, are still unreached. Yet, each of these former French colonies do have a Baptist Convention and the infra-structure in place, for the Baptist Christians of the nations, to continue the work of reaching their unreached. At this point, as we understand it, no new missionaries will be assigned to people groups less than 100,000 strong, for the IMB is targeting the "Greater Lostness". There are many people groups made up of 1 million people or more with no Christian witness whatsoever. To be good stewards of their

Appendix A

missionary personnel, with a great burden for the lost of the world, the larger groups will receive missionaries, while the task of reaching the smaller groups will be handed over to the national Baptist conventions and U.S. churches (more about that in a moment).

Is this partly a financial decision? Of course. If we had unlimited resources and missionaries, there wouldn't be choices about "where" to place personnel. They'd be placed elsewhere.

It sounds impressive when people say the IMB has over 3,000 career missionaries and over 2,000 two-year termers (5,700 total). But when we place those statistics against the U.S. membership in SBC churches, which is 16 million—-the number of missionaries pales by comparison. In fact, 0.03 percent of the membership of SBC churches have surrendered to be missionaries. So few, from so great a cloud of witnesses . . ..

We are astounded, as we travel from church to church, to share the powerful work of Christ among Ayizo, at the people we encounter (nearly in every church) who say, "When I was young God called me to be a missionary, but…" During my teenage years, I was sure I would be a missionary in Africa, but…" And they give us the reasons they were swept away from God's call to make choices that have been comfortable and nice, but stained with regret. Jeff and I wonder if our job, and the job of the missionaries across the globe, would be so difficult if everyone who had been and are being called, actually went. While I'm pausing from my intent to grant in-depth information on our mission's scene, Jeff and I want you to know how thrilled we are with how you give to missions through your churches, through special gifts, through the SBC Cooperative Program, and especially through the Lottie Moon Christmas Offering (which supports 45 percent of the entire work in the world—-excluding the U.S.). Your giving is our financial resource to go into all the world for Christ. There are obviously many in our churches (of the 16 million members) who do not take this task—-of sending and supporting world evangelism—-seriously. Just tossing a little extra into the offering plate for the special mission's emphasis doesn't fulfill Christ's mandate. Each of us needs to plan through prayer, what kind of commitment Christ would have us to make to win the world through our finances. How we, as stewards of the money Christ allows us to have, distribute and use those funds, shows where our lives are centered. What percentage of your budget is set aside to be used to reach the unreached of the world? One of our favorite pastors, Brother Jim McDaniel of FBC Brinkley, AR, teaches that we should give to the Lottie Moon Christmas Offering what we spend on Christmas gifts for our family and friends. Good thought. Is your heart beating in sync with Christ's? Has his love and passion for the unreached gripped your life so deeply that you daily cry out against their going to a Christ-less eternity in hell? (A real, horrible, eternal place and not just a story). Jesus said, "you spend your money according to what you truly love." ("Where your treasure is there will be your heart also.") If you've never really given in Jesus' name for the world, try it. You'll be surprised how Christ will open up your life, in Him, in greater measure!

Back to the premise of this letter! Due to the reasons mentioned above, in the foreseeable future, people groups less than 100,000 in Burkina Faso, Cote d'Ivorie, Togo, and Benin will not be receiving new missionaries—-which is a significant number of groups.

One part of the plan to reach these yet-unreached peoples has been offered to Jeff and me. Jeff has been asked to work with the Baptist Conventions of these four countries as a liaison between the West Africa Area Offices of the IMB and our African Christian brothers who lead the conventions. Besides building lasting relationships of love, trust, and counsel, one of his primary jobs will be to flame a passion in them to reach their unreached for Christ, which, of course, would naturally cause us to have a burden for **all**

Appendix A

These unreached groups take us beyond Benin's borders and beyond our present zeal for the Aziyo.

Although we'd sensed God would be "expanding our boundaries" we were shocked at this proposal. We'd thought of working with other people groups in Benin, but not taking on a work this extensive.

We asked you to pray, and turned our hearts toward prayer. We know West Africa. We know that this new work would be very difficult and involve much travel. We had no desire to change our direction. We love working in the bush—-being totally hands on all the time—-witnessing, starting churches, training workers. We actually are comfortable in our work with the Ayizo and looked forward to returning to that work. This great change wasn't what we'd been planning.

But God . . ..

After seeking God's face—-His will—-for weeks He confirmed to us through many Scriptures and godly counsel that this task was indeed God's appointment for us. We've been praying that God would grant us the nations as our inheritance (Psalm 2:8), and He made it clear to us that this is part of His answering our prayer! Jeff, through relationships with men in leadership in these four nations will be able to have an affect on seeing all their people groups won for Christ.

We can't go into this huge responsibility alone. Are you willing to step into this adventure with us in prayer? You came on board to pray for the Ayizo. But just as God has expanded our vision and responsibility, He would do the same for you to take us together "To the Ayizo and Beyond . . .." You've been so faithful in the task of prayer and now God is offering to you a much larger, much greater prayer responsibility . . ..

We will slowly phase out of our work with the Ayizo, but will continue to live in Benin. The volunteer trips already planned will not be affected. In fact, we will have contact with a larger range of people groups, in these nations, that will need you to come prayer walk through and evangelize.

That leads me to part two of the plan to win these nations/people groups to Christ—-you.

Across West Africa we will be searching for churches and associations who will take the responsibility for an unreached West African people group to lead to Christ. This will be called "Engaging" a people group. As Christ burdens churches for a specific people group in West Africa, that group becomes theirs in a covenant relationship. Whether these unreached people hear about Jesus or not will be completely the church or association's responsibility. Through prayer walking, evangelism, leadership training . . . they will win the unreached, and train the new Christians in Christ. No group would be alone in setting up and understanding this task. There is already a team of missionaries in West Africa specifically designated for aiding with Engagement. Contact us for more information!!

We don't know any more specifics than we've already shared with you. The job will evolve as we get back on the field (which we are still **planning** to do the third week of January 2006.

We will continue to travel every weekend up to Christmas—and will send you that schedule in another email!

Blessings in Christ!!

Barbara and Jeff

Appendix B
Autobiography of Charles Mugisha Buregeya

EARLY CHILDHOOD

My spiritual journey began on the day I was born. My mother went to the Jinja Hospital to take my older brother for treatment of measles. My brother died in the hospital and I arrived, unexpectedly, on the very same day. I was born one month early, and my health was very poor. My parents were afraid I was going to die and live eternally in hell since I was not baptized. Since both of my parents belonged to the Roman Catholic tradition, they went very quickly to find a priest to come and baptize me. I was baptized the day I was born.

As a young boy, I loved God and I loved church too. By the time I was in the second grade, I knew how to read my local language, and I read and memorized the Catholic catechism. I not only memorized it, but also taught other kids to memorize the catechism at school. We used to have an Italian priest called Father Joseph. I loved Father Joseph and always wanted to assist him. My dream was to get an opportunity to serve in mass at the main parish. I also dreamt that one day I would go to Seminary and become a Catholic Priest. As a young boy, I felt that the best thing I could do in my lifetime was to become a priest, be near to God, and serve the spiritual needs of other people. I believed that the way to heaven was through the Catholic Church, and the priest played a very important role in who would go to heaven due his power to minister forgiveness.

I attended special classes, on the subject on Holy Communion, in preparation to participate in the Lord's Supper. The priest taught us that whenever we participated in the Lord's Supper without penitence Jesus would come in our hearts angry. But if we had penitence before Holy Communion, Jesus would come in our hearts happy. I always went for penitence and confessed my sins to the priest to be able to make Jesus happy in me.

TIMES OF WAR

In 1982, when I was 15, war broke out in Uganda and separated me from my parents for over a year. During this time, I lived in a danger zone with rebel army men fighting for the government. I served and did intelligence work for them. At times, I would be required to spend all night by the roadside guarding the community. This may be hard for Americans to understand, but much guerrilla warfare uses children to fight battles in Africa. During this period, I came very close to God, but I was not born again. I didn't understand the need to accept Jesus Christ as my personal Lord and Savior. I knew Mary and other saints and I loved God and believed that God answered prayers of all those who call upon Him. I called upon God for protection and to help me reunite with my lost parents. God answered me and protected me from death, as many of my friends died. I was able to reunite with my parents in a miraculous way. God used other army men to smuggle me out of the danger zone to a place where I was able to reunite with my parents. Even before I became a born-again Christian, I believed that God loved me in a special way, and that He was always there for me.

During the time of war, I saw a woman preaching about getting saved, but I did not understand what she was saying. I suspected that she had a mental problem. In general, I thought born-again

Appendix B

people had a mental problem, although they seemed to be good people. I never responded to her message. But at the age of 16, I started doubting the teachings of the Catholic Church, mainly the confession of my sins to a priest. I had sins that I could not tell another human being. I was struggling with my prayer life; I started hating written prayers and praying to the saints.

SEARCH FOR GOD

One day I was reading the written prayers the priest had taught me to follow, but the prayer book had no room for me to convey my need and feelings to God. I broke out in tears, put down the book, and started crying to God expressing my need and feelings. I started praying to God with the assistance of the prayer book. I needed a breakthrough in my search for God. My whole village did not have any born-again Christians; none of my family members were Christian. In fact, my mother was very much involved in witchcraft to help her solve family problems. The whole family was in trouble; we had lost nearly everything during the war. My father was in a hopeless situation and got deeply involved in alcohol. We needed help, but no missionary came in our village. No one was available to help us with our spiritual lives when we were searching for peace and answers to the problems.

HOW JESUS FOUND ME

In 1984 at the age of 17 years, I heard about a pastor from another village named Kyaggunda who had a church school and needed someone to teach young children how to read and write. I felt confident I could teach children. Where we lived, before the wars, we had good schools. Our new village was poorer, with no educated people, and not good schools. This pastor was trying to introduce education to children deep in rural Uganda, where people did not know how to read and write. They had lived in a circle of illiteracy from one generation to another. I contacted the pastor for a job in his school. The fact that I was offered a job to teach, at my age, was a miracle, but little did I know that God was going to use this job to change my life and introduce me to the true Gospel of salvation in Jesus Christ.

After working for a few months for Pastor Francis Bukenya, I went to his home on a Sunday to ask him to pay me during school holidays. Fortunately, the pastor was away on a preaching engagement and could not meet me until he had finished preaching. The pastor's wife asked me to accompany her to their church, and at first I refused. I was not interested in going to their church since I believed they were the type of Christians with mental problems. After a little struggle in my mind, I decided to follow her. When we reached the church, I changed my mind and told her that I would not go inside the church, but will wait for the pastor outside. The pastor's wife said something that changed the direction of my life. She said "the devil is hindering you from going into the church". Deep in my heart I responded by asking what kind of power does the devil have over my life? I decided to enter their church for the first time. Little did I know that this was going to become my church and a place where God was going to call me to serve Him.

I went to the same church for two Sundays before I gave my life to Jesus Christ. Each of those Sundays I heard the Gospel preached, but the message was not very clear to me. The pastor was preaching from the book of Revelation, and I did not understand the message. I had never read the Bible, apart from the scriptures the priest read to us in the Catholic Church. During the week before the third Sunday, I was very much convicted about the issue of giving my life to Jesus and asking him for the forgiveness of my sins. I returned to church on the third Sunday of March 1984 to hear the Gospel and also to give my life to Jesus. Unfortunately, the pastor never made an altar call, but I took a very bold step to write a note asking him to pray for me to give my life to Jesus Christ.

DAYS OF PERSECUTION BY MY PARENTS AND FRIENDS

I told my mother about my decision to be saved. My mother did seem concerned. A few weeks later my dad returned from a trip and I informed him that I had given my life to Christ. My dad did not understand the gravity of my decision because no one in our family had ever given his/her life to Jesus. I started changing very quickly and could no longer go with him to carry alcohol to his friends or family parties. My dad got angry and started persecuting me for my faith, but this became time for me to grow. The more he attacked me the more I grew in love with Jesus. I loved to talk about my new faith. A few months later I won four of my neighbor's children to Jesus and they followed me to church. Both my neighbor and my dad got angry with me about my new life and how I was sharing the Gospel.

I became isolated from the rest of my family and went to stay with my pastor. During this time, the Lord taught me to read the Word and to pray. I would spend many of my lonely evenings praying. We also used to meet with other Christians and have all night prayer meetings. I got very much involved in all night prayer meetings with other young people. My life was on fire of Jesus; we started traveling long journeys on foot to take the Gospel to the regions around us. It was during this time, I felt the Lord calling me to ministry and the mission of winning people to Christ. I loved doing evangelism and seeing people give their lives to Jesus. Evangelism was hard during this time with long journeys on foot and very little money to live on as we traveled. But our hearts were filled with joy although few people came to Christ. We were introducing what many people called a new "teaching", so they doubted us. Now, when I look back, I see many people who have come to Christ due to our faithfulness to proclaim the love of Christ. Four of my brothers and sisters and some of my cousins are now Christians as well, many, many other people.

TIMES OF CONFUSION, DOUBT, AND TEST OF FAITH

God started using me very early, but I was spiritually immature. I think many times I confused hearing the voice of God and my emotions. God brought a teacher who was leading a Bible College, to teach me how to understand the difference between my emotions and hearing the voice of God. Later, I went to his Bible college and God used this man to bring my spiritual walk in order, and also to move me towards maturity.

The time I spent in Bible College was a time of great heights, but also I experienced days of doubting my relationship with God. God started stretching me and taught me to live by faith. I did not know what it meant to live my life by faith. God put me in situations where I was forced to trust him, and not my parents, to provide for me. I did not have enough funds to go to college and many times I did not have books.

There were times when I did not have food, my shoes had holes, and during rainy seasons water could get into my socks. I used to have only one good pair of pants; this was the pair I wore when I went out to preach. I would wash it at night and then dry it quickly by ironing it. I was very confused and wondering why God was not helping me. I was praying and calling upon him, but the heavens seemed closed to me. I thought I had sinned and repented a lot, but still nothing was happening in my life. I doubted whether God was there, and if God was there, why was He not hearing me.

This was the darkest time in my spiritual life, and my friends could not help me. I felt that God had left me alone to suffer and my future looked dark and bleak. However, many times after doubting God, He would send help to me in a very miraculous way. Then

Appendix B

I could come back to God and repent of all the vain words I had said to Him in prayer. God challenged me by providing for me after I had been angry with Him and doubted Him. During this time I learned to fast and pray, for long periods. I came closer to God than ever before. God started opening doors for me to preach. My ministry life was growing in the midst of my pains. I remember once during a school vacation, my pastor sent me to a small village church to do my internship. I had to walk for nearly a whole day in the wilderness alone to go to this church. While serving at this church, we reached out to another nearby village and nearly a whole community turned to Christ. I was undergoing a lot of physical pain, but in the middle of my weakness, God was working.

FINDING DIRECTION IN THE MIDST OF PAIN

In the midst of my struggles, I started asking God how He wanted me to serve Him and where He wanted me to go. By this time, my relationship with my father had improved and he was supportive of my Christian life. I had a family and a home to return to with plenty of food. But I knew God was calling me to go to a place I did not know. I felt like Abraham, with God saying, "Leave your people and go to a place I show you." On my knees, I sought for direction from God to show me the place. I believed that my success in ministry would be determined by going to the right place, at the right time. During my college vacation at the end of my second year, I got very sick while staying with my parents. I suffered from malaria for weeks without a doctor or medicine. I started calling upon God for my healing because I knew God heals. I had seen God heal people through prayer, and I knew God loved me and could heal me. I prayed, but I didn't improve. Instead, I became worse and my life was moving toward death. One day while sleeping on my bed, alone, I prayed and asked God to deliver my pain by not healing me, but taking me to heaven. I rested on my bed prepared to go to heaven. A few minutes later God in His power came into my bedroom. I had a life-changing encounter with God. The presence of God covered me. This experience is not easy to explain in words. I can explain it by saying it was good to be in the presence of God, but could I stay for a long time. God spoke to me and told me that it was not time to die, but I was going to live and go to the nations of the world and preach the Gospel. God spoke to me about going to a place called Gaba and told me from that place He will send me to the nations, which now has come to pass.

GABA: SPIRITUAL WARFARE IN MINISTRY

I started the first youth ministry in our small church of about 15 people, together with the Senior Pastor and other friends. We worked very hard to grow the church, but nothing happened. Many people, in this area, were fishermen and very superstitious. They believed that evil spirits controlled the area. Some preachers had previously tried to plant churches in the area but failed and abandoned the village. Little did I know that I was about to get involved in a huge spiritual war in Gaba. I found out that many African witches had built their shrines near the lake, because they believed their spirits work better at the lakeside. There was much demonic worship and many shrines, where they gave animal sacrifices to the spirits. One day they even came to our church and left an animal sacrifice to scare us away. This was a time of great battle and our help would only come from the Lord; God is higher that their gods.

We decided to start seeking the face of God and to break down the power of the devil in our community. We started conducting all night prayer meetings every Friday night and sometimes in the morning. I joined the battle to cast out the power of demonic worship in the community. I had never engaged in such a direct spiritual war like this before. I had been taught about spiritual warfare, and

I believed a spiritual warfare existed. On a small level, we had prayed for people with spiritual oppression and seen them delivered, but I had never been in a direct confrontation with demonic powers. The first center for witches was about 50 meters from the church. They could hear us praying and we could hear them calling upon their spirits. Whenever their spirits came, we could hear them celebrating, and whenever their spirits were hindered by our prayers, we could hear them singing songs of hopelessness. This battle between the praying church and witches continued for a long time until the witches started becoming weaker and weaker, and they finally lost ground. Finally, we had a major breakthrough in the battle. The World Bank gave a grant to our national water corporation to build a new water pumping station. The Water Corporation decided to build their new water pumping station and housing for their workers in the area where most witches lived and worshipped. The National Water Corporation compensated them for their land and asked them to leave immediately. In a very short time, all their homes were destroyed and they were paid to leave. After the witches left, the heavens opened up in the community and people started receiving Christ as their Savior, and coming to our church.

When the witches left the community, we thought the battle had come to an end, but another battle with the government soldiers started. The government did not want us to pray in the night. They did not understand the nature of prayer. They worried that government rebels could hide themselves, in the church at night, and carry out the dangerous activities of attacking the people on government posts. Of course, this was not true and our church was not involved in politics at all.

PERSECUTED FOR PRAYING

The government soldiers started persecuting us. One night they took me, with other people, out of the church, at night, and beat us. One girl denied her involvement with our group so she wouldn't be beaten. Another woman was raped that night. The soldiers allowed us to go back home but told us never to pray again. I was beaten, and my body hurt, and I had conflicting thoughts that caused me to doubt. Yet, deep down I remembered how God had been faithfully providing for me. I did not have room to keep entertaining doubt about what God can do in such hard times. The more they persecuted us, the more I was on fire for the Lord. I lost my natural feelings of fear against death or abuse from my enemies. The next day every one was afraid of going back to church to pray at night, and I encouraged them to go back.

At the same time we went back to church, the soldiers arrived to beat us again. I lead the prayer meeting that night and I refused to stop and talk to them. They came over and pulled me to come out of the church. I became very bold and told them, "Today we can't leave the church." I told them to do whatever they want, but that we were going to remain in the church, the house of our heavenly Father. We began praying right in front of the men who were persecuting us (praying for them as well). Finally, they backed off but head counted all of us. They commanded us to stay in the church until they can come again and take us in the morning. We prayed all night, and in the morning they came to take us to the local court. That morning after asking us many questions about our prayer life and the church, they commanded us to stop praying during the night and pray during the daytime only. Praying during the day was fine, but we wanted to pray during the night when the remaining witches worshipped. We asked why they allowed the witches to have loud night parties in the community but wanted us to stop praying. Many evil activities were going on at night in the community and we felt God was calling us to watch the community in prayer. After arguing back and forth, we prevailed and they allowed us to pray up to this day.

During this battle with the soldiers, I was greatly encouraged not by one person or any one leader, but by the unity of our ministry team in the church. We worked together, prayed together, and stayed together for some time and overcame evil together. The church membership grew from the 15-20 who prayed together to over 600 people, and is still growing every week. The church started a school that now educates over 600 children, many of them poor and orphaned. The defense officer that persecuted and supported the closing down of the prayer meetings came to the Lord and his children attend our school. Some of the children of the witch doctors attend the school as well. Our church has become a center of spiritual growth, physical healing, and social progress in the community. The village of Gaba is completely transformed.

FRESH DIRECTION

Towards the end of 1999, I felt God bringing another direction in my life. God moved my heart away from the church I had served for 11 years. The church had grown and my life improved, but I became uncomfortable to stay any longer. I had married Florence, a wonderful Christian woman I met in college. The people of Gaba loved my wife and me, and thought we would stay forever. I was not where God wanted me to go and we were emotionally torn about God's new direction.

I had always dreamed of starting a new ministry in Rwanda, where I had seen a lot of need among my people. But I was not sure whether this was the right time. In the process God put on my heart to go to seminary. I started praying about where God would want me to go. My former college had a one-year program toward a graduate program with a university in South Africa. Several times, I wanted to fill the forms, but my heart was closed towards this program for reasons I could not understand. I made arrangements to go to Rwanda to visit and also to sense whether this was the time to go to Rwanda and start a new ministry. That night when I had packed up for my journey, ready to go, the Lord spoke to me and stopped me from going to Rwanda. I decided to obey the leading of the Holy Spirit. The next morning, I drove back to my church where I was not expected, since the other staff members knew I had gone to Rwanda.

Upon my arrival, I met Dr. Tim Robnett from Multonomah Biblical Seminary in Portland, OR, with his friend from France, Dr. Bill Thomas. Dr. Robnett needed a translator for the Sunday service so I helped him to translate the message into the local language. I didn't realize that the Lord stopped me from going to Rwanda so I could meet Dr. Robnett and hear about Multnomah Biblical Seminary. God eventually brought me to Multnomah through miraculous means.

While attending Multnomah, we founded Africa New Life Ministries, with a vision to help orphaned and poor children of Rwanda, train Christian leaders, and conduct evangelistic missions. We developed a child sponsorship program so that individuals can donate $25 per month to send one Rwandan child to school and have their basic needs met. In summer 2001, we returned to Rwanda to start our first school. We rented and renovated a building for a kindergarten, and recruited teachers and volunteers. On September 17, 2001, New Life Nursery School opened to help orphans and children from poor families get pre-primary education. The New Life Center now has 125 kids in pre-school (many still waiting for sponsorship), 39 kids sponsored to attend local primary school and 11 kids in secondary school. Parents in the area are so blessed by the school and child sponsorship program. One parent remarked, "Thank you for all you're doing; my kid now learning English and French; no one in our family has ever gone to school; none of us can read or write; my kid is going to save the whole family."

Appendix B

I have just finished seminary with a master's degree, and our second child has just been born around two weeks ago. In the next few months, we shall be working on raising support for ministry projects and to provide for my family while on the mission field back in Rwanda. In November of 2003, we shall return to live in Rwanda and develop the children's ministry, evangelize, plant a church, and also develop a leadership resource center in the city of Kigali, the capital of Rwanda.

LaVergne, TN USA
10 December 2010
208241LV00002B/2/P